The
Complete Book
of Fishing

The
Complete Book
of Fishing

A. C. BECKER, JR.

South Brunswick and New York: A. S. Barnes and Company
London: Thomas Yoseloff Ltd

A. S. Barnes and Co., Inc.
Cranbury, New Jersey 08512

Thomas Yoseloff Ltd
Magdalen House
136-148 Tooley Street
London SE1, 2TT, England

Library of Congress Cataloging in Publication Data

Becker, A   C   Jr.
  The complete book of fishing.

  Includes index.
  1. Fishing. 2. Fishes—North America. 3. Cookery
(Sea food) I. Title.
SH441.B35   639'.2   76-18477
ISBN 0-498-01973-X

Photos by the author except where otherwise credited.

PRINTED IN THE UNITED STATES OF AMERICA

And this one is for my grandson,
Carlo Vincent Savino,
as a guide to a lifetime
of fishing and outdoors enjoyment

Contents

Introduction

In the beginning there was no such thing as sports fishing. Man fished for existence and existence alone. He caught fish to fill his belly, not to inflate his ego. Sports fishing didn't come into being as such until the Industrial Revolution so streamlined man's work that he had leisure time on his hands.

Yes, there are references in literature to sports fishing in yestercenturies, but it is all in the light of catching fish with artificial flies. Obviously the oldest specialized form of sports fishing is fly-fishing, but if you examine these historical references to fly-fishing as a form of sports fishing, you will find that this art of fishing was practiced by a fraction of a fraction of a percent of the population of the time.

An activity doesn't become a sport until it is practiced by a relatively large number of people for the purpose of recreation and/or enjoyment. Today sports fishing is a recognized, legitimate sport. It wasn't so back in the eighteenth and nineteenth centuries.

Perhaps in the beginning, sports fishing in North America was basically a matter of getting a baited hook into the water and waiting for some finny creature to take it. Yes, that angler caught fish and sometimes he or she caught a lot of them, including some of record size.

That was before the population explosion and its accompanying spread of civlization and urbanization. The face of the land changed and as the Industrial Revolution—the same IR that gained us leisure time—with its concrete and asphalt jungle encroached on wildlife habitat, man's trek for his game and fish stretched more and more miles from home.

Today's fishing is no longer a case of tossing a baited hook into the water. Today's fishing—sports as well as commercial—has become both sophisticated and complicated. Man has discovered that the sea is not a never-ending reservoir of fish. There has been a drop in fish populations—not all species, but certainly in those species that had a limited range to start off with, had relatively low reproduction, or had their nursery grounds drastically altered by man's spinoff—pollution and/or greed.

The purpose of this book is to help people become better anglers, and in so doing, I've divided the book into three sections—fishing techniques, popular fish species, and preparation of seafood for the dinner table.

The section on fishing techniques is designed to help all fishermen, whether they toss their baits in saltwater or freshwater, and whether they fish from a boat, a pier, a jetty, or get right down into the water and fish wade style.

The section on fish species covers only the most popular saltwater and freshwater fishes found in North American waters. Listed in this section are descriptions of the species, characteristics, their range, best methods of fishing for them, and their sizes. The section also includes a thumbnail where-to-go sketch on each state, Canadian province, and Mexico.

The section on seafood recipes wasn't in he original book plan. It came into being as a result of talking with so many people who referred to seafood dinners as "fish fries." In searching out recipes and new ways to prepare fish, I encountered a large number of people who liked to fish but who were less than enthusiastic about eating their catch. What was their objection? Almost to a person the answer was "fish tastes too fishy."

It was with this in mind that Part III, "How To Cook Seafood," came into being. After all if what one eats tastes good, the diner is sure to return again and again. And that means that person is going to go fishing again and again.

PART I

How To Catch Fish

1

Fish Shapes

Fish are like men and women—they're not all shaped alike and they all don't act alike. This indeed should tell the angler that he or she is going to faced with problems. Fish don't all act alike nor do they react alike where baits are concerned. A fishing style deadly for one species of fish can be entirely wrong for another, and unless the angler knows this, one is certain to waste a lot of time and go to a lot of trouble for small rewards.

The point can best be illustrated by considering several fish species, their shapes, and their behavior. I'll approach it with personal experiences with several species, considering first their behavior to baits and lures. I have had northern pike in freshwater fishing follow a lure as much as fifty to sixty feet before making a pass. In the case of saltwater fishing, I have had Spanish mackerel, king mackerel, dolphin, bonito, and tuna trail a trolled bait or lure for hundreds and hundreds of yards before actually making a strike.

Now back to fresh water to consider the behavior of two other fish species—largemouth bass and black crappie. I have yet to have either of these species follow a bait or lure more than a few feet without either striking or turning away. I've had the same fish do it time after time on the same lures as well as variations in lures and retrieves. Channel bass and spotted sea trout (speckled trout to Gulf Coasters) react similarly in salt water.

What's the answer? Why do some fish follow a bait for a long distance? How can one distinguish between "traveler" and "homebody" fish?

The answer lies in the overall shape of the fish, the size of their gills, the shape of their fins and tails, and the rigidity of their dorsal, anal, and pectoral fins.

Discounting such specimens as the flatfish, eels, and snakelike fishes, most fish species are generally torpedo shape. Some are more so than others. Note the slim, streamlined shape of the members of the pike family as opposed to that of the sunfish clan, which includes the popular largemouth bass. Over in salt water we find deep-bodied fish like the giant sea bass, channel bass, black drum, and sheepshead as opposed to the streamlined beauties of the mackerel family, the sailfish, marlin, and the sharks. Almost without exception deep-bodied or blunt-shaped fish are notable "homebodies"; those with the slim, trim lines are either travelers or migratory species.

Fish are able to breathe, or absorb oxygen from the water, by means of gills. Homebody species have larger gills in proportion to their overall size than do the species that are travelers. The homebodies need the larger gills in order to obtain sufficient oxygen to live in that they have to work their gills to breathe, whereas the migratory fish gets its oxygen supply by swimming fast. You can keep a homebody fish alive and healthy in a tank; you can't do this with a migratory fish unless the water is swirled to create a strong current that in effect when the fish faces into it, is equivalent to swimming fast.

Now let's go to the fins and tails. Migratory species have strong fins supported by hard, rigid spines.

The fins of nonmigratory fish may have hard, sharp spines, but the fin rays that connect the spines are soft and feathery. The homebody fish have soft-rayed, squarish tails; the migratory fellows have hard tails, deep V in shape.

Generally speaking, nonmigratory species have mouths that are large in relation to overall body size. Another difference is found in the teeth. Most homebody fish have small, rather dull teeth; on the other hand, traveler species have pronounced teeth that are razor sharp.

A fellow can use identical techniques and catch both migratory and nonmigratory fish, but he will almost always catch more of one type than the other. Those in the minority could be called fish caught by chance rather than by design. For example, about sixty percent of my fishing is in salt water and the bulk of it is for speckled trout. I use gear designed for these fish, special baits and special techniques. Although I catch more speckled trout than any other species, I still pick up channel bass, Spanish mackerel, flounders, and such. These are strays that just happened by when the bait was in the water. I have changed baits and techniques to fish specifically for flounders and have been rewarded mostly with flounders. Nevertheless a stray speckled trout or two, channel bass, or some other species were also caught. They were simply fish that chanced by when the bait was dangling in the water.

The point is that if you seek a specific fish species, tailor your baits and techniques accordingly. Don't trust it all to chance.

Fish shapes, mouths, fins, tails, etc., call for alterations in baits, lures, and techniques. The angler who is successful is the one who knows the meanings of the various physical parts of fish and then fishes accordingly.

Note the following.

Nonmigratory fish work best to slow-moving baits or lures and generally feed on or near the bottom. They are more apt to pick up and mouth a bait rather than strike savagely. They will not pursue a bait lure more than a few yards.

Migratory fish work best to fast-moving baits and lures fished near the surface. Most are armed with wicked teeth and strike savagely to kill their prey on the first pass and then circle back to pick it up and dine more leisurely. The exception comes when these species travel in schools. They then strike savagely to grab their prey and quickly dive toward deeper water to take their victims away from the competition. They will often follow baits and lures considerable distances before striking. Often this "follow" time can be shortened if the angler, upon observing what is happening, works his lure in such

a manner as to make it appear frantic to escape the area. Quite frequently this hastened action will result in a strike right in the shadow of the boat.

Fish that are bluish, gray, or whitish in color are migratory in nature and are surface feeders. As far as the fish are concerned, these are protective colors that make the species less likely to be seen when viewed from above. Except for the small bait fish that may be seized by birds, fish are preyed upon from below.

Fish brownish and dark in color and fish with dark spots, stripes, or blotches are bottom fish that lurk around obstructions, in the rocks and rip rap, in bottom vegetation, or in holes in the bottom. These fish are bottom feeders and they are caught on the bottom. Their colors and markings blend in with the bottom as protective markings to shield them from predators that may be lurking above.

The more a fish's lower jaw protrudes, the more likely it is to hit surface lures and baits. Good examples are tarpon and members of the mackerel family in saltwater, and the pike family in freshwater. Fish with underslung jaws and mouths that open downward are bottom feeders. For example, note the channel bass, black drum, and whiting in salt water; the carp, the paddlefish, and catfish in fresh water.

Some fish have specialized bills or fins that play a significant role in their lives. Take the billfish—the sailfish and marlin. The long spike that extends out from the upper jaw is a weapon used to stun fish. The billfish slams baitfish with the bill and then turns back to pick up the kill. This characteristic has led to specialized fishing in which a trolled bait is released when it is struck by the bill. The sawfish has an outlandish-looking saw up front that is used as a tool to root the bottom to stir up marine life. The paddlefish, a freshwater species, is another with a special tool. That big top lip spatula stirs up mud from which the fish sifts its food. If one is to catch fish, one has to fish accordingly. After all you wouldn't go lion hunting with bird shot.

Most people believe that fins are for swimming. This isn't completely true. Fins are for balance and maneuvering. A fish moves through the water because it wiggles snakelike. The dorsal and anal fins are for vertical balance. The pectoral and pelvic fins are for horizontal balance as well as steering. A fish also uses these fins to change directions upward or downward much like the diving planes on a submarine. The fins can be either spinous or soft-rayed. Most soft-rayed fish are good jumpers, while the spiny-rayed species are more apt to be found near the bottom. Fish with spiny-rayed fins usually have proportionately larger fin areas than do

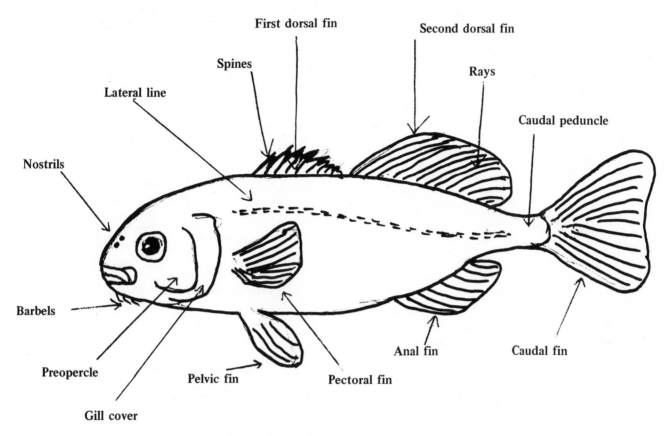

First dorsal fin
Spines
Lateral line
Nostrils
Barbels
Preopercle
Gill cover
Pelvic fin
Pectoral fin
Anal fin
Second dorsal fin
Rays
Caudal peduncle
Caudal fin

the soft-rayed species. The dorsal fin can be a single continous fin or contiguous fins, which can be adjacent to each other or slightly connected. Tail or caudal fins are found in many shapes—rounded, indented, forked, square, double truncated, pointed, etc.

Fish with large fin areas are able to start and stop quickly but are not able to maintain speed over any distance. These fish, however, are capable of intricate maneuvers. Fish with streamlined and small fin areas are capable of swimming fast and traveling great distances, but they are unable to do close-quarter maneuvering. A comparison of largemouth bass and mackerel striking characteristics will serve to illustrate the point. The largemouth bass eases within strike range and then grabs its victim in a sudden strike. If the fish misses, it can turn on a dime and still grab the victim. The largemouth bass is able to remain still and suspended in the water for long periods. The mackerel must always be on the move, otherwise sufficient water will not flow through its gills for it to filter out oxygen to maintain life. The mackerel moves through the water fast, and it makes a fast pass at its

intended victim. If the mackerel misses on the first strike, it cannot spin on a dime to get a second chance. Instead it must make a sweeping curve. The largemouth bass with great maneuverability is able to pursue and capture erratic-moving victims. The mackerel on the other hand is unable to do this and must depend on speed and surprise to capture its victims.

Fish with eyes on top or near the upper part of their heads are species that feed from below. Those that inhabit coral banks or live in considerable marine vegetation have eyes on the sides of their heads. Eye placement is such that the fish has approximately 180 degrees of vision with each eye. The only time the fish has binocular vision is when objects are straight ahead. It has monocular vision when an object is off to either side, above or below eye level. There is an overlap of the 180-degree vision range in front of the fish, and as a result the fish has a blind spot behind it. If the fish had 180-degree monocular vision with each eye and there was no overlap or binocular range, the fish would then have 360-degree vision with no blind spots.

TYPES OF TAILS

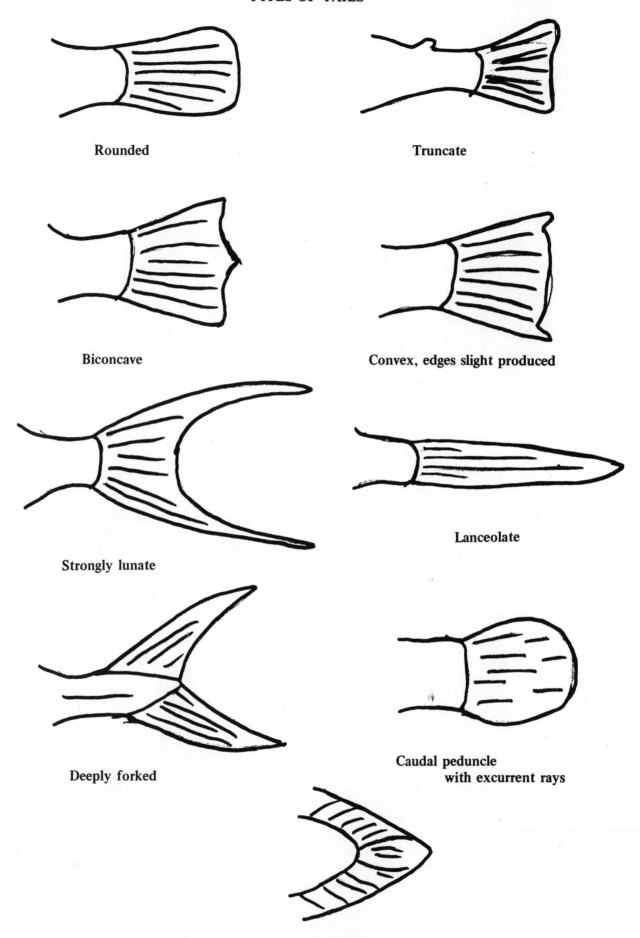

Rounded

Truncate

Biconcave

Convex, edges slight produced

Strongly lunate

Lanceolate

Deeply forked

Caudal peduncle
with excurrent rays

Dorsal and anal fins continuous with caudal fin

TYPES OF MOUTHS

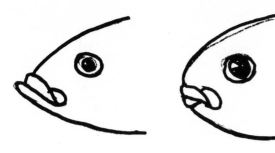

Terminal mouths   Dorsal mouth

Inferior mouths

BODY SHAPES

Migratory species   Non-migratory species

Billfish species

Flatfish

2

The Five Senses

If we expect to enjoy reasonably consistent fishing success, we must have considerable knowledge of the fish itself. The rifle range offers a good analogy. The rifle, the target, and the urge to shoot are simply the introduction. Hitting the target consistently means knowing the range, the windage, the ballistics of the cartridge, and finally the timing and coordination in squeezing off the shot.

And so it is with fishing. There is more to dangling a baited hook in the water and trusting to blind luck. We need to know the fish itself, how it acts and reacts to various stimuli. We, meaning us humans, learn through our senses—sight, smell, taste, hearing, and touch. The young child needs to touch the hot stove only once to learn that it is a no-no. This is knowledge through education, even though the sense of touch was involved. There are some things we do instinctively as a result of our senses. As an example when a bright light is flashed in your face, you instinctively shade your eyes. You don't have to think to make this reaction.

Fish, too, act and react as a result of their senses. Most of their reactions involve instinct and lean strongly toward survival. Because of their small and poorly developed brains, fish are unable to reason, although in laboratory studies, it has been proved they can be trained to react to various stimuli.

Now let's go to the individual senses and correlate each with catching fish. In doing so, however, it is important to remember that the system of senses is like a coin—there are two sides. One side can be used to work for the fisherman; the other side against him.

SIGHT

The eyes of most fish, and certainly all the species caught by sports and commercial fishermen, are well developed. The eyes are large. They can be focused, and located on each side of the head, each eye has a vision range of approximately 180 degrees. Not only that, the eyes are situated in such a protruding manner that a fish can see to the rear. No doubt this is nature's way of protecting the fish from some of its enemies.

The eye of a fish contains all the parts of the human eye with one exception. The eye has the cornea, lens, iris, and retina. The fish eye, however, does not have a lid. In short, a fish can neither blink, nor close its eyes.

This lack of an eyelid should send a message to the discerning fisherman. Note how fish react to light; they flee excessive brightness. This, then, should explain why surface fishing is generally blah in the ten A.M. to three P.M. period on a bright, sunny day. Rays from the sun are striking the surface of the water at angles that permit deep penetration. If the water is clear, one can see the bottom twenty feet below the boat. You can't see the same bottom in the same clear water when the sun is low to the horizon. The rays are reflected; they just don't penetrate at this shallow angle.

This in turn has a bearing on colors, and it raises some interesting questions. Which is the best color to use? Is yellow more effective than black on a surface lure? Is the color of blood in water really red?

Answers to these questions come in all shades of

gray. For a long time fish were thought to see the world around them only in black and white and the shades of gray in between. This has been proved to be otherwise, although there is a time when a fish won't see the color in its true hue. This is when the object is immediately in line between the fish's vision and the source of light. The object then will appear invariably either black or dark. You can prove this with a snowball. The snowball viewed in your hand is white. Hold that same snowball up toward the source of light, and the back side of it—the side you're looking at—will appear dark. If the light source is weak, the back side will actually appear to be black.

It is thusly so with fish when they view an object floating on the surface. Those parts of the object *out* of the water may be invisible to the fish because of light refraction, but that part *in* the water will appear to be either dark or black, the degree again depending upon the light source. Consequently when lying at rest on the surface, the yellow plug with the red head is just a dark object to the fish when viewed from below. Suppose the plug is a diver and it is put into motion. Its wiggling dive carries it down to a level with the same fish, and now the colors come into play. How well the colors stand out depends upon the intensity of the light in the sky—early morning, late afternoon, or midday— and the clarity of the water itself.

Keep in mind that water filters light, and this means the deeper the water, the less light penetration. As light rays are filtered out, certain colors lose their properties and appear as other colors. Blood on the surface of the water is red. Many feet below the surface, blood appears green instead of red. Color movies made in underwater research bear this out.

Sunlight is a form of radiant energy, so let's consider a sunbeam and how it is affected by water. It appears white although it is made up of all colors of the spectrum that we can see plus the invisible parts, infrared or heat and ultraviolent that produce sunburn. Each form of radiant energy has a specific wave length—violet and ultraviolet have the shortest wave lengths; red and infrared have the longest. Colors as we see them are produced by the length of the light waves that are reflected by whatever we are viewing. The violets, indigos, blues, and greens are on the lower end of the spectrum and have short wave length—violet and ultraviolet have the shortest wave lengths; red and infrared have the longest. lengths.

What happens when these rays penetrate the water and become visible as they reflect off lures? The long light waves are intensely absorbed, and on a clear day in sea water, the red, orange, and yellow rays disappear in the first thirty-five to forty feet. The blues, greens, and violets are less absorbed and visible to greater depths. So we have a situation of the color in water becoming progressively greener, then bluer and darker the deeper the object sinks.

In any consideration of colors in water, one must always remember that because of the high index of refraction of water, much of the light from the sun is reflected rather than absorbed, except, of course, when the sun is at or near its zenith.

The absence of eyelids is a clue to where fish are likely to hang out. In open waters they go deep when the light is bright. Yet there are times during the brightest part of the day one catches fish near the surface. How can this be explained? The answer here lies in looking for a shadow and what cast it. Let's look at fresh water and the largemouth bass for some answers. This fish's habitat is generally cluttered with drowned trees standing tall above the surface, banks rich in timber stands, steep hills or cliffs. Bass invariably lie in the shadows cast by the environment. Cast to the shadows and you'll catch bass; cast only the sunny side and you'll wind up with a sore arm.

Now look at saltwater fishing, blue-water fishing far out of sight of land. Nothing to cast shadows there. This is true if you're looking for objects that stand high above the surface. But how about that patch of floating seaweed, the logs washed to sea by the rivers, and the general flotsam and jetsom found on our oceans? They may not cast shadows as such, but they certainly provide shade beneath. I wouldn't have to work for a living if I had a dollar for every fish I've caught from under a log or the edge of a seaweed patch. I never pass up fishing around a buoy. Ease in quietly and cast to the shadow side. A word of warning. Don't tie up to the buoy; it's against maritime law and practically a hanging offense.

Much of the animal life in this world is without color vision. Almost all birds have color vision, often so acute that even shades of a single color can be identified. Most four-legged animals, however, are without color vision; they go through life seeing the world only in black and white and those gray tones in between. Those creatures lacking color vision have eyes without cones, minute nerve ends activited by color wave lengths. Fish eyes have cones and are able to distinguish differences in colors if the light source is sufficient. In addition to cones, the eyes of most fish also contain rods, which come into play as the light dims. When the light dims to the point where the cones cease to respond, the rods then come into play. It is then that hues lose their meaning and objects appear bright or dark depending upon the location and intensity of the light source. This is the reason color is meaningless in night fishing.

Most fish species depend upon sight to a certain degree in feeding. Translated into fishing itself this simply means that clear water and good fishing generally go hand in glove. If you are a lure devotee, reasonably clear water is a must. When the water is off-color, sandy, or downright muddy, you have to appeal to one or more of the other senses to catch fish.

Always keep in mind that the fish is not where you see it nor are you where the fish views you to be. What appears but isn't is caused by refraction, a deflection of a propagating wave, such as light or sound, as it passes from one medium through another. In the case of fishing we are concerned with sight, which is light, and light is bent as it goes from the air into the water. Let's look at how the fisherman and the fish see each other.

The fisherman standing on the bank sees the fish but not exactly where the fish actually is, for vision is "bent" as it enters the water. Consequently the fish is closer to the fishermen than it appears to be. If the angler happens to cast a bait in such a manner that it strikes the water where the fish appears to be, everything is okay for that will place the lure beyond the fish in such a manner that it can be retrieved back over the fish. A lure that strikes the water short of where the fish appears to be may literally "hit the fish" on the head and spook it to the other side of the lake. So this must be kept in mind in all fishing when the fish is visible to the fisherman. The cast that appears to be right to the fish or a little beyond is the proper cast. Those short casts are the ones that will get one into trouble.

Okay, so jump overboard and look at the world from the fish's point of view, and we have an entirely different situation. The fish sees the man but in a place other than were the fellow actually is, and this place is in the reverse of where the fisherman sees the fish. This will explain why fish are so easy to spook. The man will appear much closer to the fish than he actually is and furthermore he will appear to "tower over" the fish, and if the man happens to be wearing clothes that intensely reflect light, the fisherman indeed will appear to be some giant monster.

The calmer the water, the better man can see fish and vice versa. A wind-rippled surface will work to the advantage of the fisherman in that refraction will diffuse the image to the extent that it may appear as nothing more than a distorted shadow or cloud. Furthermore, a rippled surface isn't a silent one. There is a wash-lapping sound involved that can an aid in helping to cover sounds made by the fisherman, especially if he is a wade-fisherman.

Now from sight let's proceed to smell.

SMELL

The sense of smell is almost without question the most important in the life cycle of a fish. I say "almost without question" because we can't get the fish to talk back to give us definite answers. Consequently it is impossible to make a hundred percent positive statement. We can only assume and reason, and in support let me offer this observation. I've caught fish consistently from water so turbid that you couldn't see your hand six inches below the surface. And these same waters remained in this murky state for weeks on end. If fish depended mainly on sight for food, then why didn't the fish in these murky waters die of starvation? They had to either smell or feel out their food, and I doubt if any marine life is going to remain still to be fondled when the fondler is something that is going to eat them.

The acute sense of smell of the shark is thoroughly documented. A shark can detect one part of blood in from ten million to one hundred million parts of water. Not all fish have such ultrasensitivity to smell. Human blood scent attraction for sharks has been known for years and proof is the result of many tests conducted over decades. Yet in the case of other fish species, studies of their reactions to smell have taken place only in recent years. Probably the only reason for such exhaustive tests in the case of sharks is the dangerous nature of the fish in relation to man. After all, has anyone heard of a rainbow trout or a largemouth bass or a flounder attacking man?

Moves are being made now toward using manufactured scents as means of attracting gamefish, and there are dozens of companies making preparations ranging from salves to vile-smelling fish oils to completely odorless and tasteless liquids that can be applied to baits and lures. I have tried a number of these preparations in enough tests to state conclusively that they work. They do attract fish, although their track records are not exactly up to some of the advertising claims. For example, I did some exhaustive testing of a liquid that when applied to a lure was supposed to attract largemouth bass. I carried out the tests in several small, private lakes in East Texas. The water was clear and my vantage point was high enough so I could see the fish. I used identical lures, one treated with bass scent, the other without. The lures were lowered into the water at the same time and about ten feet apart. Fish of all species—bass, bluegills, crappie—eased up to investigate each lure. Those that came into the scent range of the treated lure reacted by excitedly striking at the lure. Big fish took it in a mouthful; the small ones pecked at the sides of the lure. I caught far more fish on the treated lure, but they were not just bass. They included big bluegills, crappie, and in two instances catfish. Almost all of the fish caught on the untreated lure were bass.

I'm not knocking scent at all. Rather I think it is fine, although I suspect that some manufacturers may just add a little different color to the scents that are supposed to catch other fish species. In fact, in my personal tests the bass, crappie, and bluegills reacted to lures treated with muskellunge-pike-walleye scent with the same alacrity as they did to the bass scent. And there's not one musky, pike, or walleye in those East Texas test lakes.

One doesn't necessarily have to purchase a preparation made specifically for attracting fish. I conducted additional tests and came up with some interesting notes. I poured some plain old codliver oil on the water. No bass responded, but the bluegills in particular almost churned the water into a froth by their wild feeding. When they got through—and it didn't take them long—there wasn't a vestige of oil left glistening on the surface.

I did the same thing with machine oil, and I got a violent reaction from the bluegills. They sounded and vacated the immediate area like the field leaves the starting gate at the Kentucky Derby. This right here ought to explain the kind of fishing a fellow is going to have if his outboard motor leaks fuel or residue. The glistening oil slick snaking out behind the boat is not going to attract fish.

You can buy plastic worms—the deadliest of lures when it comes to dredging out trophy-size largemouth bass—with "built-in" scent. Interestingly enough these scented worms have an odor and taste not unlike licorice. You can add this same smell and taste to your lure or bait by putting on a drop or two of oil of anise, which can be purchased readily at any drug store. I know some professional guides who rub oil of anise all over their hands when they go fishing.

In the course of authoring outdoors books—this is my seventh and fourth on fishing—I have delved into books and scientific journals written by numerous authorities. Many years ago I used to view some of the theories as being crackpot. I don't make these snap judgments any more. I prefer to set out to either prove or disprove the issue before hanging a label on it. One case in particular stands out.

The matter was brought to my attention on a bass-fishing trip on Toldeo Bend Reservoir in East Texas. We had been fishing for several hours. My guide had three or four nice bass, while I had still to get a strike much less a fish. Finally the guide remarked to me, "I think maybe you sweat too much to catch many bass." To say the least that really sounded crackpot. But I responded to the question with an open mind and asked him to explain it. He couldn't other than to say that he had read it someplace.

During the next several weeks I spent time in libraries going through books, scientific journals, and reports for verification of his statement. And I found it. First in connection with scent studies made with sharks. Tests showed that whereas the scent of human blood brought sharks charging in, the acid in human sweat repelled the same beasts. Further research brought to light that the amino acid on human palms when exuded with sweat produced serine, an acid that is repellent to fish. Everyone doesn't sweat the same. Whites sweat more than other races. Not only that white adult males secrete more serine than do youngsters or white adult females. Personally I sweat something furious.

Now to eliminate the serine I carry along a bar of nonscented soap, and during the course of a fishing trip and especially in the summer when I sweat like the proverbial horse, I frequently wash my hands. And lures, too, if they happen to come in contact with my sweat-drenched clothes. Is it a crackpot theory? I don't think so. The only thing I've changed in my fishing procedure is to wash my hands frequently with plain bar soap. I still make waterhauls once in a while, but only a fraction of what I used to make when I didn't wash away the sweat. More recently I took another step. I carry along a bottle of oil of anise. I rub it over my hands, and I've found it especially helpful in masking serine when handling a lot of lure changes and hook baitings.

On the subject of scent, it is appropriate here to point out that bar soap—the plain, unscented laundry kind—is attractive to fish. It makes great bait for freshwater catfish.

HEARING

Ranking third in importance is hearing. That's right, hearing. Fish both hear and feel sounds, and they can be attracted by certain sounds.

The silent sea isn't silent at all. It's a veritable agropolis of noises, only a few of which are caused by the elements. The crashing of the waves, the rustle of water as currents swirl around obstructions, and manmade noises from boat engines only form the backdrop for the noises and sounds that come from marine life itself.

If you happen to be inquisitive, you might consider walking tidal flats on a still night and especially so on the low tide when clam and oyster beds are likely to be partially exposed. Keep your eyes alert and listen to the clams and oysters snap their shells shut as you approach. You'll hear fish scurrying in the shallow water. Go a little farther. Lower a stethoscope into the water, and it is not at all uncommon to hear the various drumming, thumping, and croaking sounds made by various fish. These noises are thought to be signals to attract together fish of a kind. It is also thought in some circles that some of these noises may in effect be mating calls. After all in the above water animal world, all forms of wildlife ranging from the four-footed to the winged sound mating calls. It is not unreasonable for fish to do the same.

Fishermen have been calling fish for a long time. In fact, the first surface lure was actually a fish caller. It alerted fish by the splash it made hitting the water. Any succeeding noises the angler caused the lure to make were additional fish-calling sounds. Consider the sounds these lures make. The "chug" or "vop" is much like that of a fish taking food from the surface. The "gurgle-gurgle-gurgle" caused by lures with inverted and winged lips is a noise similar to that made by small animals swimming. Then there are the lures with propellers. When retrieved the propellers, disturbing the surface with a "plip-plip-plip" sound, make a noise startlingly similar to that made by a crippled minnow.

Okay, so how does a fish pick up these sounds? It can pick them up through its inner ear, through the swim bladder, which is an organ that allows the fish to adjust to water pressure at different depths, or felt through the lateral line, the nerve fiber line that runs down each side of a fish's body.

It takes less noise than one would suppose to attract fish. This is because of the element in which the fish lives. Water is about eighty times denser than the air above it and it transmits sounds five times as effectively. Therefore the lure noise need not be really loud to be effective. The only thing here is that the lure must be worked slowly so that the fish has sufficient time to locate the source of the sound and then home in on it. Too frequently fishermen in their impatience to hurry to make another cast literally jerk the lure out of the water just when the fish makes visual contact.

The sound-transmitting properties of water make fish extremely vulnerable to sudden, harsh, and foreign sounds. Knocking the oars against the sides of the boat, wading the flats like a bull moose in rut, or running the motor wide open in shallow or enclosed waters produces noises the send fish finning for more placid waters.

TASTE AND FEEL

The remaining senses to be considered are taste and feel, and since they are so closely related, they will be discussed as one. After all you really can't taste that steak unless you can feel it in your mouth.

If a lure or bait isn't to a fish's liking, the finny fellow will spit it out just as quickly as it was mouthed. The fisherman asleep at the switch is going to miss these kinds of pickups. Taste in effect dovetails with the sense of smell. If the fish likes the smell, you're in the home stretch, for the taste ought to be the same, but if the fish does spit out a correctly scented bait, it is because the feel is all wrong.

Personally I don't lean much toward catching fish solely on the basis of feel. Frankly, I feel that if the fish gets the bait in its mouth to taste it and feel it and then spit it out and you fail to set the hook, then you must accept all the blame. Pure and simple fishing is not for sleepyheads. People who consistently catch fish work at it and work at it hard. But it's fun-work, a kind of labor I don't object to at all.

3

Tides and Water Levels

Tides in salt water and water stage levels where fresh water is concerned are controlling factors in fishing. True, fish can be caught and are caught on all tides in salt water and on high and low stages in fresh water. The degree of success, however, varies a great deal. Fishing can be both good and bad in the same location on any given day. If the fisherman is there when the fish congregate to feed, then he is certain to have a good day. Yet this same area a few hours later will produce virtually nothing. Fish don't feed continuously, although there are times when it may seem that way, just as there are times when it appears the fish will never feed again.

Tides and water stages play important roles in these feeding periods. Where salt water is concerned the general rule of thumb is that fish are most active and most likely to feed on rising tides and high-tide stands. Freshwater fish tend to be more active and more voracious feeders on high-water stages, although the degree of action is not as pronounced as in the case of saltwater fish.

Let's consider salt water and fresh water separately.

SALT WATER

Tides rise and fall on a regular schedule as they follow the moon in its orbit around the earth. Tides rise and fall twice in the time between two rising moons, a period of twenty-four hours and fifty minutes. The time between two rising moons is determined by the rotation of the earth on its axis and the revolution of the moon around the earth. In relation to the sun, the moon revolves around the earth once in about twenty-nine and one-half days, or about twelve degrees each day. Between the moon risings, the earth makes a complete rotation and then turns this additional twelve degrees. This additional twelve degrees of rotation amounts to about fifty minutes.

The moon's gravity pulls the nearest water away from the solid part of the earth, and at the same time pulls the solid earth away from the water on the opposite side of the earth. As a result the pull of the moon causes two bulges—or high tides—on the oceans.

Tide ranges differ from day to day according to the position of the moon and sun. When the two are pulling along the same line, as is the case with full moon and new moon, the tide rises higher than usual and is called a spring tide. When the two forces pull at right angles (moon at first and third quarters), the tide does not rise as high as usual and is called a neap tide.

The differences in the way the tides act are a result of the shape, size, and depth of our seas and oceans. The Atlantic Ocean has tides that flow and ebb twice each day. In the Pacific Ocean there are some islands that have mixed tides—two highs daily with only a little ebb between and then a very low tide. There are times in the Gulf of Mexico where there is only one daily tide—one high and one low each day. The Mediterranean Sea, on the other hand, has very, very little tide at all.

The rise and fall of tides vary, depending upon the time elapse between tides and the height of the tide stand in relation to mean low tide. High and low tides are not equidistant apart. For example, a high at midnight will not necessarily be followed by a low tide at six A.M., another high at twelve noon, and a second low at six P.M. and so forth. The tide differences between highs and lows may range from as little as a hour on up to fifteen to sixteen hours, depending upon the location in the world and the sun and moon phases. The nearer one goes to the Equator, the smaller the difference in tide heights between high and low. It is usually a matter of only a foot or less. Yet up north in Newfoundland and far south at the tip of South America, the differences can amount to as much as fifty feet.

If the saltwater fisherman is to be consistently successful, he must have daily tide information on the area he fishes. This material can be obtained from tide tables published annually by the National Ocean Survey of the U. S. Department of Commerce. The Survey publishes four tide tables books covering the world's oceans and seas. The books, by titles, include: *Tide Tables, Europe and West Coast of Africa (including Mediterranean Sea); Tide Tables, East Coast, North and South America (including Greenland); Tide Tables, West Coast North and South American (including Hawaiian Islands);* and *Tide Tables, Central and Western Pacific Ocean and Indian Ocean.*

These publications are quite detailed and include such information as daily tide predictions, lists of reference stations, tidal differences, tide heights at any time, local mean time of sunrise and sunset and moonrise and moonset. All of these are factors that the serious saltwater fisherman should study and take into consideration when he plans a trip. This information will not positively guarantee him fish, but it will give him an astronomical head start on the spur-of-the-moment fisherman.

It is estimated that ninety-five percent of the sports saltwater fishing in North American today is done in inshore or coastal waters. This means waters where tide differences are visible to the eye—at low tide the sand bars stand out in bold relief and on high tide the salt waters flood well back into the lowland marshes.

As the tide rises and the water creeps over the flats and into the salt grass marshes, new marine fodder in both animal and vegetable forms is exposed. Tiny baitfish ride in with these tides to feed on this fodder. These baitfish, in turn, are pursued by the gamefish that the sports anglers seek. Although the water is often too shallow for gamefish to swim over the flats, they keep to the channels and guts where they are quick to pounce on baitfish that may stray or be swept off the flats. The fisherman who knows the locations of these channels, guts, and depressions is in for some exciting action on the incoming and high tides.

These same gamefish retreat to the safety of deep water when the tide turns and begins to fall. The larger of the baitfish retreat, too. Many of the tiny baitfish, however, fail to fall back with the receding water, and they in turn are trapped in pools and holes where they face the added hazards of water evaporation and depletion of oxygen due to excessive heat in the summer, or ice and freezing to death in the winter, or falling victims to marsh animals and shorebirds that venture on the exposed tidal flats.

Generally speaking, inshore saltwater fishing is best in a period that begins about two hours before the high stand until about an hour after the turn of the stand. On a day of just one high and one low, the good fishing stand may stretch over five or six hours, depending upon the time length between high tide and the turn of the stand.

Most saltwater fishermen, however, prefer days with two highs. There's more to it than the obvious advantage of two fish feeding and activity periods. There is the added advantage of being able to pick the tide period that best fits the weather conditions. For example, consider the summer day with two highs—one at six A.M. and the other at two P.M. Obviously the morning period will be superior in the light of the heat that prevails at midday and through a good part of the afternoon. The reverse is likely to be the best fishing tide on a cold, wintry day.

Tidal movements are much more pronounced on days on which there are two highs and two lows than on days with just a single high and low tide. The stronger the surge of the tide, the more pronounced the fish activity period. This, however, is true only up to a point. In areas like Newfoundland bays and the tip of South America where the difference between low and high tide may be as much as fifty feet, the tidal surge is much too swift and dangerous for hook-and-line fishing.

Beginning fishermen are often astounded at how often big fish are caught in surprisingly shallow water. It all has to do with the tides and knowing which tides to fish.

Gamefish follow the food supply. Just how far they venture into shallow water depends on water temperature and clarity, wave action, light, and noise. Fishing is invariably poor on water temperature extremes, and in either case gamefish do not move far into inshore waters. Gamefish move closer to shore when the water is clear than when it is turbid. Except for a few fish species that feed in the breaking surf, most fish do not follow the tide in close to the shoreline when the water is rough. Under such conditions they seem to be content to roam just outside the line of seaward breakers. Under cover of night big gamefish often come into water so shallow that their dorsal fins stick above the surface. Down through the years I've caught a lot of thirty- and forty-pound channel bass and black drum in water two feet deep. You won't find this happening in the light of day unless it is in the first few minutes after dawn. Bonefish on shallow flats and cruising sharks are exceptions.

Noise deserves a paragraph all by itself. Fishermen must always keep in mind that water is a good conductor of sound. In fact, sound in water travels amost five times faster than it does in the air above. Where shallow water is concerned, sound alone can be the deciding factor as to whether a fellow catches fish or not. The bottom itself being far denser than the water above is also a good conductor of sound. Hence the fisherman who makes undue noises in shallow water is certain to send the fish finning for the horizon. The general absence of sound at night is the reason many big fish venture into extremely shallow water after dark.

A great many successful fishermen turn only to wade-fishing when shallow water is involved. They may use a boat to get to the fishing grounds, but after that they turn to wading, and this is true even though the water may be deep enough for a light boat with a small outboard motor. The bottom in shallow water simply acts as a sounding board. The only way to quietly fish shallow water is by wading. Wade-fishermen move over the flats in slow motion personified, ever looking for telltale swirls, ripples, or wakes that indicate the presence of gamefish. Then they seek to maneuver themselves into intercept courses that will put them within casting range of the fish. And they do it without any alarming sounds that may spook the fish.

Tides have no effect on true offshore or deepsea fishing. There are a few offshore migratory species that frequent a sort of "twilight zone" between offshore and inshore waters. These fish—Spanish mackerel, cobia, and jack crevalle to mention a few—normally work outside the channels, passes, and rivers that empty into the sea, but on occasions when tides are extremely high these species venture into the entrances of bays. These species, however, do not work into shallow water in the true sense of being very shallow. For example, some big fish species like channel bass, striped bass, and black drum in the thirty- and forty-pound class will work into shallows just a couple of feet deep. The migratory "twilight zone" species like the Spanish mackerel, cobia, and jack crevalle may be found close to shore but seldom in water less than eight to ten feet deep.

FRESH WATER

Although not subject to tides as such, bodies of fresh water, whether they are lakes or rivers, are subject to changing water levels.

These levels in fresh water may remain constant for many days, even weeks, or they may change almost daily. The contingency factors here are the weather and the primary use of the water. Quite obviously water levels will rise in rainy seasons and will fall during periods of prolonged droughts. Abnormally fast snow melts and ice thaws will cause sharp rised downstream in those bodies of water that don't freeze over. Water level fluctuations under these conditions—nature by the way—can be dramatic, ranging from floods to the proverbial trickle. These extremes severely alter the ecology of the area and result in disastrous fishing. Floods destroy spawn, move adult fish into isolated pockets and hollows that dry up when the flood recedes, and silt over breeding grounds, trapping and isolating adult fish in holes and deeps that are likely to become stagnant, and congregating masses of fish in relative small water areas that draw poaching netters like carrion attracts vultures.

Water areas affected by power-generating, flood control, and irrigation-control dams have far less dramatic water level stages, although the levels are likely to fluctuate more often.

On the lake or reservoir side of the dam the water level may rise of fall anywhere from a matter of a few inches to a few feet, depending upon the surface acreage involved and for what purpose the water is used. Over on the river or stream side of the dam, the water stages can be measured in many feet. It depends here on how long water is passed through the dam's control gates and in what quantities.

The water that comes rushing into the stream or river when the dam gates are opened invariably stirs fish into action, often into frenzied feeding. The new water pouring into the stream brings with it a lot of marine fodder. In addition the force of the rushing water on the stream bed and shoreline dislodges and sweeps into the main stream a great amount of additional fish fodder. For want of a more expressive term, you can call it "fish supermarket" time. The places to try during the fast-rushing water periods are alongside of and behind boulders, logs, or anything that breaks the flow. A fish uses a lot of energy constantly fighting the current, so they move to the downstream side of obstructions that break the current. They dart out from these shelter spots when food particles are carried by in the rushing water.

When the dam's power valves are closed, the

water level in the stream or river will fall rapidly, and in a short time the flow will be quite slow, perhaps even snail-pace. The area will be dotted with exposed rocks, boulders, logs, etc., interspersed with a lot of quiet pools. These pools are the places for the fisherman to try, but the action is likely to be rather slow if the fisherman tries these holes too soon after the river recedes. After all the fish have just had their feeding spree in the rushing water. Furthermore, they will be strongly inclined to rest following their bout with the strong water flow. The time to work these pools is four, five, or six hours after the closing of the dam's gates. In cases where water is released downstream only every few days, then the angler should try each of the pools on the days when the dam's activities are shut down.

Water levels in the lake or reservoir proper dictate when the fisherman should try his luck. Here, however, he must correlate the water level with weather and season of the year conditions.

Normally when the water stand is high in an impoundment, the areas to fish are the shorelines, coves, and particularly the brush stands near the shore. New areas covered with water mean new food supplies and fish make the most of this. This holds true for spring, early fall, and generally mild temperatures. When the water level is down, the channels, cuts, and holes are the places to fish. As for as the seasons are concerned, fish will invariably go to deep water in the cold of winter and in the heat of midsummer. Fish are cold-blooded creatures that take on the temperature of their environment, and like all cold-blooded animal life, they react to temperature changes. They get loggy at either extremes of temperature, and this is reflected in their feeding habits in a marked slowdown in foraging and feeding.

4

Reading the Water

Successful fishermen are just that because of their ability to read the water. They just don't go fishing any place where there happens to be water, for they know the water can be like the land—areas populated and teeming with life and other vast areas devoid of life. In short, there are deserts in the water just as there are deserts on land. Fish can be found in these water "desert" areas but only when they are passing through in migration. To make this point clear very few people live in the Mojave Desert but a lot of folks cross it going to and from California.

The bottom is the key as to whether an area is a desert or not. One rarely finds gamefish in waters where the bottom is soft, oozie mud. A few fish like catfish and carp like mud bottoms, but in general gamefish favor firmer, cleaner bottoms.

Soft, mud bottoms in salt water—bottoms that fishermen should avoid—are usually formed where river, stream, or bayou discharges meet sea currents. The result is the silt-laden waters pouring out of the rivers and stream come to a stop when they collide with sea currents. The suspended silt then sinks to the bottom and forms a marine desert. In recent years the situation has been aggravated by pollution, and in addition to bearing silt, the water discharge from inland often carries industrial, chemical, and raw sewage pollutants. Marine vegetation is killed by all this junk that settles to the bottom and a new marine desert is formed.

Electronic gear today has taken the guesswork out of what is on the bottom, but this kind of equipment isn't in every fellow's tackle box. The serious boat fisherman, whether he plies fresh or salt water, is almost certain to have his boat armed with this electronic fish-finding gear, but there are a great many other fishermen, however, who can not afford such equipment. This gear is a waste of money if the fisherman plies his sport from a pier, in the surf, wading the bays and streams, fishing from the bank, or for that matter occasionally goes out in a livery boat. These devices are useful only in a boat. This electronic gear will tell the boatman what kind of bottom lies below and if there are any fish in the zone between the boat and the bottom of lake, bay, sea, or whatever. In the overall fishing fraternity the boat fishermen are in the minority. A rough guess is that pier, surf, bank, and wade fishermen probably outnumber the boat anglers twenty or thirty to one. Maybe even more. Consequently it behooves these "have-nots" of electronic gear to have the skill to read the water. It sure saves a lot of time, wear and tear in useless casting and cuts waterhaul trips to a minimum.

Before going into reading the water it might be well to make some observations about waterhauls. By definition a waterhaul is a fishing trip on which the angler catches nothing or at least none of the fish species he seeks. They are by no means reserved for tyro fishermen. All fishermen, including professional guides, make them. Of course they don't talk about them, for after all the guide who admits to waterhauls is going to cause some prospective customers to have doubts. Frankly I think this is the wrong approach to take. Real fishermen know waterhauls will occur, and when these things happen, they accept them as part of the sport. Those people who look to a guide as an absolute guarantee of fish every time are the ones who cause the headaches. Guides would be better off skipping the folks who don't know the meaning of waterhauls.

The only reading-the-water rules that hold true for all bodies of water are those concerning color and breaking waves. The darker the blue of the water, the deeper it is. Breaking waves in an absence of wind or in just light winds indicate shallow water. These are the starters when it comes to reading water.

Water can be read easiest when seen from an elevation. It's easiest then to distinguish colors that indicate cuts, channels, bars, flats, and shoals. In flatland country or on the beach you can get that elevation by standing atop the car. Okay, so you do that and note some deep cuts and holes indicated by a deep blue color and the adjacent flats by a lighter green-blue. Now comes the problem of where to fish. Again consider the habits of the fish sought, the time of day, and the season of the year. Bottom feeders are most likely to be found in the holes, channels, and cuts along the stepoffs of these depressions. The exception comes when waters are at flood stage, and this holds for both fresh- and saltwater fishing. Flood stage water open new vistas for foraging fish, and if the flooding is pronounced enough, the bottom feeders will react accordingly by fanning out over the area.

Fish are remarkably similar to people. The seek out an environment where the living is pleasant. This is where time of day and season of year enter the picture. In hot weather fish will be found deep, especially during the heat of the day. They range to shallow water at night or in the cool of the dawn. In cold weather they are quite likely to move into relatively shallow water if there is a bright sun, for even in midwinter a warming sun can raise the temperature of shallow water a degree or two.

Ability to read the water is an absolute must if one is to score in fishing the surf. Here fish move along in the troughs between the bars, and then move from trough to trough through the narrow cuts and channels that frequently bisect the sand bars. The troughs are easy to find. They are the darker colored stretches of water that lie between the lines of breaking waves. There is always considerable wave action over sand bars with relatively little wave breaking over the troughs. The cuts and channels are indicated where there is a break in the line of waves.

These cuts, troughs, and depressions are the places to fish. Surprisingly big gamefish, brawlers like channel bass, black drum, and striped bass, often lurk in these troughs feeding off the marine life that is tumbled off the sand bars by the breaking waves. The best fishing action will be found in these troughs, while for all intents and purposes, those who fish atop the bars in affect fish in spots relatively free of fish.

Unless maintained by man for navigation purposes, rivers, streams, and bayous will not be of uniform depths. Of the three mentioned, the bayou is the one that is likely to be closest to a uniform depth. This is because water flow in bayous is slow.

Stream and river flow can vary from slow to raging torrents. The deep and shallow places are easiest to locate when water flows slow. A placid, flat surface indicates water of some depth. A rippled surface indicates sand bars and shallow water. Water also moves faster in shallows. Boulders, rocks, fallen timber, etc., have an effect on stream and river bottoms in that they build up sand bars and cause channels to reroute. River and stream fish payoff spots are in the deep holes where channels are gouged out on the outside bend of turns, around boulders and timber jams, and alongside of sand bars that border fast dropoffs. Fish along the banks of bayous. Fish often lurk here picking up tidbits that drop our of the trees or are blown off the banks.

The fisherman working a lake from the bank can get an idea of water depth by noting what appears on or above the surface of the water. Tiny bits of grass reaching above the surface indicate shallow water—a flooded grass flat. Floating moss and water plants indicate water less than five feet deep. Tree limbs poking above the surface indicate deep water. The fisherman can judge the depth by noting the height of the trees on the bank in comparison with how much of the drowned trees stick above the water.

Ability to read water will clue a fisherman as to the kinds of bait to use. Clear water is best for the fellow who prefers to fish artificial lures since most of this hardware needs to be seen in order to be taken by fish. Only a specialized few artificials can be used with any degree of success in off-colored water. These lures are the surface disturbers, the lures that make noises when put into motion. They attract fish by making sounds that stimulate fish into action.

The fisherman must resort to natural baits when water is murky or turbid. These baits have odors and are able to attract fish by smell. The fisherman will also find that bottom fishing is more productive than surface or midwater fishing when the water is cloudy. Surface feeders get their food mainly by sight, and when the water is badly off-color, they simply move to where water clarity is more to their liking.

Whether a fisherman is reading the water for surf, bay, river, or lake fishing, he should always watch for signs of marine life—surface as well as on the bottom. A water surface scarred by the ripples and vees caused by small baitfish is indicative that the area is worth trying, for wherever you find baitfish, you usually find gamefish. Bottom marine life can be crabs, small crustaceans, snails and the like. Waters completely void of baitfish and marine bottom life are also void of gamefish. Oxygen depletion, heat, extreme cold, contamination, and pollution can cause these watery deserts.

It is easier to catch fish in a small body of water than in a large one. This is true because no body of water is totally saturated with fish, for whenever the fish population gets that high, there is natural attrition in the form of massive dieoffs. There is still another reason why fish aren't found everywhere. It is simply that every acre of water within a given area is not suitable for fish habitation. Whether it is the open sea, an enclosed lake, or a flowing river, the water area is like that of the land. There are places where land life congregates and there are places that this same life avoids, except to use as a transit zone—a highway if you want—to move from one place to another. So it is the same with fish.

It has been proved time and again that at least fifty percent—maybe even as much as seventy-five percent—of a given water area is uninhabited by fish. The fisherman must recognize this fact and fish accordingly. Don't fish blind; go to the places where fish are know to congregate, feed or pass by on a fairly predictable schedule.

It is easier to catch fish from a small rather than a large impoundment because the fisherman in moving about gets out of the unproductive water quicker than he would if fishing a huge water area. Look at it like this. A wader can completely cover the shoreline of a twenty-acre lake in the course of a morning's fishing, consequently he is bound to find someplace where the fish are active. But how about the twenty-five thousand-acre lake? How much shoreline can he cover in a morning? Or even in a full day? It works the same say for the boat fisherman as it does for the wader.

5

Fishing the Barometer

"Spect we kin git along fishin' now. They'll bite 'cause the cows are beginnin' to graze."

An old guide, as country-fied as they used to come in the Texas rolling hills country, made that remark to me many, many years ago. I was thunderstruck by the statement and thought surely he had to be jesting. But he was serious, dead serious, and right after the statement, which was really a long speech for him, he tugged at my jacket sleeve to hurry into the boat. To make a long story short, we went out on Lake Travis and proceeded to have a ball catching first largemouth bass and later white bass. Several times during the course of the fishing trip I asked the fellow why he said the fishing would be good as long as the cows grazed.

The only answer I got was: " 'cause it's jist so".

A statement like the fish will bite because the cattle are grazing is not a pronouncement one is likely to take lightly. It just raises a lot of questions that all lead up to the same word—why? I asked questions. I got some laughs and I also got some answers; some made sense, while others had to be pure nonsense.

There was just one fly in the ointment. Over the next year or so, I made several dozen bass fishing trips, and on each I made a special point to note what livestock was going in the adjacent fields. Interestinly enough I found out that in the majority of the cases that when the fish were hitting the nearby livestock was feeding too. In turn I made notes of the fishing dates, the catches, and the exact times these things occurred. Then I compared my notes with the Solunar Tables for the corresponding dates. The Solunar Tables were developed by the late John

Alden Knight and are based on sun and moon positions for a given date for given locations. He came up with a pattern of fish activity periods, which were further classified as major and minor. Over the years Knight's tables, which are still produced today by his heirs, have proven to be quite accurate. There are a lot of people who swear by the tables and fish accordingly.

Anyway, a comparison of my notes with the Knight tables showed the fish-biting-cattle-grazing periods generally coincided with the recommended fishing time times on the Solunar chart. There were exceptions, which at the time I could not explain with satisfaction. So I continued the note keeping on more fishing trips, only I added one other factor; that being the barometric pressure and its tendency on the fishing day. Again all of this information was compared with the activity periods listed in the current Knight Solunar Tables. And now I had more of the answers. The fish failed to bite and the cattle were bedded down instead of grazing during the table periods listing favorable fishing when the barometer for that particular time was (1) low and unsteady or (2) falling rapidly.

The things I'm writing about here were carried out in personal experiments back in 1946 and 1947. A lot of water has flowed into the ocean in the ensuing years, and at the same time a lot of research has enriched us with new information and knowledge. Today science recognizes as a fact the influence of atmospheric pressure on all living matter. It's a fact that people, animals, and fish tend to be most active when the barometric pressure is high and steady; loggy and sometimes depressed when the pressure is low or falling. The barometer is the instrument that tells us whether the pressure is high, normal, or low. The quick assumption to make is to go fishing when the pressure is high and stay home when it is low. That's a good assumption for a starter, but serious complications are likely to develop if other pressure variables are not taken into consideration.

Checking the barometer once a day won't do you much good, other than to let you know the pressure for a given hour on a given day. The fisherman needs to know the tendency of the pressure. Is it steady? Is it rising or falling? Is the rise or fall fast, slow, or unsteady? You get this tendency by taking barometric readings at regular intervals, say checking it every hour. Does this mean one has to check the glass—that's what seamen call the barometer—every hour of the day to get the picture for fishing? Not at all. A check over three or four hours can be sufficient for as much as a twelve- to forty-eight-hour period, but you can do this only when additional information is added to the maze. The new information is the long-range weather forecast, quickly obtainable from any weather station.

If your barometer is high and steady and the long range forecast indicates two days of good weather, it is reasonable to assume the fishing will be favorable during those two days. This kind of information is necessary if one is to plan intelligently for a weekend or even a week of fishing.

In this modern day and age there is no reason for anyone to be out of touch with civilization unless one's plane crashes in the middle of the Amazon jungle or one's ship dashes to pieces on the coral of some uncharted Pacific atoll. Radio stations the world over broadcast the weather at regular intervals. But even if your radio goes on the fritz, you can still predict the weather with reasonable accuracy if you have a barometer and its accompanying wind-velocity-wind-direction chart.

Following is the information on the standard barometer table, giving weather tendencies for various pressure-wind-direction-wind velocity variables.

In the way of explanation a wind listed as SW to NW means it is blowing *from* either the southwest or *from* the northwest. Barometric pressure is considered to be steady if there is no change over an eighteen- to twenty-four-hour period. If a small change is noted within this period, then it is either slowly rising or falling. A marked change over an eight- to twelve-hour period is described as rapidly rising or falling.

WEATHER PREDICTION TABLE

Wind direction	Barometer tendency	Probable weather
SW to NW	30.20 or above, falling slowly	Fair and clear
S to SE	30.10 to 30.20, falling slowly	Rain within 24 hours
S to SE	30.10 to 30.20, falling rapidly	Rain with increasing wind in 12 to 24 hours
SE to NE	30.10 to 30.20, falling rapidly	Rain in 12 to 18 hours
SE to NE	30.00 or below, falling slowly	No rain in summer, rain within 24 hours in winter
SE to NE	30.00 or below, falling rapidly	Rain within 24 hours in summer, rain or snow in winter
E to NE	30.10 or above, falling slowly	Rain to continue for 24 to 48 hours
E to NE	30.10 or above, falling rapidly	Rain and wind with clear and cold following in 36 hours
S to SW	30.00 or below, rising slowly	Clearing and fair for several days
S to E	29.80 or below, falling rapidly	Severe storm with clear and colder to follow in 24 hours
E to N	29.80 or below, rising rapidly	Severe gale and wind, snow and colder in winter
Going to W	29.80 or below, rising rapidly	Clearing
SW to NW	30.10 to 30.20, steady	Fair with little change for 24 to 48 hours
SW to NW	30.10 to 30.20, rising rapidly	Fair and warmer with wind in 48 hours

In addition to fishing I log a lot of outdoors time hunting waterfowl, gamebirds, and small game. Atmospheric pressure plays a dominant role in hunting, too. The game, both winged and furred, bed down and remain quite inactive on low pressure or rapidly falling pressure. This would seem to be untrue in the case of waterfowl since all popular pictures of duck and goose hunting depict the nimrod out in the foulest of weather. Foul weather and low pressure or falling pressure go hand in glove.

I've hunted waterfowl since I was twelve, not just once or twice a season but dozens of times within a season. In fact, there have been seasons when I hunted four and five weeks straight without missing a day, although in recent years I've slowed my pace to about once every three or four days. Ducks and geese do a lot of moving on low-pressure days, but only if outside influences cause them to take to wing. The outside influences are hunters. When waterfowl find sheltered waters they will stay put in the foulest of weather unless hunting pressure forces them to move. Good duck hunters know this, and they hunt the protected waters. Their shooting chases out some of the ducks, but these same birds in seeking out shelter often return to the same waters a half hour or so later. As long as sheltered areas are gunned, there will be a lot of waterfowl movement. But just note how little movement there is when there are no hunters.

Wildlife—finned, furred, and feathered—seems to have built-in barometers, for wildlife has the uncanny ability to sense weather changes and act accordingly. It has to do with the barometric pressure since it makes and controls weather.

Fish have predictable reactions to certain kinds of weather changes. Usually just a few hours before a major weather front moves through an area fish will go on a frenzied feeding binge. It seems their built-in barometer tells them rough and foul weather is coming so stock up on the vittles. That barometer, however, apparently doesn't tell them how long the weather will be foul. Otherwise why should they stock their bellies for a front that will pass in just an hour or so?

Atmospheric pressure over an area is low as long as foul or unsettled weather prevails. It might last for a few hours or for several days. Invariably when the low pressure period is lengthy and when the change comes and the pressure begins to climb like a 727 reaching for altitude, fish react by going on new feeding sprees. The old salts who fish our coastal water know this, and they are the first ones out to wet lines immediately after the passage of a storm or hurricane. I have had some fantastic fishing experiences resulting from going fishing as soon as the weather cleared following the passage of hurricanes on the Texas coast.

It certainly behooves the fisherman to time his fishing jaunts to coincide with periods before and after major weather changes. One has to partake to really believe just how wild and fantastic fishing can be in these before-and-after-the-storm periods. Writing about them doesn't do justice at all.

6

The Right Temperature

Temperature is important in fishing, although I don't feel it is so all important as some fisherman make it to be. By way of illustration, I know some largemouth bass fishermen who won't wet a line unless they can find a depth at which the water temperature is exactly sixty-eight degrees, which is generally considered to be the temperature at which bass feed most often. Personally I feel this temperature angle can be stretched a little both ways. Referring back to personal experiences with largemouth bass, I have enjoyed excellent catches in water in the temperature range of sixty-five to seventy-five degrees. I have found that the more one goes below sixty-five or above seventy-five degrees, the more sluggish the fish become.

The colder or warmer the water, the longer the lapse of time between feeding forages. When the fish do feed, they are slow and pickish. They barely nibble at the bait, and when lures are involved, they just seem to bump them with their noses. You can catch fish under these conditions, but you must be alert and really work at the fishing. In the case of cold the fish become sluggish and do little moving around. On the other end of the scale and where warm water is involved, fish are reluctant to feed but they move around considerably, apparently seeking out water levels where the temperature is more to their liking.

You can stick your hand in the water and decide whether it is too warm or too cold for good fishing. I've done this many times, but while I think the system has merit, I feel it may be more of a crutch a fellow uses as an excuse not to go out when it is cold or hot. We Americans have a strong tendency to rationalize excuses for not doing things. It would be so much easier to say "I don't feel like going fishing" and letting it go at that. Instead we have to do it the hard way, and just why I don't know.

So much for the dip-your-hand-in-the-water system. It has merit and will serve as a workable guide if you're without scientific means of determining water temperature. The serious fisherman, however, ought to invest in a thermometer that will give him exact information on the waters he fishes. Don't expect to do wonders with the ordinary garden-variety thermometer. It will suffice to give you an accurate reading for the surface water, but how about five, ten, fifteen, or more feet down?

Water is like the air above in that the temperature varies. The air is warmest at ground or sea level; it gets colder the higher one goes. Water is generally warmest at its surface and then gets cooler the deeper one goes. Temperature changes cause expansion and contraction. Water expands as it warms; contracts as it cools. As water contracts it becomes "heavy" and sinks; hence cold water is found down deep. This, however, is true only up to 39.5 degrees Fahrenheit. When water begins to get colder than 39.5 degrees, it begins to expand and get lighter. It comes to the surface, and if the temperature keeps dropping, it eventually becomes ice.

In a given body of water, one can find layers with different temperatures, and in the case of flowing water and currents in our oceans and seas, some of these layers stand out in bold relief to the fellow who uses instruments to measure temperatures at various depths. I can illustrate this with some temperature readings I made on Toledo Bend Reservoir, Texas' biggest manmade lake, in the early fall of 1972. The temperature from surface to five feet down was eighty degrees. Then came a three-foot layer of seventy-nine-degree water, and under this was a six-foot layer of seventy-six-degree water. The water was forty feet deep and on the bottom the temperature was seventy-four degrees. Several years earlier I took some temperature readings in the channel at the entrance to Galveston, Texas, harbor. The water was thirty-five feet deep. Except for a five-foot-thick current wending through the channel about fifteen feet down, the temperature from surface to bottom was seventy-eight degrees. The temperature in that five-foot-thick current was seventy-four degrees.

Obviously you can't get these temperature differences at various depths without devices manufactured expressly for this kind of work. There are a number of fish thermometers on the market, and depending upon their complexities, they range in price from about twenty-five dollars to one hundred dollars. For general fishing the twenty-five dollar battery-operated models do a good job.

How often does one take the water temperature? This depends upon the body of water—standing or moving—and how often the fisherman moves. Temperatures are likely to change frequently when moving water is involved, and doubly so when the fisherman himself does a lot of moving. One may have to take several readings an hour. Where waters are still a reading every few hours will suffice.

Now let's take a hypothetical case. Your start fishing in the morning, and up until midmorning the air temperature is a pleasant seventy-five degrees. And then in comes a norther that drops the air temperature over the next two hours to sixty degrees. What happens to the water? The first water to be affected will be at the surface, but it won't cool nearly so rapidly as the air. In fact, it probably won't drop more than a degree or two in the time you're fishing. A more appreciable drop is not likely until the following day.

It's important to know the temperature range within which the fish you seek are likely to be most active. This knowledge can save you a lot of time, money, wear, and tear.

Except when legislation sets seasons on certain species, fish seasons in general are determined by the temperature. One can catch Spanish mackerel, king mackerel, and billfish the year around in the tropical waters lapping Central America, but as one travels north first into the Gulf of Mexico and then up the Atlantic Seaboard, these same fish become seasonal, the length of which depends upon how far north one ventures. In the Gulf of Mexico and Atlantic waters bordering Florida, the season on these fish roughly spans six months. It shortens considerably in the more northern waters of the Atlantic.

Another point to consider about the species mentioned is that they are fish that feed on or quite near the surface. This makes them far more susceptible to minor weather changes than are the fish species that roam the bottom. I have caught Spanish mackerel day after day just a few miles off the Texas coast. Then along comes a light summer norther. It may only drop surface water temperature a couple of degrees, but that drop, slight as it may be, can stop mackerel runs as effectively as closing the window shuts out the rain.

A long winter can delay the start of the migratory fish runs in temperate zone waters just as an early fall can cut off these runs prematurely. For years the old salts at Galveston, Texas, my birthplace and home, always predicted the season's first good Spanish mackerel run to come on Easter. And, you know, except for those Easters when waters were too rough for boats to venture out, Galveston had the predicted mackerel runs. This prediction began to hold true less and less with the beginning of the sixties. In the early sixties the mackerel runs used to start about a week after Easter, by the time the seventies rolled around, the start was closer to two weeks after Easter. It all dovetails with what scientists and weather experts have been saying all along—we're seeing a cooling trend, perhaps even a return to an ice age in the far distant future.

Vexilar, Inc., manufacturer of electronic fishing gear such as thermometers, fathometers, and allied sonar devices, has compiled a list of preferred feeding temperatures for a number of saltwater and freshwater fish. The following tabulation lists fish species, the preferred feeding temperature according to Vexilar's reference sources, and the temperature ranges within which I have consistently caught the same fish species. Blanks on some species indicate either Vexilar or I have no readings.

Several electronics fishing gear manufacturers offer thermometers with sensors that can be pushed down a fish's throat and right into its stomach to take a reading. Then the sensor is lowered over the side until it reaches a depth where the temperature is the same as that recorded in the fish's stomach. This, then, is the depth at which to fish.

Fish species	Vexilar preferred feeding temperature	Personal range of consistent catches
Albacore	64	62–72
Amberjack	65	65–80
Barracuda	67	65–80
Bigeye	58	—
Billfish	58	55–85
Bluefish	68	68–75
Bluegill	69	68–80
Blue marlin	74	—
Bonita	64	65–75
Brook trout	50	55–65
Brown trout	50	48–52
Calico bass	65	60–68
Channel bass	—	55–60
Channel catfish	72	70–80
Chinook	54	52–56
Cod	45	40–50
Coho	54	50–60
Crappie	65	65–75
Cutthroats	47	45–50
Dolphin	75	72–80
Flounder	67	65–70
Arctic grayling	—	40–44
Jack crevalle	—	75–85
Kelp bass	65	—
Kokanee	50	—
Lake trout	47	45–50
Largemouth bass	68	65–75
Mackerel, Spanish	—	78–85
Mackerel, king	—	78–85
Muskelunge	63	60–70
Northern pike	63	50–70
Panfish	65	65–80
Permit	65	65–75
Pollack	45	—
Pompano	—	70–80
Rainbow trout	47	45–50
Red snapper	57	55–75
Salmon	52	—
Sauger	58	—
Sharks	70+	70–95
Skipjack	73	70–80
Smallmouth bass	62	62–70
Smelt	50	—
Splake	49	—
Sockeye	52	—
Steelhead	47	45–50
Striped bass	55	55–60
Sturgeon	66	—
Tuna	73	70–75
Walleye	58	55–70
White bass	70	70–75
White marlin	68	—
White sea bass	67	65–70
Yellowfin tuna	67	65–70
Yellow perch	68	65–70
Yellow tail	65	65–70

7
Fishing Natural Baits

You can't catch fish without bait on the hooks, a statement almost but not quite one hundred percent true. Occasionally fish do strike bright, shiny hooks absolutely naked of any vestiges of bait. True, there is no bait on the hooks attached to an artificial lure, but here is a case where the lure itself, both in appearance and in action, is made to resemble something the fish takes as food. How to catch fish on lures is discussed in the chapter "Fishing with Lures." Right now the topic is how to fish successfully with natural baits.

Again we must go back to the basics of knowing your game. If a fish's main diet is one thing, and you insist on using something different for bait, you have only yourself to blame for poor pickings. Let's take a saltwater and a freshwater fish as examples. First the sheepshead in salt water. It will take a number of different baits, but if one wants to catch them by the dozens, then go with their favorite—the little sand fiddler crab. Fresh water catfish are occasionally caught on minnows and worms, but if you want to catch them by the dozens, then go with those dough stink baits.

When one mentions fishing with natural baits, one visions shrimp, squid, and various minnows and mullet for salt water, and minnows, crawdads, and worms for freshwater fishing. These are by far the most popular and most easily obtainable baits, but in reality they are only starters in the game. There are a lot of other baits that are far more effective for certain species of fish. Let me illustrate the point with Gulf Coast flounder fishing. Each year in later September and extending well into November, flounders mass on the bottom of cuts and channels

connecting Texas and Louisiana bays with the open Gulf of Mexico. These flatfish are caught by slowly dragging the bait across the bottom. They can be caught by slowly dragging the bait across the bottom. They can be caught on either live shrimp or live mudfish as bait. At the time of this writing live shrimp sold for four dollars a quart with the count running about seventy-five to the quart. The tariff on live mudfish at the same time was a dollar a dozen. It takes neither a mathematical genius nor a computer to show that live mudfish cost twice as much as live shrimp. So on this basis it would appear flounder fishing with shrimp is the most economical way to go. Not so. The flounder runs occur at a time when waters are still warm enough to teem with persistent baitstealers like hardhead catfish, porgies, etc. These creatures dearly love to feed on shrimp, and you may find yourself feeding baitstealers instead of catching flounders.

These same nuisance fish don't truck with the mudfish, hence your bait gets down to where the flounder action is and you come home with a hefty stringer of flatfish. My flounder fishing buddies and I figure on using three mudfish or ten shrimp for every flatfish landed. There is no argument about which is the most economical way to go.

If it is necessary to fish with live bait, the fisherman must know how to handle the bait or be prepared to see a lot of it die before it ever gets near the hook.

So this makes the container the starter. It should be clean and free of rust, paint, or chemical residue, or bits of dead bait from the last trip. Personally I recommend plastic containers instead of metal.

Metals rust or corrode, and any such abrasive spots inside the container will cost you bait. Minnows and shrimp swimming around in the container will suffer cuts or bruises when they scrape against these rough spots. Often these injuries are serious enough to cause death. You won't have this problem with a plastic container.

How large a container is big enough? My rule of thumb is to figure bait capacity at about sixty percent of what the container manufacturer recommends. If the bucket says one hundred-minnow capacity, I'm going to only put in sixty, maybe seventy-five if they are unusually small. One of the main reasons bait dies in the container is overcrowding. Whether the bait is shrimp or minnows, overcrowding causes the inmates to become frantic. They dart about bruising each other and using up oxygen at an abnormal rate.

There are chemical actions and mechanical means of putting oxygen into the water. There are several brands of chemicals molded in tablet form that when dropped into the water release steady streams of oxygen. Even better are the little aerators that operate off flashlight batteries. These are highly efficient little pumps that drive a good supply of oxygen into the water. A fresh battery has sufficient juice to run one of these aerators for approximately twenty-four hours. The costs vary from three to eight dollars, depending upon the make of aerator. I bought a five-dollar model that gave me six years of hard service before finally giving up the ghost.

If you can't find any of the chemical oxygen tablets and your aerator goes on the fritz, you can still salvage the situation to some extent by dropping some ice cubes into the container. The lower water temperature will cause the bait to become less restless and as a result use up less oxygen. A word of warning about the use of ice. Don't dump a lot into the container all at once. Try to lower the temperature gradually, for a sharp, sudden temperature change either up or down can kill every inmate in the bucket.

When arriving at the fishing spot, the impulse is to quickly change the water in the container, filling it with a fresh supply from the waters in which you plan to fish. This is the right move to make, but only if the temperature of the water is close to that of the water in the container. If there is a marked difference, put the entire container in the lake or sea and allow it to gradually go up or down to level off with the outside water temperature. Needless to say this will not work with flow-through containers. It is better to put the container in the water at the side of the boat rather than at the stern. You don't want any fuel drippings from the engine to contaminate your bait container.

In transportation as well as on the fishing grounds, one should frequently check the container for dead baits. Remove them immediately, for as soon as they die, they begin to decompose and foul the water within the container. This can trigger a chain reaction that can kill everything in the bucket. This is especially true in the case of shrimp. Curiously shrimp are cannibalistic. When they feed on their dead kin, something stirs them to go on killing sprees. They will spike their neighbors and feast on them. If a fisherman is to be so careless as to let this happen, he might as well just buy dead shrimp to start off with and save money.

Galveston, Texas, sports fisherman Vince Stiglich Jr., shows how to hold a castnet in preparation for casting. These nets are popular for getting small baitfish.

Dip bait out of the container with a minnow or some sort of bait net. Don't use your bare hand. You can knock about and injure the bait, or if your hand should come in contact with the outboard motor, you may get contaminating oil and gas in the container. The results will be sure death for all the bait.

When fishing with live bait, the size of the bait should always be matched to the size of the hook.

Use small hooks for small baits. After all, the purpose of using live bait is to have the shrimp or minnow dance about lively to stir nearby fish into action. Don't shackle this action with a big, heavy hook.

Be gentle in placing live bait on the hook, and don't bury the hook in any vital part of the body or head. You want the bait to remain alive and kicking as long as possible. Live shrimp can be hooked just under the spike atop the creature's head or through the second or third body section from the tail. Live minnows can be hooked through both lips; through the fleshy part of the back just behind the dorsal fin, exercising care not to strike the backbone; or through the fleshy part of the body immediately ahead of the tail.

The fruits of a well-thrown castnet. These small mullet make excellent live bait.

Properly thrown castnet opens in a circle. Leadline causes it to sink rapidly to trap marine life.

Now we come to the part of casting the bait out to where you hope the fish are. If you cast in the accepted manner of flipping out an artificial lure, you're going to snap the live bait right off the hook. So you must exercise care in the cast by starting it slowly and then building up speed with more of a swinging motion than a pure casting motion.

Live bait can cost three to four times more than corresponding dead bait of the same species. Whether to go live or dead bait, however, depends upon the fish species sought. Use as an example the spotted weakfish, also called speckled trout, in salt water. These fine gamefish dearly love shrimp, but they go for the live ones quicker than dead shrimp. Put two fishermen of equal ability fishing side by side, one using live shrimp and the other dead, and invariably the fellow using the live shrimp will outcatch his buddy several times over. Here, then,

is another case of the most economical fishing being that of using the more expensive bait.

Most of our gamefish, fresh water as well as salt, prey on live creatures. This means they become accustomed to feeding on fresh, firm matter. Most species that feed by scent, and certainly all of the scavangers, food primarilly on dead matter. Consequently this means the gamefish angler will score most often using live bait, and the fellow seeking the scent-feeders will do best with dead bait. This is true only up to a point in seeking the gamefish. The exception comes in trolling for the billfish and offshore big game fish. There is just no way of trolling a live bait and keeping it alive. In this kind of fishing a whole dead fish is threaded on and then sewed on the hook in such a manner that it will appear to be alive when trolled through the water.

Let's go back to those species that are likely to take either live or dead bait, and analyize why better results are had on the live bait. First off, as soon as marine life dies, it rapidly decomposes with all the vile odors that emanate from decaying flesh. This in itself will repell a lot of gamefish species. Only sharks and the true scavangers seem to enjoy dining on such putrid matter. So we have in the case of dead

Live shrimp should be hooked just under the horn on the top of the creature's head. This will permit the shrimp to swim in a natural manner.

bait scent alone the attracting factor for fish. You have scent with live bait, too, only it is the normal fresh marine scent and not that of decaying matter. Examine a little closer and you have two other plus factors working for you. The live shrimp, minnows, or worms also attract fish through sight. Their movements catch the attention of the fish and it fins over to investigate. Even if the live bait is too far from the fish to be seen, it is still effective, this time through sound. Shrimp make a crackling sound when they jump through the water, and frantically swimming minnows set up vibrations. A fish through its lateral lines, which in effect are built-in

sonar, can pick up these cracklings and vibrations and then home in to the source.

There will be times when live bait can't be obtained for love or money. Then we must resort to dead bait or artificial lures, and since some people are inept at lure fishing, they must use dead bait or stay at home. The fisherman then must thread the bait on the hook in such a manner that when retrieved through the water it will "act alive." He should also keep the bait well iced until each piece is put to use. This way he can stall decomposition.

Natural baits, whether alive or dead, can be made more effective through the use of chum, which is nothing more than scattering extra marine fodder into the water. It can come in the form of tossing out a couple of extra baits every now and then. A more effective way is to have a chum bag or chum pot. The subject of chumming is covered in detail in the chapter entitled "Chumming for Fish."

Next to the minnow the most popular freshwater bait is the lowly worm, the night crawler that may range from a couple of inches to six or eight inches in length. Properly cared for these rascals can be kept for days. Naturally care means feeding the creatures. No problem here, for there are worm feeds available in many tackle stores. The worms are kept in a container filled with a compound known as "worm bedding." This, too, can be purchased at most tackle houses. This bedding must be kept moist, not soaking wet, and must be protected from temperature extremes, particularly excessive heat. A hour of direct sunlight can kill every worm in the bucket.

There is an art to threading a live worm on the hook. Many fishermen mistakenly try to spike the hook through the worm in several places and attempt to cover most of the hook itself with the worm. This is incorrect. Drive the hook through the worm once, the place of entry of the hook being about a third of the way back from the worm's head. If care is taken not to make a big hole or tear the worm's body when inserting the hook, there need be no worry about it slipping back over the barb and escaping. A worm so impaled on the hook will be a lively fellow, and that's what you want to attract fish. The worm spiked in a half dozen places and wrapped around the hook like a boa constrictor won't be very active and will have considerably less fish-appeal than the more wiggly fellow.

8

Fishing with Lures

Lure Fishing was the third book I wrote. It was completed after almost two years of research, and during that time there were several occasions when I was on the verge of scraping the whole project. Why?

Because what I knew to be true kept coming out in various shades of gray. I have always contended that all artificial lures will catch fish. There is no question that some are better fish catchers than others, but nevertheless all will catch fish. In seeking to prove this point in print I kept running into a facet that as a result of research eventually became a fact. This fact is pure and simple: artificial lures often catch more fishermen than fish. Of course, in order for a lure to catch fish, it must first catch the fisherman. The trouble here is that the catching bit too frequently ends with just the fisherman being caught. The lure's life is shortstopped by infrequently or never reaching the water.

The book *Lure Fishing* has been accepted as a reference on artificial bait fishing. While it expounded the whys and wherefores of fishing with artificial lures, the book did not detail some of the diseases that plague lure fishing. These diseases—all in the "itis" family—stop a lot of fishermen from using lures.

The diseases generally in order of severity are (1) change-itis, (2) retrieve-itis, and (3) cast-itis. Even though the meanings of the illnesses ought to be self-evident, each requires a few words to make the meanings explicit. Learn to recognize these diseases, avoid getting them, and you will catch fish.

Start with change-itis. The fellow afflicted with this one has several tackle boxes, all chocked full with assorted lures in all colors of the rainbow. He opens a tackle box at his feet, ties on a lure, and starts to fish it. If he doesn't catch anything or have any strikes after a dozen or so casts, he decides to switch to a different color or a different type lure entirely. Again a dozen or so casts, no fish or strikes, and he resorts to another lure change. This goes on all day long, and maybe the guy even catches a few fish. But look at what is happening. He is wasting time changing lures, snipping this one off and tying that one on. This uses up valuable fishing time, and there is one truth in fishing that has never been proved otherwise—you can't catch fish unless the hook is in the water. Change-itis is an admission to not having faith in a lure, and without faith a fellow just doesn't put his all into fishing. Successful fishing is not a lazy man's sport; it is work, often hard and at times quite trying.

By all means use different kinds of lures, but always give a lure a long and fair trial before switching.

Retrieve-itis is that ailment common to the fellow who only partially fishes out a cast. He flips his lure out to a likely spot, fishes it for fifteen or twenty feet of the retrieve and then completely changes styles and makes like the Kentucky Derby in swiftly reeling in the lure. The proper way to fish a lure is to work it all the way back to the boat, pier, or wader as the case may be. Often a fish will be hesitant in striking until it sees the lure about to be pulled into the shadow of the boat or pier. This often galvanizes fish into action, and the finny creatures charge in to grab the lure before it escapes. This is very unlikely to happen with a racehorse retrieve.

The largemouth bass is America's No. One freshwater gamefish. More lures are used for seeking the bass than any other fish species either in fresh water or salt water.

Retrieve-itis is an admission to not having patience, which happens to be an absolute must for successful fishing.

Cast-itis is a malady spawned by retrieve-itis, only with this one the fisherman is hell-bent on getting in a lot of casts. When cast-itis is in full bloom, the lure spends as much time flying through the air as it does being retrieved through the water. Usually the victim of this disease delights himself in being able to make long casts, a lot of casts, and accurate casts. But he gets few fish because he fishes too fast. He could have amused himself much easier and at less expense by casting a practice plug on the front lawn.

Cast-itis is in effect an admission of indecision, restlessness, and an awful lack of knowledge about fishing.

So much for the diseases connected with lure fishing. Learn to recognize them so you can take the necessary remedies when any or all show signs of creeping into your fishing style. It can happen, and I have seen it happen even to old pros. It is most likely to happen when the fishing action is dreadfully slow

to the point of frustration, a feeling that frequently commits us to actions later regretted. Where veteran fishermen are concerned these maladies are more temporary, maybe for a day or part of a trip. Unfortunately those illnesses can be fatal where beginners are concerned. The illnesses spell few or no fish for the fisherman, and consistent and repeated waterhauls can kill one's interest in fishing.

Successful fishing with lures is a combination of knowing fish characteristics and habits, their likes and dislikes, their moods, and finally trying to think like a fish. To me lure fishing is a supreme challenge, a head-to-head confrontation in which I'm trying to outwit the fish. It is all different from fishing with natural bait, which has smell, taste, and feel appeal to the fish. The artificial lure is made of hard, inanimate objects and materials completely foreign to fish. It is a useless piece of hardware until you put life into it with your rod and reel.

Successful lure fishing is like good poker playing—your head in the game all the time. You can't cast haphazardly and retrieve in the same manner and expect to score well. You must fish out every cast and every retrieve; in fact, think fish on every turn of the reel handle.

Skilled lure fishermen can manipulate their outfits in such manners as to create a minimum of commotion when their lures strike the water. This is very important. The splash of the hardware striking the water is sudden and often harsh. The noise can startle nearby fish, and if the water is shallow, any fish that bolt in fright start a chain reaction that results in all fish in the immediate area taking off helter-skelter. This initial fright is not quickly forgotten, and the fisherman who fails to recognize this will begin to work his lure at a time when odds are against productivity. Better he should allow the lure to rest motionless for a few minutes, hoping to permit any fish remaining in the immediate area time to overcome that initial scare. Then when he does begin to fish the lure, it should be slow and gentle. Remember you must give fish time to locate the source of the sound and then swim in close enough to make visual contact. Any hurried lure retrieve would simply bring the hardware back to the fisherman and out of the water before the fish moves within striking range.

The American public, and especially the male, has a peculiar habit of buying a product, putting it to work, and then at some later date getting around to reading the directions. Usually they skip reading the directions as long as the product works properly. And so it is with artificial lures. A fellow plunks his money down for a new plug, spoon, or whatever. He ties it on the end of his line and starts fishing.

Eventually, maybe the same day or perhaps a week later, he gets around to reading the printed instructions on the lure container. It is not unusual for a fellow to discover that he has been working the lure improperly. No wonder his fishing success was so limited. Lure manufacturers don't furnish printed instructions just to take up blank space on the box. They spend a lot of time and often large sums of money in dies and molding equipment to manufacture their products. They want their lures to catch fish; this is the only way they can stay in business. So the first thing a fellow should do when he buys a new type of lure is to read the directions. Discover within the space of a few minutes what the lure manufacturer had to learn the hard way in weeks, months, even years, of testing, redesigning and retesting.

Where freshwater fishing is concerned casting accuracy is extremely important when using artificial lures. Here the aim of the game is to plunk the hardware immediately adjacent to a spot where you have reason to believe a gamefish is lurking. A short cast creates an unnecessary disturbance and puts the fisherman at the disadvantage of having to make a second cast, room for another error. A cast beyond the target is less troublesome since the retrieve will bring the lure back near or over the desired spot. The trouble here comes when the too long cast puts your hardware fast on the shoreline, in a brushpile, looped over a cypress knee, or stuck in the side of a drowned tree. A fellow discovers the importance of accuracy and cast control when he fishes for largemouth bass in some of our southern states' drowned-timber lakes. You have to fish them to really believe the mazes of tangles. But if you want to get into big bass, these are the places where the big bucket-mouths hang out.

There is less of a premium on casting accuracy in saltwater fishing. A degree of accuracy is necessary, but of more importance is the ability to make distance casts. You're fishing big waters here, and you'll need to cover as much as you can, since saltwater species range over wider areas than do their freshwater cousins.

It used to be that lures were attractive to fish in two ways—sight and sound. Science and kissing cousin chemistry have added another—scent or smell. Some lures today are treated with fish-appealing odors that become activated when the hardware is immersed in water. In addition there are marketed today many fish-appealing solutions that can be dabbed or sprayed on lures. Contrary to the claims of some makers, these solutions are no guarantees that fish will be taken. They do have merit, however, and I have used a number of them

with favorable results. If they do no more than mask out human smells, this in itself is a success.

It goes without saying that for a lure to be seen, the water must be clear. It is in this respect that lure effectiveness is most seriously curtailed. If the water is not reasonably clear, there is no point in attempting to use lures that attract by sight. The scented ones are a little better but really not a whole lot if the fish can't see the darned thing. If one must go with hardware in murky waters, then do so with noisemaker lures. These can set up enough commotion and appealing sounds to attract fish from considerable distances. They must, however, be fished slow in order to give the fish time to locate them. My experience with using noisemakers in off-colored waters has been better results in small, confined impoundments rather than spacious lakes or the open sea. My personal feeling is that on the big waters any noises the lure makes are lost in the conglomeration of other noises in the water. The sea is not silent by a long shot. Personally I feel the sounder approach to fishing murky water is to go with natural baits rather than artificial lures.

The noisemakers—these are the lures with propellers, saucered·or dished fronts, spinner blades, inverted lips, etc.—are extremely effective fish-getters if fishermen bother to understand what happens to sound in water. It is pointed out in the chapter on "The Senses" how water, because it is so much denser than air, actually magnifies sound. This means that a fish does not have to be real close to the source of the sound to either hear or feel it. The unfortunate thing about using noisemakers is that the fishermen themselves often become too engrossed with entertaining themselves with what they consider to be fish-attracting noises.

Consider a hypothetical case. The fisherman is using a chugger—a plug that when jerked makes a distinct "chug" sound in the water. By varying the amount of force applied to the rod in manipulating this lure, the noise can be made to range from what could be called a rather seductive "loop" to a loud and distinct "vop." That "vop" magnified by the density of the water can sound like an explosion to a closeby fish. It is just the kind of noise that can disturb the quiet calm to make fish head for more open waters. Yet keep in mind that this "vop" is the same noise fish make when they strike savagely at surface targets. If there happens to be a school of fish wildly engaged in surface feeding, that "vop" is just what you want. But you don't want it when the surface is calm and quiet and certainly not at the very start of the retrieve. Start the noise-making with subdued, seductive sounds, operating on the assumption that your lure plunked into the water

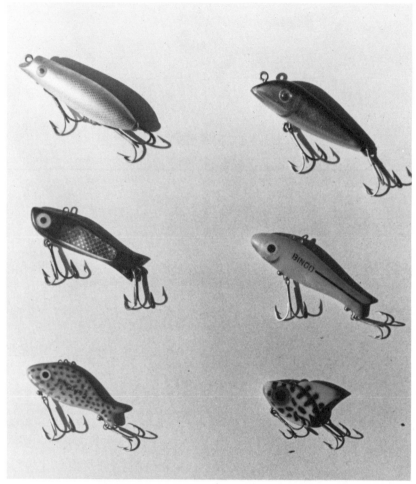

This is an assortment of plugs used for lure fishing. Long plugs have a slow wiggle, while short ones have a violent wiggle.

just a few feet from the fish. Then increase the action and the noises as the lure is worked in. If you need a parallel, consider how much more pleasant the start of a day is when you awake to the music of the clock radio as opposed to being startled by the sharp, harsh chatter of an old-fashioned alarm clock.

There's an old East Texas fishing guide who puts it even more succinctly: "It's like courtin'. Start off easy and don't rush it."

Successful and established lure manufacturers got that way because they put a good product on the market. They spend a lot of time and money in developing lures that produce results. The best lure, however, ceases to be a thoroughbred when the fisherman starts making uncalled-for modifications, the first being how the lure is attached to the line. A snap or a snap-swivel at the end of the leader can make lure-changing fast and easy. This extra bit of terminal hardware, however, can seriously affect the action of the lure. If the lure is meant to be fished

with a snap, snap-swivel, line-connecter, or any other such device, it will be plainly so stated on the instruction sheet, or the lure will come with the device already attached. When lure hooks break or rust and need to be changed, they should be replaced with hooks of identical size. Weight differences in replacement hooks can throw a lure off balance and upset its action.

Now to the case of leaders and lures. Some artificials can be used with wire leaders; others cannot because the stiffness of the wire impedes lure action. In between all of this come the many shades of gray. The plugs, spoons, and jigs that catch largemouth bass—a species that requires no wire leader—will also take such toothy creatures as northern pike, lake trout, and muskelunge in fresh water and members of the mackerel clan in salt water. These latter mentioned species require wire leaders. So what is the fisherman to do? Compromise by using a leader as short as possible—six to

43

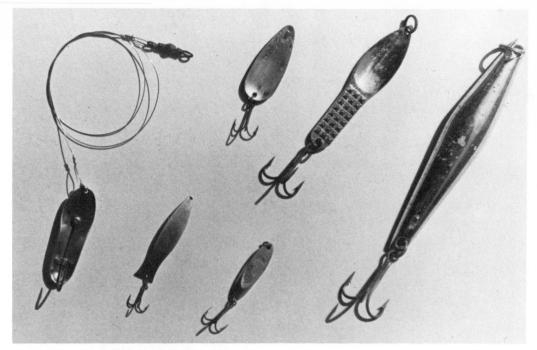

Spoons come in all shapes and sizes. Although some spin upon retrieve, most are designed to wobble. Spoon at left rigged with wire leader is for fishing for sharp-toothed fish.

Jigs have become increasingly popular, especially in salt-water fishing. The two large ones are for offshore trolling, while the two small ones at the bottom are for shallow-water fishing.

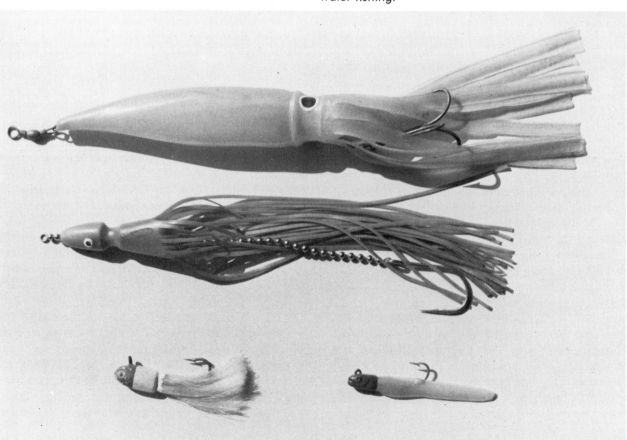

eight inches—and using a leader of braided wire that is plastic coated instead of stiffer, single-strand wire. The stiffness and added weight of the leader will affect the action of the lure, but this can be minimized by going to larger-size lures. Today most lure manufacturers put out the same type of lures in a number of sizes. In making these compromises, the fisherman will have to experiment to come up with the most suitable combination. You will run into cases where lures will work effectively on a six-inch wire leader but not on anything longer.

There are no hard and fast rules to cover the situation.

There are times when it pays to fish combination lure-natural-bait rigs. Balao sewed on a hook and nosed with a feathered jig makes an extremely good trolling bait for billfish. The same kind of rig is good for mackerel, bonito, and barracuda, only instead of balao the natural bait is either mullet or strips of cutlassfish. Spoons are ofter rigged with strips cut from the bellies of panfish.

9

The Plastic Worm

The plastic worm—it deserves a chapter all of its own.

The plastic worm: it's a blessing; it's a curse. It all depends upon who is doing the fishing, the experience of the fisherman, and finally his temperament. One has to have the right disposition for fishing, otherwise he'll never make it with the plastic worm. Disposition in this case amounts to persistence and patience. You can't go with just one or the other; you need both when plastic worm fishing is involved.

Without a doubt the plastic worm is the greatest largemouth bass lure to ever hit the market. It will dig out lunker bass when the only other way would be to drop hand grenades over the side. But a fellow has to know how to fish that wiggly sliver of plastic to give it the right appeal to attract fish. If he is heavy-handed and lacks finesse, that same worm is a curse.

Today's plastic worm is a far cry from its prototype of many years earlier. Today's wiggly not only comes in the rainbow of colors and almost as many lengths, but it also looks, feels, smells, and tastes like the real thing. A bass doesn't need any imagination where the plastic worm is involved. Why, then, if this thing is so all-fired real is it so difficult for some folks to fish?

The answer seems to lie in how the bass takes this bait.

In the early days of plastic worm fishing, the accepted technique was to throw the reel into free spool when the fisherman felt a pickup. One of the first magazine articles I marketed on worm fishing was built around the theme "count five, then strike." The technique here was to allow the fish to run with the worm for a few seconds before attempting to set the hook. The "count five, then strike" theme wasn't mine. I picked it up from guides. The system worked, but it didn't have a high batting average. I would guess I hooked about one out of every ten pickups. That's a pretty lousy average, but when you have situations where the bass hit nothing else offered, then one out of ten is like money in the bank.

During the ensuing years a lot of study went into worm fishing. Folks experimented with bass in aquariums. Some of the more adventuresome researchers went down in diving gear right into bass habitat and watched proceedings. And they made a startling discovery—a bass doesn't take the worm in the same manner in which it strikes other baits. When it came to baits like minnows, crawdads, and small panfish, bass struck savagely. A sudden strike and gulp the victim was gone, apparently right down into the fish's belly. It wasn't that way at all with the worm, plastic as well as real. Instead of striking hard, the bass picked up the worm, sometimes quite gently, by the tail and rather slowly ingested it. The fish very obviously did not swallow the worms immediately, for in many cases, the fish spit the whole thing out after a few seconds. Something was wrong to make the fish reject the bait. Sometimes the fish came back to pick it up a second time; more often it just swam off and left the worm alone.

The observations quite obviously pointed out that a "count five" or for that matter any count before striking was the wrong way to go about it. No wonder I used to miss nine out of ten pickups. The recommended technnique today is to strike and strike hard when you feel a pickup. None of this waiting around, for it only allowed the fish to spit out the bait. I still miss pickups but no longer on a ratio of nine out of ten.

Now why should the fish grab some kinds of baits savagely and another kind almost gingerly?

I can only give an opinion on this. All of the marine life picked up in a sudden strike and gulped straight to the belly had mobility. It could move fairly fast and was capable of taking evasive actions. Now look at the worm, night crawler, or whatever you call the wiggly. It does a lot of wiggling, but none of it is fast. It can move about in the water, but its movements are rather slow with no evasive darting whatsoever. In short, the bass does not have to grab the worm quickly. The worm just doesn't move fast enough to escape. So the fish can take its time. Perhaps the fish savors the taste in its mouth, and this may be the reason the worm, sometimes even a live one, is rejected and spit out.

Good results in worm fishing call for knowing how to thread the plastic on the hook. Before tying the hook on the line, slide a slip sinker (worm sinker) up the line. Be sure the point of the sinker faces toward the rod tip. Many worm sinkers on the market today are hollowed out a bit at the butt so they nestle neatly against the worm head. Insert the hook about a half inch into the worm head, entering at the center top. Extend the barb out through the middle of the side of the head and make sure that the hook eye is imbedded about a quarter inch into the worm head. Now turn the hook around until the barb faces the worm and insert the barb into the body. This gives you a weedless lure, and this is important when you have to fish the worm down in drowned timber stands and brush tangles. When the barb is inserted into the body it should be in a straight up-and-down position. Make sure the worm is kept in a straight line from head to where the barb is inserted. Twisted or S-shaped rigs only cause the worm to spin unnaturally when retrieved.

When you fish the worm, always keep in mind how a worm moves in the water. It crawls slowly on the bottom, along brush limbs, over rocks, etc. It moves at a speed best described as snail-pace. If there is a current running, let it carry the worm along. You need all the patience of Job and a little more to be a success at plastic worm fishing.

Perserverence comes when you have a pickup and miss setting the hook. Usually the snatching away of the worm in the attempt to set the hook will spook the fish to some degree, and that fish might refuse to have any more to do with your worm. So what should you do? Go on the assumption that the bass isn't alone. Figure he or she, as the case may be, has company. The game here then is to get the company interested in the worm. When it comes to lunker largemouth bass—fish generally in excess of six pounds—there is seldom more than one or two in a given hole or around a particular brush pile or stump. It's a different story with the school-size fish of a pound to two pounds. I've caught as many as forty-five all on plastic worms on a single trip and all from the same hole. School bass sometimes mass in almost unbelievable numbers. Let me point out that when you get into such situations, the fish generally abandon caution and aggressively strike the worms, often hard enough to hook themselves. Apparently they do so to beat the competition to the goodies. In all fairness, however, let me point out that such situations are uncommon.

I prefer to catch my bass on lures other than the plastic worm. The most fun with largemouth bass is when they are taken on flyrods with popping bugs. Next in line for thrills is catching them on surface plugs, then spinners, next the floating-diving plugs, deep-runners, and spoons. When it comes to furnishing thrills—and this is a personal opinion—the plastic worm runs dead last.

To begin with, the worm is the only artificial lure that can be fished in brush tangles on the bottom, which happens to be where bass usually lurk. When you hook a fish in that tangle, you have to pull it clear in a hurry, otherwise it is certain to swim around a snag. So this means fishing with a stout rod—they call them "lunker sticks"—and heavy test line. You feel a pickup, sock it to the fish to bed the hook, and then reel furiously to snatch the fish away from the brush. The heavy gear doesn't allow the fish much opportunity to display its fighting tactics. The largemouth bass is one species you never have to worry about ripping the hook out of its mouth with too much pulling and jerking. This fish has a mouth with flesh like boot leather; bed the hook and it will stay.

All of this doesn't mean that I don't use plastic worms. If conditions dictate using the worm, I go with it and the heck with the other lures. I just like to catch fish.

When the plastic worm made its debut, it was offered in only about a half dozen colors. The early preference was natural finish because fishermen figured a thing so lifelike as to action and feel should be even more alluring to bass if the color was that of its real live counterpart. As worm fishing became more of an art, a rule of thumb came into being. Today we have worms in all colors of the rainbow plus two-tone jobs, polka dot finishes, flourescent, etc. The general rule is to go with dark-colored worms in deep water or in dark and cloudy water, and to use lighter colors in clear water and especially in shallow water along the shoreline.

Not only are there hundreds of established lure makers turning out plastic worms, but there are molds and supplies for the fisherman who wants to make his own worms.

Most of the worms float when not rigged. This is very important to successful worm fishing. The hook and slip sinker will carry the worm to the bottom, but the tail portion will float up and dance in the current. This floating tail action is most attractive in luring bass. It is also the part of the worm that the fish takes first.

Some plastic worms today are made with so-called built-in "scent." In addition to looks, feel, and action, the appeal to taste is there, too. This built-in scent is usually nothing more than the addition of oil of anise to the mixture that is used to mold the worms. The aroma is that of licorice, a scent or taste that is not unpleasant to bass. More important than that, however, I feel the scent is extremely effective in masking certain odors and tastes that are repulsive to bass. These are such things as gasoline, oil, and the tobacco taste from your smokes. If you happen to be a heavy sweater, the anise flavor will neutralize the acids produced in the sweat. Fish find the acids from sweat very repulsive.

It is impossible to say a particular length is the right one for worm bass fishing. This is a variable that must be determined practically on a day-to-day basis. There have been days when I've had bass hit six-inch worms and absolutely refuse any other lengths. The next day they go for giant nine-inchers or perhaps shorty three or four inches. And there are times when they will take all lengths. You just have to experiment to determine the menu for the day.

Uncertainty is the one certain thing about fishing.

10

Quantity or Quality

The two fishermen were less than fifty yards apart. Each had fish on his stringer. One had a mixed bag that included a few speckled trout, croakers, whiting, and catfish. In all his stringer included a dozen and a half fish and prior to dressing the total catch weighed almost twelve pounds. The other fisherman had three fish on his stringer—two speckled trout, the biggest of which weighed 5¾ pounds, and a five-pound channel bass. His second speckled trout was a two-pounder. His string of three fish prior to dressing weighed 12¾ pounds.

He had less fish than the other fellow, but he had larger fish. It goes without saying that his bigger fish gave him a lot more sport than the Joe enjoyed with the most fish. The fellow with just three fish had a lot of other pluses too.

There is that one job connected with fishing that anglers universally dislike. It's the chore of cleaning the catch. Obviously the fellow with three fish had a lot less work to do than his counterpart with the eighteen fish. Furthermore his larger fish permitted him to fillet his catch into choicer table cuts. Not only that, all of his fish were choice ones. The fellow with the eighteen fish had species ranging from the choice speckled trout down to the not-so-desirable saltwater catfish.

In a nutshell the man with eighteen fish had quantity, while the fisherman with the three had quality. What has just been reported took place in a wide, expansive Texas bay about a month before this chapter was written. I was the fellow with the three fish, while a friend, who desires to remain anonymous, caught the eighteen. We used identical rods and reels and general fishing techniques. The only difference was in the baits used.

And therein lies the story of quantity or quality fishing, or what I choose to call selectivity in fishing.

Now back to the baits used. The fellow who caught the eighteen fish did so using live shrimp for bait. I caught my three fish on artificial lures. The two speckled trout were taken on spoons, while the redfish hit a lead-head worm jig. The only difference in the fishing was that I used artificial lures and the other fellow used natural bait.

When it comes to fishing, whether in fresh water or in salt water, there is one tenet that holds true. The fisherman who uses natural baits will always catch the most fish. Obviously if the fellow figures having kids is cheaper by the dozen and he has to feed that dozen, then he should by all means stick to natural baits.

But in this day of sports fishing where fish species, size of fish, and quality of fish count the most, the fellow who goes with artificial lures will in the long run catch the most "bragging" fish. True, there will be days when water conditions are such that artificial lures will be completely ruled out. There will be days when the only fish caught are those taken on natural baits. But when water conditions are right, the fellow throwing the artificials will end up with the biggest or quality fish.

Pitching artificial lures at fish gives the fisherman still another advantage other than just quality fish. The plugs, spoons, and jigs give him selectivity. The example can be seen back in the beginning of this chapter. I was fishing particularly for speckled trout.

The redfish I caught had to be considered a bonus fish since it was the wrong time of the year for reds to be back in the bays. In addition to the three fish caught, I lost two other trout that threw the spoons before I could work the fish into the landing net. I had a couple of other "bumps" that most likely were trout. I doubt seriously if the "bumps" could have been croakers, whiting, or catfish striking. Why? Simply because these species very rarely take artificial lures.

The fellow who caught the eighteen fish would very much have preferred to catch only speckled trout or redfish. He is a good fisherman in his own right, but he does not like to use lures. He says the reason is that he tires easily because of so much casting. He prefers to use natural baits in a style of fishing where scent plays a major role in attracting fish. His style of fishing is to cast out and allow the bait to remain either on the bottom or suspended a few feet beneath a float.

You can't do this in lure fishing. The plug, spoon, or jig that is allowed to lie motionless on the bottom is as attractive to fish as last week's stock report is to the stockbroker. In order to catch fish on lures, one must impart action, and the only way that can be done is by pumping the rod and turning the reel handle. This means a lot of casting and a lot of reeling. It's a style of fishing that requires a lot of patience. Lure fishing in a nutshell is a lot of work and at times hard work. But then isn't there a lot of work involved in anything that is really worthwhile?

The advantage of selectivity offered by lure fishing becomes evident when waters teem with a number of fish species, and it becomes most impressive when an area abounds with the so-called bait-stealer species. These are the times when the bait no more than strikes the water and schools of bait-stealers like porgies and catfish in salt water and perch and bluegills in fresh water clean the hook of every vestige of bait. In such cases the natural bait fisherman catches a lot of these fish, but he does a lot of reeling in and casting out again because of having to rebait the hook so often. There may be choice fish species around, but the trouble here is that the bait-stealers clean the hooks before the choicer species ever get near the bait. Any of the quality fish caught under these conditions are taken because the bait almost hit the fish in the mouth when it struck the water.

This, then, is the ideal situation for the lure fisherman. Whether he uses plug, spoon, jig, or combination thereof depends upon his knowledge of fish species in the area and what they are most likely to hit.

The lure fisherman will have these bait-stealers follow his hardware. He may even on occasion catch one. If he is observant, he is likely to note that the bait-stealers that fell victims to his lures were robust fellows, big for the species. This in itself should be a clue to the fisherman as to the reaction likely from the choicer species he seeks. Small-size fish have a tendency to nip at the bait, whether it is natural or artificial. The larger, lunker fish go for the whole bait. Nevertheless the lure fisherman will have a chance at the fish he seeks since he still has something resembling bait in the water and not just a bare hook. In gin clear water a lot of fish, especially some of the smaller game species, have been caught on bare hooks. The only trouble is there are very few bodies of water around where the water is that clear the year round. Too frequently the water is off-color just enough to screen from the fish sight of the bare hook streaking through the water. The average artificial lure, however, is big enough and has enough flash to be seen from some feet away even in water that may be mildly milky.

The professional bass-fishing tournaments that came into vogue in the late 1960s will illustrate the point of quality vs. quantity. The fellows competing in these meets go for big money stakes. Their scores are totaled on the number and size of the fish they catch. They, of course, have to observe limits, so naturally they go for the biggest fish. Contest rules restrict the contestants to artificial lures. The fishermen could catch a lot more bass on natural baits, but as so often happens, most of the bass that go for natural baits are small to middling size fish. These fish don't win tournaments. So when it comes to digging out the big whoppers, skilled bass anglers invariably resort to artificial lures, and nine times out of ten these lures are variation rigs of the plastic worm.

I hear fishermen frequently complain about the price of artificial lures—a buck, two or three dollars for a chunk of plastic armed with hooks. That same amount of money could buy dozens of live minnows or live shrimp. Now we come to the separation points. Those live minnows and shrimp are good for just one fishing trip, and even on that trip you'll have some of them die. The artificial lure, on the other hand, can be used day after day, week after week to catch dozens upon dozens of fish. It will last and catch fish until you lose it to a snag, to a big fish, or have it "borrowed" by a friend. In the long run lure fishing is quite inexpensive. The initial cost may be high, but the cost decreases each time the lure is used. The three-dollar lure costs three dollars on the first cast, a dollar and a half on the second cast, a dollar on the third and so on. Get the point?

A surf angler hauls in a whiting from the Gulf Coast surf.
Note additional fishing rigs set out in sand spikes.

Surf fishing is to salt water what fly fishing is to the crystal clear mountain stream. It appeals to a special breed of fisherman; it requires specialized tackle; it requires an infinite knowledge of the species of fish sought, and it demands unusual patience and skill. It is a phase of fishing that is not either suitable for or enjoyed by the average fisherman. A descriptive comparison would be to call general fishing pop

music, and surf and fly fishing symphonic scores.

True surf fishing is big game fishing without need of a boat. It has countless thousands of devotees along the Atlantic Coast where the targets are channel bass, striped bass, and black drum. The surf army is only slightly less along the Gulf Coast where the prey are almost exclusively channel bass and black drum. Only down on the Gulf of Mexico, folks call the channel bass a redfish. Those southern folks have provincial names for their fish, and they aim to keep it that way. The Pacific Coast, too, has its forces of surf casters who flay the waters there for stripers and California yellowtail. The real stronghold of surf fishing, however, is along the Atlantic Coast.

Before you spend a dime for surf fishing gear, take a personal inventory—an honest inventory—to determine whether or not you are suited for this kind of fishing. If you have an abundance of patience, enjoy fishing at ungodly hours and for hours on end, and can laugh at being chilled to the bone in wet clothes, then surf fishing is indeed your cup of tea. Surf fishing is definitely not for the meek, mild, or lazy.

With that out of the way and assuming you live close enough to a seaboard to enjoy surf fishing on a regular basis, let's move to the matter of tackle.

The engraved image of the surf caster is that of a fellow putting his back, shoulders, and arms into a cast that bends what looks like a ten- to fifteen-foot rod into parabola. There is more to it than meets the eye. Yes, arm, shoulder, and back muscles are needed and they must blend into perfect coordination to get those long casts. So the need for the long, whip-tipped rod. But you can't arbitrarily designate a ten-, twelve-, or fifteen-foot rod as being the correct length. The proper surf rod length is generally arrived at by trial and error, and the economical way is to make the trails with borrowed gear. The point here is that a twelve-foot rod that is perfect for one fellow might be totally unsuited for another. Physical size does not have much to do with it. I have seen five-foot-eight fellows weighing 135 pounds handle fifteen-foot rods with all the skill and finesse of a French fencing master. Your coordination, not your size, will determine what is best for you.

A typical beach scene when the fish are running in the surf. Note fishing boats working the waters just beyond the surf.

There are several reasons for surf rods being long. First, it must have a tip with considerable whip since that flexing action is necessary to propel the heavy terminal tackle a considerable distance out to sea. In other chapters pinpoint accuracy rather than distance has been stressed. You still need reasonable accuracy in surf fishing, but in this specialized kind of angling, distance is an absolute must. Second, a long rod gives the fisherman the advantage of being able to keep the tip high to hold the line above some of the breaking surf. This is very important in keeping the surf from "rolling" the line back to the beach. And finally, that long rod gives the fisherman both the leverage and cushion to control big fish. The long rod is deadly in giving the fisherman an instrument with which to turn the direction of a fish's run. The whippy tip that made the long cast possible also cushions against any sudden runs or surges the fish might make in its bid to win back freedom. Without this shock absorber many big fish would gain freedom as a result of broken tackle or hooks torn from their mouths.

Naturally the reel should make for a perfect marriage with the rod. It can be either conventional wind or open face spinning. Again this is determined by which the fisherman can operate best. The closed fan spin-cast reel is not suited for surf fishing. This particular type reel is not suited for making long casts, and the closed face hood itself tends to act as a receptacle for the salt and sand that lines tend to pick up when used in salt water. Whether the reel is conventional or open-face spinning, it should have a line capacity of at least 250 yards of thirty-pound test line. Different makes of line may test the same but the lines can be of different diameters. Go with small-diameter line. It offers less resistance to the rushing surf and currents, and it is less likely to be rolled back upon the beach. It will also permit use of a somewhat similar sinker than comparable test line of a larger diameter. Small-diameter line is invariably easier to cast, and as a result can gain you a few extra yards in distance. Believe me, I have seen times when a couple of extra yards meant getting fish.

Surf terminal tackle consists of wire leaders, hooks ranging from 1/0 to 5/0, special sinkers scaling from two to eight ounces, and an assortment of swivels and snap-swivels.

Swivels are necessary because the surf and currents often roll terminal gear. Without swivels you will end up with your fishing line twisted into kinks and ravels. Surf conditions at the time of fishing will determine how many swivels to use. When the surf is running high, it is usually good to attach sinkers and hooks with snap-swivels.

Surf conditions will determine how much sinker weight to use. Surf and currents can vary from day to

Rigs aren't always hand-held in surf-fishing. Because of the long waits between strikes, rigs are put in sand spikes.

day. One day a two-ounce sinker will hold your line in place, while the next day you may need eight ounces of lead to keep the baited hooks seaward. The wind must be reckoned with also. You may have to increase the sinker weight some when casting directly into the wind.

Leader material can range from heavy test monofilament to stainless steel wire to plastic-coated cable or to uncoated cable. Again this will be determined by the waters fished and the species of fish sought. Monofilament is suitable for fish without sharp teeth and for fishing in waters free of rock beds. Leaders should always be inspected at points of connection with lines, hooks, and leaders. Always keep in mind that you are fishing in salt water, which attacks and plays havoc with metals. Rust on a leader indicates a possible point of weakness. Check it out to make sure that it isn't more than surface rust. If the leader itself or the connecting hardware is deeply pitted by rust, then discard in favor of new material.

In practically all surf fishing the species desired work along and feed in the troughs that run parallel to the beach. Sometimes this might be just outside the seaward breaker line; other times it may be in any of several troughs between the seaward breaker line and the shore. Again you locate where to fish by experimenting, keeping in mind that what held true yesterday may not be true today. In short, if you don't get strikes in one trough, try another and then another and so forth. It is a business that can really try one's patience.

There is an art in surf casting in order to get the baited hook in the desired trough. Sometimes you can cast to the trough right from the water's edge; other times you may find it necessary to wade out knee or waist deep in order to reach the desired spot. You must note the pattern and roll of the breaking surf. Your cast must be timed and made in such a manner so that the terminal tackle lands in the water *behind* the breaking wave. If it strikes in front of the wave, the force of the break is almost certain to roll it many yards beachward; hence your bait ends up yards away from the trough in which you wanted to fish. When the terminal rig strikes the water *behind* the breaking wave, the sinker has time to go to the bottom and dig into the sand before the next wave comes rolling along.

The cast should be made so that the terminal tackle drops on the sand bar *outside* of the trough you desire to fish. After it has settled to the bottom and after several succeeding waves have rolled over the area, take a few turns on the reel handle to ease the bait to the edge of the sand bar where another breaker can churn it into the trough. Big gamefish

Not all surf-fishing is done from the sandy shoreline. Where waters are warm enough, many surfers wade right out into the suds.

are often quick to grab food that comes tumbling down from the sand bar overhead so to speak.

Generally speaking surf fishing is best when the surf is heavy enough to churn marine life free from the bottom. Surf fishing can be horribly unproductive on those days when there is no surf at all and the water is quite clear. Some gamefish species like the channel bass won't move in close to the shoreline when the water is clear. They are bottom-rooters that feed voraciously when the water is sandy. Channel bass are extremely spooky where clear, shallow water is concerned. A shadow over the water can send them finning out to sea. These same channel bass will spend much time in shallow water if it is sandy.

The surf caster may encounter his game at any time during the twenty-four-hour period, although he will find the best odds for good action at night or early in the morning. He must dovetail his own time with the proper tides, which have a tremendous influence on surf fishing. The best tides are the incoming or high ones.

Patience will be tried sorely, since hours can go by with nary a nibble. It helps to stick the rod and reel in a sand spike, plop into a beachchair, and wile away the time with a good book. Set the reel on click and in free spool. When you have a pickup, you will know it from the buzzing of the click. Engage the spool, set the hook, and battle your fish. The use of a sand spike or two can allow you to fish several rigs at the same time. It is quite safe to do since it is indeed very rare to have pickups on all baits at the same time.

True surf fishing for such species as channel bass,

The author with a string of spotted weakfish (speckled trout) caught from the Texas surf.

striped bass, black drum, etc., is not a 365-day-a-year sport. You can fish the surf every day in the year, but you are not going to catch these fish day in and day out. Your trips must be timed to coincide with the seasons when these fish make their runs in the surf.

There are two surf run periods each year: a short run of about a month in the spring, and a longer one of two to three months in the fall. The fall runs, invariably the ones with the most action and excitement, put a special demand on the fisherman. This is the time of the year when the weather is more often than not unpleasant. In fact, at times it can be downright frigid, and unless one fishes from a pier, there is no way to keep from getting wet.

But there is an interesting thing about this kind of fishing. Flying spray from the wind and crashing surf forms in rivulets on your foul weather gear and always manages to gravitate to the bottom of your boots or waders—and always on the inside. Your toes get numb from the damp cold, your eyes water and your lips chap from the biting wind, and your nose runs. You vow this will be the last time for this kind of "damned foolishness." Then your line begins to pay out. You have a pickup. You see line spool off the reel as you delay a few seconds before setting the hook. The purpose of the delay is to allow the fish to get the bait well into its mouth. The seconds seem more like minutes. Then you flip the lever to engage the reel's gears, lean the rod well forward, and when the line begins to get taut, you rare back sharply to set the hook. You feel life at the other end of the line as the fish surges in a startled bid for freedom. The line sizzles off the reel as the drag whines in protest. Then just to make sure you dip

the rod and sock the fish again with another strike. Got to make sure the hook is bedded deep in the flesh.

The surf may be shallow but it can yield big fish like this thirty-pound channel bass.

How long you battle the fish depends upon the size of the fish and how it uses the surf and currents in its attempts to win freedom. You just have to wear the fish down, for you know one of the easiest ways to lose a fish in the surf is to attempt to horse it to the beach. Your battle with the fish goes on; you pick up line and then the fish sizzles it off in a run seaward. Here is where that long rod is worth its weight in gold. The springy tip cushions the shock of the run; the long tip allows you to walk a few yards parallel down the beach so you can apply pressure from an angle in order to turn the run. How many times this kind of action repeats depends upon the size and stamina of the fish. Finally you start picking up more line than the fish takes out on succeeding runs. Its back and tail show in the sudsy water. A black spot the size of a half dollar stands out boldly and identifies the fish as a channel bass. You estimate it to run forty pounds; later the scales will only register

54

A landing net is helpful in handling fish when wading out into the surf. The above fisherman has just netted a large flounder.

thirty. The force of the surf and currents simply magnified the fish's strength.

Whether the scrap lasted fifteen minutes or a half hour, you end up wet and sticky with sweat, not spray; your toes are no longer numb; your eyes are keen and sharp, and someplace in the interim the runny nose stopped. You look at your fish and decide it wasn't "damned foolishness" after all.

That's surf fishing, the symphony of saltwater fishing.

Wade-Fishing

Of the many styles of fishing, wade-fishing is one of the most productive and enjoyable, but only so if the fisherman knows what he is doing and how he should go about the art. You might say this is true for all styles of fishing, and so it is, but it is far more valid and meaningful in wade-fishing than in most other styles. Probably the only style that calls for more expertise and finesse is fly-fishing, which happens to be an ultraspecialized kind of fishing and a style of angling that is relatively expensive.

Wade-fishing calls for getting right down in the water with the fish. If one is a hearty soul and the waters are temperate to warm, he might not object to getting wet, and in some cases literally soaked. If he finds this objectionable, he can always don boots or chest-high waders to stay dry.

Wade-fishing is remarkably similar to upland game bird hunting. For that matter, it has one thing in common with all types of hunting—the importance of stealth. You can't charge into either sport like a bull moose in rut and expect to score. In hunting you enter the field or forest with as little noise and commotion as possible, the object being not to frighten the game out of the area. It is the same with wade-fishing. Enter the water slowly and quietly; don't make waves. Where upland bird hunting is concerned, the successful hunter is the one who works an area slowly and thoroughly, probing every patch of cover where game birds are likely to be concealed. So it is with wade-fishing; work all surrounding waters carefully before moving to new territory.

The wade-fisherman has a tremendous advantage over other styles of fishing. If he is competent, he can ease right into the school of fish, and if he knows how to read fish movements in the water, he can tag along with the school for hours.

Everybody is fishing in this scene—the waders, the boaters, and even the seagull.

The secret to successful wade-fishing lies in the word *competent*. It takes more than knowing tackle and how to use it, and knowing fish species and their characteristics. Competence itself calls for the fisherman to think; he can't daydream and expect to have success.

For a starter the fellow must dress properly for this method of fishing. Don't let this frighten you; it doesn't mean a bundle of cash for fashionable wear. In fact, the only out-of-the-ordinary expense will likely be for hip boots or chest-high waders. And again these items are not really necessary if your wade-fishing is done in warm climates. Dressing right for wade-fishing means wearing apparel that won't frighten fish out of their wits. Remember

This wade fisherman is putting his catch on his stringer.

you're right down there in the water with the fish, and even though you may not see the fish, the water may be clear enough for the fish to see you. Consequently the wrong clothes can make you a fish-spooker instead of a fish-catcher. The worst color you can wear is white. It can stand out like a beacon and fish can see it from a considerable distance. Down through the years I've found cotton khakis the best wade-fishing wearing apparel. The color does not reflect light, and it is even less visible when it is wet.

Note I mentioned cotton khakis and for good reason. If you wade sans boots or waders, you're going to get wet, and a half-day or a full day of wade-fishing can get mighty toilsome when you tote the extra weight of wet clothes. Cottons just don't soak up water like woolens, and cottons are considerably cooler than synthetics. There is another advantage in cotton gear in that it dries fast. This is darned important when your fishing trip is one of several days. You don't need a hot sun to dry out the cottons. Just hang them out in the wind. You can dry them in an hour in the sun, and in the matter of about three hours at night. All you need is enough wind to make them flap. Even in a dead calm, cottons will "drip out" overnight.

Footwear for wade-fishing can be boots, waders, wading shoes, tennis shoes, or for that matter those old street shoes that have seen better days. Although I have waded bare-footed, I don't advise it. It is much too easy to injure one's feet on half-buried pebbles or shells and in these modern days in particular on broken bottles and rusty fliptop tabs and rings left by that beast *Litterbuggist americana*.

There's an art in the way the wade-fisherman should walk. Naturally you don't walk along as you would strolling the streets or spanning the well-beaten path between your desk and the junior executives' washroom. The proper way is to go slowly, of course, but instead of picking up your feet as in normal walking, shuffle or slide your feet along. There are several good reasons. The fellow who wants to be a fish-catching wader obviously has to concentrate on his fishing. He can't be hamstrung with having to watch his feet to note where and where not to place them. Here, then is where the shuffle comes in, for this manner of locomotion is quite by feel. For example, if your toe bumps a rock or some sort of obstruction, you can feel around and pass the object by moving one way or the other with no more bother than making a slight detour. You don't have to divert your attention from fishing. Now look what happens if you walk normal fashion, picking up and setting down each foot. If your foot comes down on the side of a rock, stump or sunken log, you slip and ker-splash—you take a spill. The very least bad thing then is the big splash that will certainly spook nearby fish.

The shuffle method will warn you of holes and

This wade angler holds a hefty spotted weakfish he caught working a flat.

57

The author with a five-pound flounder caught wade-fishing around a flooded grass stand.

stepoffs. Even with boots or shoes on you can still feel with your toes. I'd rather "feel" the edge of the stepoff with the toe of my boot rather than to step in it blind and go "ker-chung." Always remember that the bottom ahead could be inhabited with marine life, some of which could inflict painful foot or leg wounds. Without exception this bottom life would rather run than fight, but if you insist in walking natural and step down atop the critter, it is going to fight back—the instinct of self-preservation. You meet this same marine life when you shuffle along, but when nudged—or to be emphatic "goosed"— with a toe rather than stepped on, the critter will make off in a cloud of sand and silt rather than strike back.

You can get this point with emphasis if you wade-fish saltwater flats. These are areas with considerable stingaree populations. I've encountered and goosed out of the way literally hundreds of stingarees in over three decades of wade-fishing, and I have never had one lash back. I can't say the same thing about the stingarees that I have stepped on; every time the critters wrapped their whiplike tails around my leg. Now let me point out the circumstances. None of these incidents occurred when I was wade-fishing; they always happened on duck hunts. You don't shuffle along slowly chasing a crippled duck. You've got to move fast, and that calls for picking 'em up and setting 'em down. I escaped injuries because I wear heavy waders when I hunt ducks. Several of those stingarees punctured my waders with the barbs near the base of their tails. The heavy waders protected my legs.

Wearing the right clothes, moving along slowly and quietly and shuffling instead of walking are really just the starters in successful wade-fishing.

It doesn't make a lot of difference which way you move in still water. It becomes another ball game, however, in waters where there are currents. Keep in mind that every shuffling step raises a cloud of silt and sand, and in view of this, it is advisable to wade against the current, especially if you're using artificial lures or live bait. It behooves you to keep your terminal gear in waters where the visibility is greatest. Wading downstream can end up with you fishing in water clouded with stirred up silt and sand.

Now do it the other way around when wading a swift flowing stream that has a hard bottom and one in which the water is clear. Wade downstream and cast in such a manner that the water flow will swirl your bait or lure by boulders, logs, etc. Fish are like people; they don't waste energy without a good reason. It requires a lot of energy for a fish to go upstream or for that matter to stay in one place if the fish is out in the flow of the stream. This same fish can conserve energy by lurking in the relatively slow water behind obstructions that break the stream's flow. They lurk there waiting for bits of food to swirl by. Tight line fishing is the very essence of successful action if you are wade-fishing downstream in a fast moving river. If you can't feel that bite, you won't know when to set the hook, and if the fish doesn't like the taste or feel of what it picks up, it will spit it out without the fisherman ever knowing he had something working his bait. This will happen if the fisherman allows slack in his line.

A fisherman can work with the current in wade-fishing if casts are made out and in such a way that the bait or lure will not be obscured by any stirred up silt or mud. This is an especially effective way to wade the saltwater flats when live bait is used or when the fish species sought are bottom feeders. The style, then, is to fish with a float, rigged in such a manner that the bait dangles a few inches off the bottom. The current carries the float along and the fisherman by making casts of varying lengths can cover a lot of bottom. It is in effect a kind of drift-fishing in which no boat is used. It may take a half dozen casts with the ensuing float-drifts to cover an area before the angler shuffles along to new water, but this manner of fishing with the float carried along by the current is extremely deadly when one goes for flounders and other members of the flatfish family. These fish lie on the bottom and have in common a peculiar characteristic of "eating in bed" so to speak. They forage for food like other fish, but they also spend a lot of time letting the food

When the fishing is good, wade fishermen line productive spots like pickets in a fence.

come to them. A flounder nestled down and camouflaged to look like a part of the bottom itself and with only its eyes protruding waits for food to pass within inches of its mouth. Then it rises off the bottom in a cloud of sand and silt, grabs the food and then nestled back down in its bed to feed in leisure. Tyro fishermen often mistake a flounder on the line for a snag, for quite frequently a hooked flounder won't move out of its bed until the fisherman actually drags it free. A hard jerk against what seems to be a snag sometimes ends up with a broken fishing line.

Always remember in wade-fishing that when you start to catch fish you are right in the school or at least darned close to it. Be super cautious. Sudden noises or noises out of character with the environment will spook fish. So will any shadows that may fall across the water. Whenever possible the

Bays, especially those with grass stands, offer excellent wade-fishing action. The coves and points are the prime places to work.

wade-fisherman should fish into the sun. Granted reflections dancing off the shimmering surface of the water may be unpleasant to the eyes. This is an inconvenience that can be minimized by wearing a long-visored cap and sunglasses.

Wade-fishing always involves shallow water, and a fishing rule of thumb for shallow water is that the action is best at night, early in the morning, or late in the afternoon. When the sun stands high overhead, fish move out to deeper waters, which are usually well out of the wader's casting range. This early-morning or late-afternoon fishing means a sun low in the sky, and this low angle can result in your body casting extremely long shadows across the water. There are going to be some sudden, fast movements in this shadow; after all how else does one make a cast without arm and body movement. If these moving shadows fall across fish, the result is startled fish that hurriedly scurry out of the area, and if that shadow lies in front of you, it usually means fish finning beyond your casting range. Better to fish into the sun to keep that shadow behind you.

Clear water often means a fellow can see the fish he hopes to catch. This is likewise true in off-color water in shallow depths and where bottom feeders are concerned. Bottom feeders rooting along in quest of food often stand on their noses as they dig out choice morsels, and it is not uncommon for their tails to stick out of the water. The skilled wader will note the direction in which the fish appear to be working, and he will cast so that his bait or lure strikes the water beyond and ahead of the direction of fish movement. Then he works his bait back on a path that will intercept the fish. In this manner the angler places the bait in an area that fish will soon invade. In making his cast he must be careful to thumb his reel expertly so that the bait or lure will strike the water with a minimum of commotion. Fish are more sensitive to splash noises in shallow water than in deep water.

The mark of an inexperienced wade-fisherman is to cast right at the fish. If he hits a fish with his bait,

and this happens frequently when a big school is working in shallow water, the hit fish will take off like a scalded cat. Fish are always extra cautious in shallow water, and any fish that fins wildly for the horizon simply starts a chain reaction that results in the entire school vacating the premises. Lo and behold our noble wader is then left in undisputed possession of barren water.

A wade-fisherman's skill is determined by how many fish he can take out of a single school of fish. Many can consistently take one, maybe two. Others, a decided minority, can work a school with the same deadliness with which the Sioux culled through General Custer and the Seventh Cavalry in 1876. The secret lies in how the fisherman plays his fish and how he leads it to net. The man who takes a lot of fish from a single school is the one who plays his fish gently. He never horses the fish, and he keeps his rod tip low, sometimes even dipped into the water to keep the fish from splashing around on the surface. A splashing, jumping fish offers an exciting picture but it also makes enough racket to cause the rest of the school to move to more placid waters. There are a few exceptions where fish species actually home in on noises. Some of these are barracuda, the sharks, and cobia.

Whether the wader is fishing a saltwater bay, a flowing stream or river, or a placid lake, he will have two distinct advantages if he can fish with the wind blowing from behind him. The most obvious is that in casting, it's easy to control casts for accuracy and distance when fishing with the wind. The second advantage is one of making the most of a characteristic of fish. They may be under water, but they can sense wind direction from the movement of surface waters, and a general characteristic of most fish species is to work into the surface flow. Even a dumb fish knows that flowing water also brings food. This is true to a marked degree in freshwater fishing where tall trees or heavy shoreline brush is involved. Fish move in close to feed off the tidbits the wind shakes out of the trees and brush.

Birds are working fish ahead and those boaters are headed for them. Birds are the key to excellent offshore fishing. *Courtesy Mercury Motors.*

regurgitate that matter, and start all over again. When you find a school of "gone crazy" bluefish, you will find great numbers of birds working the area. The Spanish mackerel and king mackerel are other saltwater species that leave wakes of food bits. A good example in fresh water is the white bass, also called sand bass and striped bass in some parts of the country.

Birds, of course, aid the boat angler more than the wade-fisherman. After all the boat gives the fellow mobility, and with care he can move and maneuver right into the area where the birds are working. The wade-fisherman, on the other hand, can get to the birds only if they are working waters shallow enough to wade, and even then he can only get to the birds if they are working in the right direction. In this case the right direction means either right to or angling toward the fisherman. His job then is to wade quietly out to an area that will intersect the birds' line of movement. If the school of fish feeding beneath the birds meanders, the birds will do likewise; consequently the poor wade-fisherman may be left "high and dry."

Birds, however, can be worked by one type of land-based fishing. The case here is surf fishing. There are areas where one can drive for miles on sandy beaches. In between dodging washouts, logs, and the usual flotsom and jetsom the sea casts upon the beaches, the fellow can watch for flocks of birds working the bars and troughs running parallel to the beach. Note the direction in which the birds are working, drive several hundred yards ahead of them, and then wade out to do your surf fishing. Again you're in a spot that will intersect the line in which the birds are working. In surf fishing this is a

Call birds the fisherman's friend.

Whether one fishes salt water or fresh water, the presence and actions of birds can guide a fellow to some mighty fine action. Birds have excellent eyesight, many times superior to man's, and from their lofty viewpoint they can see well down into the water. They are not about to tackle the gamefish like largemouth bass, northern pike, striped bass, Spanish mackerel, and the likes. They are, however, always alert to swoop down to pick up any small baitfish the big gamefish chase to the surface. Consequently when the fisherman finds working birds, he usually finds fish. *Working birds* is a fishing term that covers a flock of birds weaving and milling low over the surface and frequently dropping down to the water to grab food tidbits off the surface.

These birds are not always taking small baitfish. Often they are picking up tidbits of fish or marine life shredded to bits by wildly feeding schools of gamefish. A notable example is the bluefish. These fish often feed in dense masses and slash up everything that gets in their path, including other bluefish. Not only that, they will feed to capacity,

The author inspects a six-pound channel bass that was caught fishing under the birds.

fairly predictable line in that the fish sought—channel bass, striped bass, black drum, whiting, to mention a few—generally stick to working in the troughs. They don't meander about as do the same species back on the bay flats. When fish working the surf troughs change directions, it will invariably be out to sea and the reasons will be (1) they've had their fill of food or (2) something spooked them to flee to the safety of deeper water.

I've fished the Texas surf for three and a half decades for redfish—channel bass to Atlantic coasters—and I've caught a heck of a lot of big ones just by driving down the beaches and fishing ahead of the birds.

The boatman has mobility. He doesn't have to wait for the birds to come to him; he can go to the birds. This isn't as simple as it may seem. In the case of white bass in fresh water and members of the

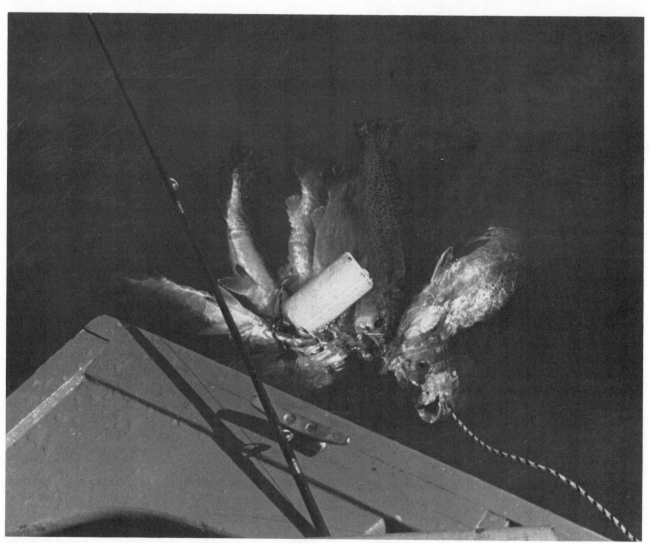

The rewards of a morning of fishing the birds, a string of spotted weakfish to five pounds in size.

mackerel family in salt water you can run right up to the schools provided you don't do it with a super horsepower motor running full speed. Use discretion and common sense. Go in under power but do so at greatly reduced throttle. Not only that, run on a tangent to the direction in which the birds are moving and intersect just a few yards ahead of the lead bird. Running at a tangent means closing the gap on the fish at a rather leisurely pace. The fish, of course, will pick up the engine sounds, but as long as these engine sounds get louder at a gradual pace, they are unlikely to spook.

A far more foolproof approach by boat is to give the birds a wide berth, swing ahead of them and cut off the engine when the boat is about fifty to seventy-five yards away. You want to locate your boat in a spot that will intersect the direction in which the birds are moving. This approach calls for taking wind and currents into consideration because the boat's drift will be determined by them.

Working a school of fish under the birds can be fast and furious. It is in no way whatsoever leisure fishing. It starts suddenly when the school moves into casting range, and it ends just as abruptly when the school passes on. You might get five or ten minutes of red hot fishing and then—nothing. If your boat happens to be drifting in the direction the school is moving, the action can last appreciably longer. When the action stops, there is only one thing to do; crank up the motor again and relocate ahead of another milling bunch of birds. Two things are a must in this kind of fishing—binoculars and plenty of fuel. You'll need the binoculars to glass the area for birds, and in this respect you must remember that you're not looking for just birds. You're looking for gulls and terns, the winged species that generally feed out over the water and often many, many miles from any land masses. Don't pay attention to the herons and egrets. These are shorebirds that feed by wading in every shallow water. The glasses will enable you to determine what the gulls and terns are doing. If they are hovering and milling, give the area a try. If they are flying a straight line, they're going some place, maybe the next county, so just forget these birds. Maybe you sight a couple dozen gulls and terns just swimming in a group. Keep tabs on these birds. They are there because fish are around, but the fish aren't feeding voraciously enough to chase bait to the surface. The birds are just biding their time until the action starts. If there are no working birds anywhere on the horizon, ease over to the swimming gulls. Fish the area, working baits and lures down deep. The odds are favorable to pick up at least a few good fish.

Open boats are ideal for bird-fishing in bay waters because they have ample room for moving around.

Most saltwater "bird fisherman" work the fish with two rods and reels. One is rigged with a float to hold a natural bait just a few feet below the surface; the other is rigged with an artificial lure. It can get hectic trying to handle fish on both rigs at the same time, but these old pros know from experience just how short the action time can be. This fishing two rigs bit is beginning to catch on in freshwater fishing, especially on the huge impoundments and mainly where white bass are concerned. The main difference is that most two-rig freshwater fishermen go with lures on both outfits.

There are a few winged species that bear close watching where freshwater fishing is involved. These include the eagles, fish hawks, and kingfishers. Eagles and fish hawks will go down and pluck some rather large fish out of the water. Any time I see one of these birds of prey wheeling over the water, I make it a point to get out there to fish the area. This is especially true if the incident takes place far from shore.

I frequently take my family to the Wildlife Kingdom Fishing Resort, an out-of-the-way haven nestled deep in the piney woods of East Texas. The area has a half dozen ten- to forty-acre lakes that offer reasonably good bass, crappie, and catfish action. There is one lake I like in particular because I can always dig a few bass out of it, even in the foulest of weather. There is a stand of drowned timber at one end. The deep part of the lake is at the earthen dam at the other end, and this is where most of the bass are caught. But there are occasions when you can't miss on bass up in the drowned timber end, and I chanced upon the secret quite by accident. I

The presence of those birds milling and working jetty waters is a good sign that the fisherman has picked a choice place to fish.

discovered whenever the kingfishers were in numbers on the branches of the drowned trees, the bass action was about to start. It seems that some mechanism within these birds told them when the bass would start herding minnows and especially small bluegills into the shallow water. The kingfishers, of course, got their share of minnows and bluegills, and I caught bass. None of the bass were trophy size; they were always one- and two-pound eating size. The trophy blacks were down in the deep end of the lake.

The trophy fish, however, wouldn't always cooperate no matter what baits were offered to them. Nevertheless waterhauls were held to a minimum simply by paying attention to those kingfishers that congregated at the shallow end of the lake and fishing accordingly. This isn't an isolated case. I've worked in conjunction with kingfishers in other lakes and I've enjoyed similar results. Trophy fish? No. But again a good many eating size one and two pounders.

The feathered fishing guides don't have to be big flocks to indicate the presence of fish, although a big flock will invariably signify that the school of fish lurking below is a big one. Just a single gull or two can reward the discerning angler with trophy fish. Most fish tend to school when they are young and small, but the bigger they get the more they break away into small pods rather than continue with the numerically big schools. Then you come to those really big lunkers, and for some reason they tend strongly to be loners or move around in small groups of two, three, or four fish. These big lunkers, even three or four of them together, don't seem to attract birds in any sizable flocks. Most likely there may be just a half dozen birds milling overhead, and quite

frequently it may be only two or perhaps a single bird.

Pay attention to what these birds do. Suppose you sight a single gull winging its way across the bay. If it is flying in a straight line with a steady wingbeat, the bird is bent on going a long way; it isn't hunting. Yet if this same bird flies a meandering path, especially dipping low to the surface every now and then, you can bet money it is hunting for food. Every time that bird dips toward the surface it is doing so to take a closer look at something. If it swoops down and pecks something off the surface, you can again bet money the bird is working a feeding fish. But should the bird plunge all the way into the water for its morsel of food, you can discount it as working over feeding fish. Something in nature tells these birds not to dive beneath the surface when gamefish are present. Those big fish are just as likely to swat the bird as the baitfish. When the fish are present and feeding, gulls and terns invariably peck off the surface; when there are no fish around, they dive.

Let's go back to that single bird. A meandering course means the bird is hunting. If the bird begins to circle, this means it has found fish. Then if it flutters a few feet above the surface but does not swoop or dip, the meaning here is that the bird is following a fish that isn't feeding. In offshore blue water fishing this can indicate the presence of a billfish or a shark. The higher the bird flutters above the surface, the deeper the fish is swimming. Birds can see deeper beneath the surface from the more lofty altitude. The bird signals the fish as feeding when it circles the area and repeatedly swoops down to snatch bits of food off the surface.

It would be nice to say that "fishing the birds" never fails to produce fish. Alas, it just isn't true. There are times when these feathered fishing guides lie, and in a way perhaps it is Mother Nature's way of evening the score with man. The big lie comes when one is fishing close to civilization—like near the docks in the shadows of the big city skyscrapers or in the busy ship channels. The gulls and terns one sees milling and hovering in these places are feeding on refuse strewn by man and not on the leavings of feeding fish. These birds are scavangers—darned good ones at that in that they help tremendously in keeping our shorelines clean—that will feed on all sort of refuse, including raw sewage.

Generally speaking in fishing the birds, small fish are caught nearest the surface and they hit more readily on natural baits than artificials. The larger fish lurk a few feet deeper, but in order to get to them the bird angler often has to resort to artificial lures. Those small fish up near the surface sometimes never let natural baits sink down to the level of the big fellows.

14

Fish the Snags

Find me a place where you can foul your hooks on snags and lose terminal tackle, and I'll show you a place where you can catch fish. This is a simple truism that holds for both fresh- and saltwater fishing. The only time this one fails is when the water is too polluted or too tepid for fish to survive.

Waters with nice clean, hard sand bottoms are great for man and his various water sports such as swimming, diving, surfing, and skiing, but these are the wrong bottoms for good fishing. Sure, fish can be caught over these bottoms, but these catches occur when the fish pass through the area. To catch fish in any quantity and with regularity you must go to fish havens, not places they only occasionally pass through. Fish are not residents of clean, firm sand bottom areas. To begin, these bottoms have nothing to which marine life—animal as well as vegetable—can attach. Second, these bottoms offer no retreats and hideouts for small marine life and baitfish to flee to escape gamefish and predators.

The seas, oceans, lakes, and rivers are like the land masses in that they are made up of areas sometimes densely populated and sometimes nearly completely barren of life. The only real difference between the land and the bottom of the lake, river, or ocean is the degree of wetness.

In order to become populated with fish, an area needs a foundation, which in turn serves two purposes. First, the area needs a base to which marine life and marine growths can attach, and second, it must provide protective cover and shelter for small baitfish. In the final analysis baitfish determine whether or not gamefish will frequent an area. Bottom foundations can be products of nature such as shell reefs, coral outcroppings, and marine

vegetation, or products of civilization such as manmade structures and wrecks.

The manmade structures most common are docks, piers, dams, offshore and tidewater oil platforms, and more recently artificial reefs. Stuff like old car bodies, tires, concrete blocks, outdated barges, and condemned Liberty ships have been sunk on many locations for the express purpose of providing fish havens. Except in a few cases where preliminary studies were sketchy, these manmade artificial reefs have proven to be highly successful. Those that failed were spotted in ill-advised locales where the weight of the reef material soon sank out of sight in the soft mud.

Structures like offshore drilling rigs and oil platforms are in effect fish-stoppers. They became focal points for myriads of minute marine life that in turn are dined upon by baitfish, which in turn keep the gamefish in the area. It is the old cycle-of-life piece. These structures have played important roles in keeping migratory and pelagic fish in areas for long periods. In effect, these structures have shortstopped and altered the migration of some species to the point of lengthening the species' stay in an area.

The guides and the old salts have a saying about fishing: if you can't stand to lose tackle, don't go fishing. These fellows know from the college of hard knocks that fishing is best when the snags are thickest. If it hurts you to lose hooks and sinkers to brush piles, oyster reefs, wrecks, etc., then you had better take up another sport, for you are not going to catch much fishing the hard, clean bottoms.

Down through the years many a landowner picked up extra money by selling dirt out of a hole on some part of his land that had a poor crop return record. Many of these little holes were enlarged to the point where the landowner thought in terms of his own private fishing hole. In time quite a number of these farm ponds became pretty good fishing holes. No record catches or anything like that, but holes good for a nice mess of panfish, a few catfish, and a good bass or two every few days. As time went by the once-clean bottoms of the ponds became littered with brush and the likes blown in by the wind. It did not take long for the landowners to discover that the places with all the snags occurred were the best places to fish. It is not uncommon today to see small ponds—square or rectanglar two- to ten-acre compounds—with brushpiles spotted in several locations. These piles are real fish havens.

We see manmade fish havens in salt water, too. They have been spotted in waters on the Atlantic, Pacific, and Gulf coasts and have been constructed of a wide variety of materials, concrete blocks, cement culverts, junked auto bodies, and old tires, to mention a few. Several fishing reefs have been made by scuttling old barges loaded with scrap; others by sinking Liberty ships. The purpose, of course, was to put something on the bottom to which minute marine life could attach. This started the fishing "chain reaction" of marine growth to baitfish to gamefish and finally to the fisherman.

In freshwater fishing in southern states, the largemouth bass reigns supreme. School-size bass are generally easy to find around the edges of the big reservoirs and often out in open water chasing shad. But when fishermen go for the big ones, the action invariably takes place down in the snags. Drowned timber and brush stands make excellent hideouts for lunker bass, but to get these fish the fisherman has to risk losing considerable terminal tackle. If he does not get his lures down in the flooded jungles, he just isn't going to score on the big ones.

15

Partyboat Fishing

The partyboat, also called head boat, is to fishing what the supermarket is to grocery shopping. It offers a fellow quantity and quality and to a degree a taste of luxury at bargain prices. Partyboat fishing as it is practiced today is found wherever there exists sports fishing that requires use of a boat.

When it comes to fishing waters requiring a boat, the ultimate is owning a boat or chartering one for exclusive use. This then allows one to dictate the day's when, where, and how in fishing. It's also expensive, like a hundred bucks a trip for a starter on a small charter boat. Everyone is not so financially endowed, and this is where the partyboat fits into the picture. It puts boat fishing in the pocketbook range of the "affluent poor." The kind of fish the one hundred dollar-a-trip charter fellow gets to enjoy can be approached for as little as ten dollars to fifteen dollars a day if the fisherman is willing to do his angling shoulder-to-shoulder with several dozen other fishermen.

A partyboat is what the term implies. Folks from the four winds gathering up in a group to go fishing. The term *head boat* is possibly a more accurate description in that each person pays a set free—so much per head—to make the trip. The term, however, has a ring that the fishing boat operators themselves don't particularly like. The *head* is the term used aboard boat for the marine toilet.

Best results in partyboat fishing are to be had when a fisherman goes about the trip with an orderly bent. Going fishing just on the urge to go fishing won't do the job. Exercise care in picking the days, first, of course, selecting the right season.

It behooves a fellow to visit the partyboat docks when the boats return from their trips, and don't spend all your time admiring the catch. It is important to view the catch and to get a rough estimate on the number of fish and approximate total weight. Next find out how many people were on the trip, and do a little simple division. The results can be startling. The following example will illustrate the point.

I spent four days in a row checking the catches on Texas partyboats operated by three different companies. Boat A brought in successive catches of one thousand pounds, nine hundred pounds, twelve hundred pounds, and seven hundred pounds. Boat B's totals were nine hundred pounds, nine hundred pounds, one thousand pounds, and seven hundred pounds. Boat C brought in catches of five hundred pounds, six hundred pounds, eight hundred pounds, and five hundred and fifty pounds. All of the fish were red snapper, the popular choice in partyboat fishing off the Texas coast. Off hand one would say the best boats to go out on would be either A or B. Well, you get some different feelings when you divide the number of fishermen into the respective daily hauls. Boat A had eighty passengers on the first and third days each, seventy on the second day, and seventy-five on the fourth. Boat B ran licensed capacity of thirty on each of the four days. Boat C carried licensed capacity of fifty on each of the first three days and forty-two on the fourth. Now let's look at the pounds per fishermen average for each boat on each trip.

	First day	Second day	Third day	Fourth day
Boat A	12.5	12.8	15	9.3
Boat B	30	30	33.3	23.3
Boat C	10	12	16	13

Offshore drilling platforms are a boon to partyboat fishing. The structures have become fish havens. The fisherman is hauling in a red snapper. *Courtesy Louisiana Wildlife & Fisheries Commission.*

takes to meet expenses just so they can say they never miss a fishing day. Boats get their fishing reputations at sea, not tied up at the docks.

Generally speaking, the price of admission entitles you to the boat ride to and from the fishing grounds, fishing space on the rail, bait, and ice on which to keep your catch. Some boats include rough dressing of your catch in the price. Without exception the boat's rods and reels go out on a rental basis with a penalty fee if the gear is broken or lost overboard. A few operations include handlines in the price of admission, but this is a kind of fishing that is unexciting and sometimes dangerous. Handlining up a small fish is like hauling a bucket out of a well. On the other hand a big fish can take off so fast that the line will either cut or burn a fellow's hands as it sizzles out.

A number of partyboat operations today assign the fisherman to a numbered space on the rail. This is okay if the procedure is to have folks switch sides or move down a dozen or so spaces every thirty to forty-five minutes. This gives everyone a shot at the best payoff spots. It's a matter of fact that fishing can be good on one side of the boat and poor on the other, good at the stern and slow at the bow, and vice versa. There is just no way of knowing in advance. There are still a lot of boat operators who run on the basis of letting fishermen find their fishing spots on a first come, first served basis. If you literally want to rub shoulders with your fellow fishermen on such a boat, then by all means grab a space at the stern or along either side near the stern. Just be prepared with having to put up with tangled lines and fish lost because of tangled lines.

So now we see that Boat B has the best track record. I did some snooping to find out why. The answer I came up with was a more experienced skipper, a faster boat, and more time on the fishing grounds. With each of the boats charging the same price—twenty dollars per fisherman—one can quickly see that Boat B offers the best deal. The only problem here is that reputations get around fast and during the peak seasons you might find the boat booked up for days. You might have to go down to the docks each day in hopes of finding a last-minute cancellation.

So now you see yourself waiting days on end for deck space to go fishing. Well not really. After you have determined the real fishing boat in the fleet, the thing to do is to make advance reservations. You might have a long wait trying to get a weekend or holiday booking, and a long wait can dull one's desire to go fishing. You can beat that long wait. Arrange to take off from work during the week and go for a Monday or Tuesday booking. Most partyboats go out half-filled on these days, and I know of a few that run with less passengers than it

The best fishing around the offshore oil rigs is down close to the pilings. This partyboat has even tied up to the rig.

You will find more elbow room up at the bow, although you will have to put up with a lot of rise and fall as the boat bobs up and down with the passing of each swell. If you prefer to fish from the side, it pays to ask the skipper or the mate a few questions. Find out how the boat is likely to lie at anchor. The wind can hold it one way, while the currents run in a different direction. It is murder to fish on the wrong side of the boat and have the current keep carrying your bait and line back under the boat.

Almost all partyboat fishing is straight down, the bait either right on the bottom or suspended a few feet off the bottom, and most of the time there are considerable currents running. This means using an appreciable amount of weight to get the baited hook down to where the fish are, and this in turn dictates the use of reasonably heavy tackle. Light gear is not suited for partyboat fishing.

The successful partyboat skippers go to places they know to produce fish, and this spells areas where there are outcroppings from the bottom, coral banks, or even the hulks of sunken ships. Again if the fellow is to catch fish on such a trip he must have tackle suited for the occasion, and again this spells out reasonably heavy gear, even if the fish involved only weigh several pounds. When bottom fish are hooked, they invariably attempt to swim into holes, under ledges, etc. Unless a fisherman has the heavy gear to immediately turn these fish and haul them into waters free of obstructions, he is almost certain to lose the fish. Coral and the shells that attach to sunken wrecks are sharp, and when they come in contact with the fishing line, the fisherman is the loser.

Partyboat fishing is not necessarily a very sporting way to catch fish; it is, however, a good way to catch a lot of fish if your plans call for filling the home freezer with a lot of fine eating seafood. A distinct advantage in partyboat fishing is all that bait in the water will keep fish schools in the immediate area. It is a manner of chumming.

Partyboat fishing is a kind of modified deepsea fishing, and since many of these trips are out to the fringe waters where big gamefish cavort, partyboat fishermen should be prepared to deal with a bonus in the game. Many a fellow who always wanted a sailfish but never had the finances to charter a boat for such, got his sail on a partyboat fishing trip. These fish are not caught as such by design. They just happen to be sails that cruised by and took a bait that was actually dangled for a red snapper or some species of the sort. But a sailfish is a sailfish whether it is caught from a one hundred fifty dollar-a-trip charter cruiser or a crowd-packed partyboat. Again this is a good reason for using reasonably heavy gear.

16

How To Troll

One of the surest ways to catch fish is to troll for it in a method that fills two tenets that spell successful fishing. These are to keep bait in the water and to cover a lot of fishable water. Trolling accomplishes both of these to the nth degree. The bait goes into the water at the beginning of the trip, and the only time it comes out is to take off fish. As for covering fishable waters, a couple of hours' trolling will traverse more territory than the wade-fisherman can cover in a couple of days.

Trolling necessitates a boat, and at first considera-tion one might think this puts trolling in a class that only the affluent can afford. Not so at all. This method of fishing is expensive—very expensive—when one partakes of it in quest of ultrabig game fish such as sailfish, marlin, tuna, and the likes, for this kind of fishing requires a small tackle shop full of specialized gear. But when it comes to garden-variety fishing, then trolling can be astonishingly inexpensive. In fact, when I was a kid and didn't have the money for an outboard, I used to troll in a rowboat. I've also trolled paddling a canoe, and both methods, rowing and canoeing, produced a goodly take of fish.

I know of no better way to initiate and stir fishing interest in children and women than to take them troll fishing. Newcomers to fishing invariably go on trips starry-eyed, dreaming all kinds of visions of great catches. Unfortunately dreams and life seldom run parallel paths. A couple of waterhauls can dampen—even kill—their interest in the sport. It behooves the tutor to put them into action to maintain their interest, and this can best be done by taking them trolling.

Time drags dreadfully slowly when the fish won't cooperate, and it becomes a study in monotony to make cast after cast with no resulting fish strikes. Trolling beats all that by covering new waters and offering the anglers new scenery. Even the boat ride itself can make a waterhaul palatable. Let's face facts, waterhauls can and do happen on trolling trips. Fortunately they don't come near as often as they do in other types of fishing. Waterhaul odds are slim if the trolling is done in an organized and systematic manner. You just can't troll around haphazardly and expect to catch fish.

Let's consider the proper way to do it, first in fresh water and then in salt water.

FRESH WATER

The most important thing in freshwater trolling is to know the water area, the surface as well as what lies below. Start with a topographic map to learn the bottom contours, the locations of the holes, chan-nels, shallows, brush piles, rocks, and so forth. Shorelines that drop off abruptly are always good trolling areas, whereas wide, expansive shallow flats are generally poor.

A good working rule is to troll deep in hot and very cold weather. Locate channels, cuts, and holes either with contour maps or electronic fish-finders and work those areas thoroughly. In more moderate weather, especially in the spring and early fall, work the edges of these same cuts and channels, as well as around brush piles and flooded timber stands. Shallow trolling with the lure running not more than a couple of feet down is quite productive in tropic and temperate zones. Troll slowly and as quietly as possible in the cuts and depressions that wend back into the flats and toward the shorelines.

Trolling is a different story again in the colder climes, where on a given day the characteristics of different species of fish can make trolling methods poles apart. Let me use a recent Canadian fishing trip in Saskatchewan province and the Northwest Territories as an illustration. When we wanted northern pike, we trolled shallow running lures near the shoreline and particularly around grassy points. We caught walleyes by trolling ten to fifteen feet down in the inlets and coves around the lakes, but when we wanted lake trout we had to troll deep—forty to fifty feet down—out in the lakes proper.

The largemouth bass is America's No. One freshwater gamefish and it is found in every state. It can be caught trolling shallow or deep, but at what level to fish depends upon the time of the year and water temperature. Always troll deep in midsummer and midwinter. Any shallow trolling done in midsummer should be at night when surface waters cool. Spring and early fall trolling for bass calls for working the shorelines and edges of stepoffs and shallows.

A study of the fins and tails of freshwater fish and a knowledge of their characteristics and habits will dictate how best to troll. To begin with, most freshwater species are nonmigratory in nature, and in the course of their lifetimes they are not likely to travel more than a few miles from where they were hatched. This means the same holes, brushpiles, etc., can be good fish payoff spots week after week.

Now look at the fins and tails of freshwater fish. Their fins are more saillike than streamlined. For the most part their tails are squarish and rather soft-spined. These fin and tail configurations spell out that these fish are neither long travelers nor fast swimmers. In the case of bass and all members of the sunfish family, the fish are deep-bodied and blimpish rather than slim torpedo-shaped. This is another clue that they are not fast swimmers.

Translate all this into the trolling computer, and it reads out slow speed, perhaps two to three miles per hour. Troll faster and you'll run away from the fish. Keep in mind, too, these fish are relative "homebodies." They are not going to follow lures across the lake. When you get a strike or catch a fish, mark the area with a spot buoy or by visual landmarks and return immediately. Chances are there are other "homebodies" around to be caught if you will just stay in the area. Fish don't always travel in big schools, but at the same time they rarely go about alone. Notable exceptions are such predators as huge sharks and barracudas in salt water and musekllunge and pike in fresh water.

It goes without saying that small motors should be used when trolling small lakes, and especially so if the water is relatively shallow. Small lakes protected from the wind by shoreline timber stands or hills can be trolled with cartop boats powered by electric motors. If internal combustion engines are used, stick with those of five horsepower or less. For that matter even when trolling a big lake, it is sound economy and good fishing sense to use a small motor. Okay, so you use a sixty-, seventy-five-, or one hundred-horsepower motor to speed your craft to the fishing area. After all time is money and you want to get them in a hurry. But when you get there, stop the big motor, tilt its lower unit out of the water and troll with a motor in the less than ten-horsepower class. Big horsepower motors just don't run smoothly for hours on end at slow speed. On the other hand the small horsepower jobs can run slowly all day long without so much as a miss or fouling of plugs. The small motor is a good investment in another way. Slowly as it may move a heavy rig, it is still great insurance of getting home if the big power plant gets cantankerous.

SALT WATER

The saltwater troller needs to know more about the characteristics and habits of the fish he seeks since their traits differ radically from those of their cousins.

Start off with the shapes of the fish themselves. Except for bottom feeders, most saltwater fish species are torpedo-shaped for speed. Their fins are hard and strong-spined, and their tails hard and deep-forked. They are fast-swimming fish, and they are fish that cover considerable distances. In the case of migratory species, the fish often swim thousands of miles. Even the nonmigratory species are strong swimmers that can move at a considerable speed. They are specially adapted to cope with strong currents, fluctuating tides, and waves—conditions common to salt water.

The two- to three-miles-per-hour speed that stood the freshwater troller in good stead won't do in saltwater. In fact, if the troll is against the current, a boat at such a slow speed might actually be carried backward. Hence the trolling speed for most saltwater fish is closer to four to six miles per hour—or about twice that of fresh water. With some offshore species like king mackerel, bonito, the billfish, etc., the trolling speed might be closer to ten miles per hour.

Bottom-feeders are just that. They root the bottom for their fodder. Consequently the odds of getting them to take trolled lures are very poor. So we end up with a situation where almost all saltwater trolling is done near the surface, even that trolling done many, many miles out to sea. And almost without exception these surface feeding species are migratory fish. This, then, restricts trolling to seasons, and in some locales to a matter of just several months in the year. The shortest trolling seasons are in the northern climes. Good troll fishing can be enjoyed practically year round in Florida waters, especially in the Keys. In central and western Gulf of Mexico waters the period of reasonably good trolling covers almost six months, spanning from late April through September. It lengthens out in lower Mexican waters and becomes a year-round practice in tropical waters.

Because of the broadness and depth of the waters trolled, engine noises are not as critical to fishing as they are in fresh water. In fact, some species—king mackerel, cobia, barracuda, and sharks, to name a few—seem to home on propeller noises. When the water is clear, these fish can often be seen following in the boat's wake, taking every twist and turn the boat skipper makes. I have a theory that may or may not hold water. There are so many boats plying our waters these days and all dump various and sundry garbage overboard that some of these fish learn to associate boat noises with food.

Trolling is most successful when done in waters known to be frequented by the species of fish sought. Most of these waters are known from past experiences, and finding the fish calls for familiarity with the area or employing the services of a knowledgeable skipper or guide. If you have a knowledge of the sea bottom and can run a true course to reach the reefs, banks, sunken wrecks, etc., then you have saltwater trolling game halfway licked. These areas harbor baitfish that attract the choicer gamefish. Successful trolling, then, is a matter of circling and crisscrossing over the area.

Texas and Louisiana coastal waters are dotted with oil rigs and drilling platforms. All have become baitfish havens and all offer excellent trolling. No pinpoint navigation to find many of these structures either. They stand forty to sixty feet above the surface and can be seen from great distances. Not only that, many of these rigs are within sight of shore.

Saltwater trolling calls for watching the water close for tide rips, floating debris, and patches of seaweed. Fish in the mackerel and bonito families like to work the edges of tide rips. Dolphin, barracuda, and cobia frequently lurk in the shadows beneath floating debris and seaweed patches.

It behooves the saltwater troller to constantly eyeball the horizon, all 360 degrees. He should watch for signs of fish boiling the surface of the water. Bonita in particular often mill wildly and churn the surface white with foam. Flocks of milling seabirds also spell likely trolling spots.

Since migratory fish to a great degree feed by sight, the saltwater troller must take water clarity into consideration. Gin-clear water, of course, is the best, but what is the best and what we have to settle for are often many degrees apart. Water that appears indigo in color is always the clearest. Water that appears greenish in color is clear enough for trolling, but when it becomes milkish-green in color, your time will be better spent staying home.

Saltwater trolling can be improved immeasurably by coordinating it with chumming, a fishing art described at length in the chapter entitled "How To Chum." This chum-trolling system is helpful in overcoming the handicap of off-color water, but in all fairness it must be pointed out that it works only when the water is mildly off-color. It's not going to work when the water resembles diluted coffee.

A question frequently asked about saltwater trolling is how much line should be let out? There is no two-plus-two-equals-four answer for this one. You have to experiment. If more than one trolling line is put out, vary the distances behind the boat, and then adjust accordingly when you start getting fish. There are some general rules that need to be observed. Lures can be trailed close behind the boat if the speed is slow, but the faster the boat goes, the more line that needs to be paid out. The point here is to get the lure or bait out of the direct turbulence caused by the boat's propeller. In offshore trolling care must be taken so the lure doesn't ride on the crest of swells where it is likely to keep popping out of the water. This works when waters are covered with dense schools of wildly feeding fish, but for average trolling it is a poor way to do it. Sometimes it may be necessary to get the trolled bait well below the surface. This can be done by rigging a trolling weight well ahead of the lure or by switching to monel line.

Trolling limits the number of people who can fish at the same time. In the small outboard two lines can be trolled with no problems. On very rare occasions a third line can be put out if the outboard is extra wide of beam and the third line is a short one right off the stern. Four to five lines can be trolled at the same time in offshore fishing from the typical offshore cruiser. Here the practice is to run two to three flat lines directly behind the boat plus two additional lines, one on each side, from an outrigger. There are times, however, when this can get pretty hairy when you get a fish on every line at the same time.

While trolling is a very effective way to locate and

catch fish, it is dangerous in that it can lull a fellow into making costly mistakes. When trolling action is slow, it is easy—too easy—to stick your rig into a rod holder and let the rig "fish itself" so to speak. Of course, you remain within arm's length to grab the rod if there is a strike, but you waste time in doing so and in the delay it is very easy to lose the fish. This is careless and lazy-man fishing. The fellow who is lazy in his trolling is a poor fisherman, indeed, for trolling like all kinds of fishing is effective only when you work at it. I've mentioned it several times before and I'll make the point here again—successful fishing is work, often hard work to the point where a fellow can work up a real sweat.

Trolling is most effective when it can be used in conjunction with an electronic depth sounder. Here the fisherman correlates his trolling to bottom structure as revealed by the depth sounder. He trolls along the edges of dropoffs and channels, around humps and pinnacles that stick up from the bottom, and if there is sufficient depth, he also crisscrosses over these same humps and pinnacles. When he gets a strike or a fish, he should note what his depth sounder shows and then swing back over the spot for additional tries. At the same time if water temperature equipment is available, make use of it and correlate the temperature with the known preference of the fish you seek. Often the difference of a degree or two of warmth will produce fish while nearby cooler waters will be barren.

Always seek to establish a pattern in trolling. Obviously no pattern can be discerned on the first fish or strike, but at least it gives one a reference point. The initial step is to pass back over the spot where you had the action, doing your trolling exactly as it was on the first pass. If you score again, obviously the pattern is beginning to take shape and it is up to you to elaborate on it. If succeeding passes over the spot fail to produce, then you must begin experimenting. Vary the trolling speed, run one line deep and another shallow, shorten a line so it runs in the backwash of the boat, lengthen another so the bait is well back out of any propeller wash. It is extremely important to note which way the boat was traveling when you got your strike. Unless artificial lures are employed, always reel in the line and examine the bait after each missed strike. Most strikes mangle natural baits to the point where they behave unnaturally. Always go with the freshest bait you have.

Trolling can be extremely exciting when fish schools are on the surface. The temptation is always great to troll right into the school. Don't! Never run through a school; you might catch a fish or two but more likely you will cause the entire school to either disperse or sound. Remember that the commotion you see on the surface is the center of the school. There are plenty of fish scattered around the outside of the surface action, and quite often these are the bigger fish. Seems in a lot of schools the youngsters tear up the baitfish, while the lunkers hang around picking off the wounded at leisure.

Work at trolling, and you will have thoroughly enjoyable sport and catch a lot of fish. Balance your tackle to the size fish you expect to catch, and you can have enjoyment supreme. Trolling with tackle heavier than necessary for the species sought is what I call "meat fishing." You catch a lot of fish but the heavy gear does not give the fish much of a chance to fight. I like to catch my fish on lighter gear because I enjoy the sport and spirit of the fish. When you troll with heavy gear, the fish is at a decided disadvantage. The initial strike and jolt when heavy tackle is employed takes a lot of fight out of a fish. It is almost like a fellow getting hit unexpectedly in the stomach.

17

How To Chum

You use bait on your hook to catch fish, so why not use another bait to attract the fish to the bait on your hook? There is a term for this; it's called chumming. It's the surest way I know of to bring fish within your casting range and to stir them into action. It's an art practiced by commercial fishermen as well as the sports gentry, and it's an art just about as old as fishing itself.

Unfortunately, as for every action there is a reaction and for every cause there is an effect, chumming as successful as it may be, too, has its drawback. Let's look at this drawback briefly and then go to the various ways of chumming, where and when, and how to make inexpensive chum.

The disadvantage of chumming is that it isn't productive of selective fishing. You may chum to better your odds to catch a particular species of fish and the chances are excellent that the chumming will aid your cause. The trouble is the stuff will also lure in just about all the fish species within scent range, and let's face it, there will be some unwanted species in the lot. This, however, is a fact you'll have to live with if you resort to chumming.

Chumming is baiting. Waterfront property owners who scatter their table leavings on the water or under their piers are doing nothing more than baiting the area. This is chumming in its commonest form. Do this weekend in and weekend out and you're going to cause some fat and sassy fish to take up residence in the immediate vicinity of your pier. In fact, where fresh water is concerned it can get to the point where the first place to try for a lunker bass or two is right under the dock pier. On second thought make that the last place to try on a trip since it would be almost a guarantee against making a

waterhaul. Some of the biggest largemouth bass I've seen have been dug right out from under the boat dock.

So much for this common form of chumming. Let's go to the more refined aspects of the art.

Chumming is the way to bring fish to an area and then to hold them there. It's a particularly deadly art connected with offshore fishing in our southern waters, especially in the Gulf of Mexico. At times Gulf coastal waters ranging ten to fifteen miles offshore are checkerboarded with shrimp boats. These boats drag huge trawls that sweep the bottom bare. These nets bring up a tremendous amount of marine life other than just shrimp, and in the process of pulling these nets through the water for several hours, the pressure of the weight of the catch will often kill much of the trapped marine life. Unless there is a definite market for it, this stuff is culled from the shrimp and dumped back overboard. In the spring and summer great schools of members of the mackerel family trail in the wakes of these boats to make the most of all the easy pickings. For years it has been common practice for sports fishermen seeking king mackerel, bonito, cobia, amberjacks, and barracuda to home in on the shrimp boats. The cull the shrimpers dump overboard is in effect chum for these fishermen. But as mentioned earlier the art does have its drawback. All this chum can at times lure in about as many sharks as gamefish, and it sure gets disconcerting to hook gamefish and then have about every other one chopped in half by a shark.

A lot of Gulf fishermen have a new twist. They pull up to the shrimp boats, and in exchange for a few cans of beer get a bushel or two of cull. Then they move clear of the area infested with sharks before they dump the cull over to form a chum slick. A good many of these boatmen pour the chum into small mesh nets and drag the nets astern as they troll for surface feeding gamefish. This in effect creates a long slick that is most attractive in attracting gamesters. When the gamefish hit the chum slicks, they turn into them and follow right to the source. Too vigorous chumming sometimes results in that same old headache of fishing behind the working shrimp boats—too many sharks.

The fine-mesh net in which the chum is suspended over the stern is called a chum bag. The chum after being put in the net is usually pounded with a club to break it up. Then when it is suspended in the water, fish oil plus small bits of crushed fish and marine life wash free from the net. If the boat is at anchor, the current will carry the slick astern. This same kind of chum bag can be used very successfully in pier fishing. Simply dangle it in the water and let the current do the rest. Whether used from an anchored boat or a pier, the chum bag works best when currents are running. The same bag doesn't have much effect when waters are current-less.

There's one kind of fishing where no chumming whatsoever should be used. That's in wade-fishing. Sure a wader can drag along a chum bag and lure in fish, but he can get into a heap of trouble if the fish that home in include such predators as sharks and barracuda. I've been wade-fishing and I've had sharks grab fish off my stringer, and I can assure you it's not a situation to be taken lightly.

Chumming can be as effective on bottom feeders as on the surface fish. The one change necessary is to sink the chum to the bottom. In this case instead of going with a net, go with a bag made of chicken wire or a metal chum pot. Either sinks real easy and will rest on the bottom, although if there is a strong current running, you might find it necessary to add a brick or two as extra weight to keep it from shifting in the current.

Those waxed cardboard half-gallon-size milk containers can be used as molds to make disposable chum blocks. Mix whatever you use as chum with water and fill the container. Pack it solid enough so you can stick a piece of clothes hanger wire down the middle. Then stick the whole thing in the freezer and store it there until ready to use. When you get ready to use it, twist a loop in the part of the wire that sticks out of the container, tie a stout line to the loop, strip the carton away, and suspend the frozen block in the water. The block will float and as it slowly melts it will form a chum slick that will be carried with the current. Depending upon the water temperature these frozen chum blocks will last thirty minutes to an hour. Those not immediately put to use can be stored in a cooler where they will last for hours. The advantage of the frozen chum block is that there are no smelly nets, pots, or cages to be cleaned when you return home.

Some folks get a big charge out of fishing for sharks. A lot more probably would if they knew how to attract these bruisers. Here again is where chumming comes in. The chum is best when you use fish that bleed a lot, for sharks can detect the scent of blood from almost unbelievable distances. You can go it one better if there is a packing plant nearby. Just go and get some five gallon cans of the usual drippings found around a slaughterhouse. Wow! Thst stuff drives sharks crazy. Many, many years ago my father and I took about twenty gallons of the stuff out with a shrimper friend who was interested in our shark fishing. We caught sixty-five sharks that day, ranging from as small as four feet on up to a couple of eight footers. Those sharks went crazy; they even attacked each other. When I think back I realize what dangers we faced. The shrimp boat was a small thirty-five-footer that rolled like a drunk sailor; we were about twenty-five miles offshore; the boat had no radio equipment, and if I recall correctly just some old inner tubes for life rings. I have no doubts now whatsoever what would have happened had any of us fallen overboard. That was way back in the early thirties, and I must have been eleven or twelve years at the time. Frankly, I wouldn't do the same thing today.

Fish live in an element where the visibility can vary tremendously within the matter of minutes. The water can be crystal clear with underwater visibility many, many feet. Then comes the tide change, a weather change, or discharge from inland waters to reduce visibility in the same water to a matter of inches. If fish had to depend upon sight alone for food, many would starve to death. Scientists tell us that the sense of smell is very highly developed in fish, and that fish have a natural tendency to pick up an enticing odor and follow it right to its source. In the case of chumming this means the fish will follow the scent right up to the chum bag.

It's interesting to note how chum is used in bluefishing along the Atlantic seaboard. Research stamps the bluefish as predominantly a daylight feeder, and a fish that leans strongly to sight as its means of finding food. After dark bluefish tend to stray from the usual formations of tightly packed schools. Yet New Jersey and New York fishermen go for bluefish on a round-the-clock basis, and they do it with chum. Apparently the scent of the chum charges these fish into breaking from their usual habit of daylight feeding and changing it to an almost twenty-four-hour binge. Marine biologists who have made studies of this claim the use of the chum changed the normal cyclical rhythms of the fish.

Chumming is a double-edged sword with the advantages favoring the fisherman. We have already seen how chumming attracts the gamefish to the fishermen. That's one edge of the sword. The other is that it attracts schools of small baitfish. These small fish move in closely packed dense schools that make a lot of noise under water, although the fisherman won't hear these noises. The tailbeats and fin rhythms of small fish carry through the water as sound waves, and sound alone is often the stimulus that spurs those big gamefish to venture in for close investigation.

What makes good chum?

Quite naturally all marine life, although some is better than others. Baitfish heavy in oil and fat are excellent since they form the most effective slicks. It's better to dice or grind up the fish rather than put them whole in the net or pot, and for this purpose some of the folks who really believe in chumming carry along small meal grinders that can be mounted on the stern of the boat. Small baitfish can be put whole in the chum bag and then pounded soft so they will ooze fish oil and tiny tidbits of matter will be carried free with the current. Crabs and other shellfish make excellent chum. Again crush the matter after it has been put in the chum bag. Oysters and conchs, shells included, make excellent chum, although it takes quite a lot of pounding to crush the shells. Clams, oysters, and conchs are as attractive to black drum and sheepshead as caviar is to the feast for royalty.

My first experience with conchs for chum bears repeating. It occurred on a fishing trip out of West End on Grand Bahama Island. Our trip was out to the reefs to fish for snapper, trigger fish, small grouper, and small barracuda. On the way out the boat skipper detoured to an area where the water was about six feet deep. A couple of native deckhands then went to work with hand dredges, and in about fifteen minutes they had almost two bushels of conchs aboard. When we reached the fishing grounds, the deckhands started to crush the conchs with wooden clubs. They would pick out two or three choice chunks of meat and eat the stuff raw. The rest—meat as well as shells—was scrapped overboard to act as chum. Later in our stay on the island I tried fried conchs and found them quite

tasty. I never could get around to eating them raw.

Up to now I have been writing about using forms of dead bait for chum. If you want to be more selective in what you lure in, you can do so by using live chum. Just be prepared to pay the price. No live bait—shrimp, minnows, fiddler crabs, or worms—comes cheap.

Live shrimp make excellent chum for sea trout (speckled trout). The manner here is to toss out a few live shrimp every time you get into a school of trout. The purpose is to hold the fish in the area. Sheepshead really take to fiddler crabs, and by tossing out some live ones, a fellow can entice the sheepshead out of their hideouts in the rocks. Gobs of live worms dropped overboard can electrify largemouth bass. The only trouble here is that the live worm chumming sometimes backfires and draws in the pesky bait-stealing bluegills and crappie in battalionlike numbers. Chumming with herring is a big thing in Pacific Coast waters.

Chumming can really spur the action for artificial lure fishermen. It serves to bring the fish within casting range of the fishermen, and then by resorting to artificial lures, the angler has the advantage of selectivity or quality fishing discussed in the chapter entitled "Quantity and Quality." Bait-stealers rarely strike at lures being worked through a chum slick, so in situations where the fisherman may have trouble with bait-stealers continually cleaning bait off his hook, he can turn to lures as a solution.

When chumming an inlet, cut, or channel, do so on the outgoing tide, for this is the time when fish lurk to seaward waiting for food to be swept to them by the current.

Interestingly enough there are a few vegetables and some grains that make excellent chum. Corn and green peas are outstanding chum for crappie and bluegills. So are bags of ground corn meal. Back in the days when my family had a fishing camp, we used to sink fifty-pound sacks of waste grain alongside our boat dock. This kind of chum was excellent in attracting shrimp. We could go down at night and by the light of a gas lantern could see swarms of small shrimp atop the bags of grain. A few throws of the castnet would get us enough live shrimp for a day of fine fishing. There was no expense involved for we simply got the grain sweepings that came out the boxcars on the sidings near the grain elevators.

18

Pier and Jetty Fishing

Most fishing scenes show anglers trying their luck from a bass boat or cabin cruiser, working the cypress stumps in a southern lake, or plying a fast-running stream backdropped by picturesque mountains. Unless it's for advertising purposes, one seldom ever sees a photo of a fishing pier. And that's to be expected, for really there isn't much glamour in fishing piers. At least glamour in a photographic sense.

Yet, if a boxscore were made up on how and where people fish, pier fishing would be right up near the head of the list. Pier fishing, indeed, fills the bill on a number of counts. It certainly offers low-cost fishing. It provides access to fishing in all kinds of weather and at night in particular, and it offers fishing in safety for the young, handicapped, and aged.

Successful pier fishing, however, isn't a matter of going out to the end and dropping over a baited hook. It, like other forms of fishing, requires know-how.

It's important to know where to fish from a pier. In the case of piers on freshwater impoundments, this will depend upon the bottom typography. In salt water it depends upon the bottom typography, plus tides and currents, species of fish sought, the season, the weather, and the time of day.

Where freshwater is concerned, fish tend to hang out around what fishermen call "structure." This is what provides fish with food and cover. Structure can be holes, channels, rocks, brush, wrecks, and manmade structures.

Consider the typical pier found on a freshwater impoundment. Its pilings will be covered with moss and algae, which in turn habor considerable aquatic life that in turn attracts gamefish. Largemouth bass, bluegill, and crappie often take up residence within casting range of such piers if the structure is suitable.

Pier fishing in salt water becomes something of a science because of the great many variables involved. This is easiest to understand when you take into consideration the construction and location of the typical saltwater pier.

The typical pier extends from the shoreline out to water of considerable depth. The seaward end of the pier is capped with a T-head. The first thought that pops into a newcomer's mind is that the best place to fish is from the T-head at the seaward end of the pier. This is fine and dandy if the time of the year coincides with the fish of the season. Otherwise there'll be some long, long waits between bites.

Fish from the T-head when migratory surface feeders are abundant. Almost without exception these fish will swim around the ends of piers rather than under them. When these fish move in close to shore, it is usually no closer than just outside of the last seaward bar or line of breakers. Since these fish are unlikely to swim under the pier, the fisherman must then fish for them from the T-head. Whether to fish from the right or left side of the T-head hinges on two variables—the sun and the current.

Fish have a tendency to swim into the current unless it is unusually swift. This suggests that when fishing from the T-head, it is advisable to cast in the direction in which the current is moving. If it is moving from left to right, then fish from the right wing of the T-head. The purpose is to put your bait out where the fish will reach it before coming in close contact with the pier itself. Close contact

The well designed fishing pier offers all kinds of fishing all the way from the surf to near blue water. This Gulf Coast Pier at Galveston, Texas, is called the biggest Fishing T in Texas.

Most pier T-heads are lower to the water than the part of the pier between the T-head and the shoreline. The reason is so that large fish can be docked easier.

means seeing the pier or moving into water on which the pier may cast shadows. Keep in mind that more of the migratory surface feeders will swim around the structure. This means the fish will start to swing wide when it comes in contact with the pier. If you're on the wrong wing of the T-head, the fish may pass well beyond your casting ability.

Now consider the sun. The lower it is in the sky, the longer the shadows the pier casts across the water. These shadows can spook fish. This is especially true when you have people walking—sometimes running—back and forth on the pier. They cast moving shadows on the water. You can beat this handicap by fishing into the sun when it is low on the horizon. A long-billed cap and sunglasses can make it bearable. And you don't mind it at all when you catch fish.

Piers offer both shallow- and deep-water fishing. The deepest water is always off the T-heads.

Some species of fish, mainly small bottom feeders, tend to range into shallow water. Usually they move in the troughs that run parallel to the shoreline. Depending upon the height of the tide and wave action, these fish are most likely to be found in the second of third seaward trough. They may venture into the first trough on unusually high flood tides. These fish work up and down the troughs picking up marine matter churned loose from the bottom and washed into the troughs by breaker action.

The time of the year and the tides also play important roles as to where to fish from piers.

Fish have a strong tendency to work in shallow water in warm weather and back to deep water when the weather is cold. This, however, needs to be amplified in view of the fact that you have temperature changes during the course of a day. The sun itself can cause these changes in raising the temperature of surface water. Consequently in the dead of winter you can have fish move from deep water to shallow water when the sun warms surface waters. This can often result in good pier fishing in the middle of the day, but poor fishing at night when the fish retreat back to deep water.

The opposite is true in warm weather. The sun can warm surface water to the degree of causing the fish to move out to deep water during the middle of the day and not return until the cool of evening or night.

Correlated to pier fishing this can mean that within a twenty-four-hour period the best fishing action can range from shallow water to the deep end of the pier and back again.

You have this same situation with tides. Fish the

deep water from the T-head on low tides, but move in closer to shore on high tides. Fish are quick to move into shallow water on a rising tide because the flooding uncovers choice tidbits to eat.

There are some species of fish that spend their lives within a relative few feet of piers. The pier pilings are covered with barnacles and marine growth that attract both baitfish and gamefish. The sheepshead is a good example. This fish loves to feed on the marine fodder attached to the pilings. Folks seeking to catch sheepshead invariably make their best catches by fishing right down alongside the pilings.

Down on the sea bottom you'll find a sink-hole around each piling. This is caused by currents that dig out the sand. These sink-holes are havens for flounders.

The material used in the construction of the pier can have a decided effect on the fishing. Fish are able to hear or feel sounds in three ways: inner ear, lateral line, and swim bladder. Water is many times denser than air, and it transmits sounds five times faster than air. Fish are influenced by noise and in many cases are attracted by sound. Unfortunately some sounds made on piers tend to spook fish rather than attract them.

Big fish can be caught from piers. This angler is hefting a thirty-five-pound black drum.

79

Two fine fishing locations. The anglers in the foreground are fishing from the end of a small jetty. In the background is a fishing pier.

Wood and concrete are relatively dead materials in the sense of conducting sounds. Metal is not. Consequently an all-steel pier can be a fish spooker because it can be a banjo of noises. Noises are deadened considerably when the steel pier pilings are encased in concrete.

Pier fishing requires some specialization in tackle. Ultralight tackle is not suited because piers are many feet off the water. A good pier rod should be six to seven or eight feet in length so that the fisherman will have ample length to leverage fish away from the pilings. Small fish can be swung aboard with the rod but a landing net or long-handled gaff will be necessary for landing large fish.

One of the big advantages in pier fishing is that so many people fish there, the area is well baited. This, of course, lures a lot of fish to the area, although a good portion of these fish may be of the "trash fish" variety.

A major disadvantage in pier fishing is the lack of privacy. There will be times when fishermen line the rails almost shoulder to shoulder. And today so many fishermen lack manners. You catch a fish, and right away a dozen guys horn in to cast to the spot where you hooked your fish.

Never pass up the opportunity to fish jetty waters. These are waters that yield fish in both quantity and quality.

You'll find jetties on all of our coasts—Atlantic, Pacific, and Gulf of Mexico. Mostly they are built to protect harbor entrances. Some are for the purpose of preventing beach erosion. You'll find jetties ranging from a few hundred feet to five or six miles in length. Most are flat-topped for a respectable

distance out seaward. After that they are walkable only if you have some mountain goat blood and can hop from rock to rock, each rock at a different slant from the previous one. People who fish from atop the jetties are referred to as "rock-walkers" or "rock-hoppers."

The "rock-walker" jetty fisherman has a lot in common with the pier angler. He'll need a long and fairly stout rod so he can keep his fish away from rock snags. How far he ventures out will hinge on the tides and how calm or rough the water is.

What makes jetty fishing so good?

It goes back to the old bit of where you find underwater structure, you also find fish. Many years ago I had a lake fishing guide scold me for complaining about losing lures on bottom brush snags. He maintained that wherever you find snags that claim terminal tackle, you likewise find fish. Man, when it comes to tackle-robbing snags, go to the jetties. There are more cracks, snags, overhangs, and whatever along a jetty than an army of centipedes has legs.

Again it must be pointed out that successful jetty fishing isn't so simple a matter as just dropping a baited hook into the water, although in all honesty, I've got to admit a lot of very good jetty catches are made just like that. If you place all your fishing hopes on blind luck, then drop over a line at the jetties. The odds of scoring are good.

The author's daughter, Laura, holds up a twelve-pound channel bass caught from a jetty.

80

Piers in fresh water pay dividends, too. These three largemouth bass—seven, three and one-half, and two pounds in size—were caught right out from under the pier.

You can change your fishing results from good to excellent by working jetty waters by design.

To begin with you need to visualize the jetty on a cross-section basis. Remember what you see above the water is only a small part of the jetty. Let's consider a typical jetty, first at its foot at the shoreline and then out where the water is thirty feet deep. Suppose the flat-top part of the jetty is six feet wide at its foot at the shoreline. The jetty slants outward and at its foot, the base might be ten feet across. Now consider the cross-section out where the water is thirty feet deep. Obviously the jetty can't be straight up and down like a wall, for a structure so made would topple in heavy seas. The properly engineered jetty at a cross-section any-where along its length will be pyramid in shape. The six-feet-across top and ten-feet-across base at the shoreline may be six feet across at the tope and one hundred feet across at the base out in thirty feet of water.

The underwater part of a jetty harbors great amounts of marine life, and this, of course, lures equally large numbers of gamefish.

Jetty fishing is best on moving water, and this holds true on extra strong currents. The same extra-strong currents along an open beach or in a bay would result in poor fishing. The reason for the difference is the great amount of marine life around jetties. Strong currents sweep this life away from the rocks and make it fair game for marauding gamefish. If you have wave action washing through the rocks, so much the better.

Yes, there is a time when jetty fishing can be agonizingly slow. That time is on slack water and when currents are absolutely nil. You can improve the situation to some extent if you know the locations of holes alongside the jetties or in the clusters of rocks proper.

The finest fishing—often it's fabulous—is usually around the ends of jetties, and in almost all cases this means the fishing is beyond reach of "rock-walkers." A boat is a must for this fishing. The reason for this great fishing has to do with the currents. You often have currents from different directions and these currents collide off the ends of the jetties. This swirls up all kinds of bait and in effect you have supermarket time for gamefish.

Much of my jetty fishing is done around the North and South Jetties at Galveston, Texas. I have on occasions caught tarpon, king mackerel, Spanish mackerel, ling, jackfish, speckled trout, and redfish all on the same trip. Catches like this always took place in the swirling currents near the ends of the jetties.

Without question jetty fishing is best and most enjoyed when done from a boat. Not only will a boat give you mobility to fish many places around a jetty, but it will also give you maneuverability when you tie into a big fish, always a good possibility in jetty fishing.

Lights make pier fishing a twenty-four-a-day adventure.

19

Pier Night Fishing

Fish quickly become accustomed to stationary lights and will not spook from the rays cast by the lights. This is particularly true with lights that are spotted to shine right down on the surface of the water. These lights attract fish and the lighted areas always teem with baitfish. Lurking right outside the cones of light are the gamefish that are quick to strike when baitfish stray into the so-called twilight zone. Consequently the well-lighted pier usually has masses of baitfish milling in the pools of light. Unfortunately the great amount of baitfish can sometimes cause problems. In addition to attracting gamefish, all of this bait also attracts a lot of the so-called bait-stealer or trash fish. In the case of saltwater fishing these are the catfish, piggies, etc.; in freshwater fishing they are the bluegills and small-size members of the sunfish family.

These small fish are masters at stealing the bait off one's hook, and it can be very frustrating having these fish strip hooks clean before the choice gamefish ever get close. This is the reason these fish are often referred to as "trash fish." They are the unwanted species that keep getting hooked when you're set on getting more sophisticated species like largemouth bass, speckled trout, striped bass, flounders, mackerel, and so forth. For that matter I've seen times when speckled trout and mackerel were regarded as "trash" when they kept striking at lures being tossed at tarpon. Whether a fish is trash or choice depends entirely upon what the angler happens to be fishing for on that particular day.

This brings to mind a Canadian fishing trip I was on some years ago. My fishing partner was Ken Foree, former outdoors editor of the *Dallas* (Texas)

Daylight hours hold no monopoly on incidents that can spook fish. Plenty of fish-spooking things can and do occur at night. This is especially so when it comes to fishing from a pier.

Wherever one fishes, whether on the Atlantic, Gulf, or Pacific coasts or Great Lakes or from any of a number of piers on freshwater lakes, you will find piers that range from no lights at all to those illuminated like Broadway's Great White Way. If these piers are all located on the same body of water, night fishing is likely to be best at the bright light piers, provided, of course, the lights are spotted in the correct locations.

Morning News. We were fishing Black Lake in northern Saskatchewan. Ken had his heart set on catching walleyes; I found the northern pike more to my liking. Every time I caught a pike, and I caught a boatload of them, Ken would mutter another oath about "those trash jackfish." Jackfish happens to be a provincial name applied to northern pike in many parts of the Northern Hemisphere.

Back to the piers with and without lights. The unlighted pier can offer some mighty choice action if a fellow plays his cards right. And it can reward him with some surprisingly big fish, for under cover of darkness a lot of big fish move into reasonably shallow water. This is especially true in the case of sharks. Fishing in the dark can be difficult even when using artificial lures. When live or cut bait is involved, a certain amount of light is needed in order to see to properly rebait the hook. Here is where playing the cards right comes into the picture. Use just a minimum amount of light, and then be extremely careful not to play its beam out over the water or on the water's surface. The stationary light is no problem since fish become accustomed to it. This is not the case with the moving light. I have been in speckled trout action in which a fish hit on just about every cast, and I have had this action stop abruptly and with finality when someone played a beam of light on the water. This is the big drawback of using a flashlight. There is always someone around to pick it up and shine it out on the water to see what is happening. And what is happening invariably stops when that moving beam of light hits the water.

The gas-operated lantern can fill the bill when fishing from an unlighted pier if the fisherman knows where to put or hang it in relation to where he is fishing. Remember this lantern remains in one place, and consequently it becomes a stationary light that can serve as an aid in attracting baitfish. This lantern will work fine as long as it is not placed behind the fisherman. The lantern *behind* the angler only throws shadows on the surface of the water, and since the fisherman does considerable moving when he casts out, these shadows, too, will be moving. The upshot, of course, will be to cause the fish to spook from the immediate area. If a lantern is used, it should be placed off to the side of the fisherman. The ideal location is to suspend it from the pier railing, or better yet, hang it in such a manner that it suspends at foot level with the pier decking. Placing the lantern between the fisherman and the place where he casts results in the rays blinding the angler. This is eliminated if the light is placed off to one side or at pier deck level.

Ideal pier lighting calls for a number of lights

The wing of a T-head can become a busy place at night when the fish are running.

spotted on gooseneck fixtures extending out from the pier. These lights should be floods and not spots. This extending them out from the pier places them where nothing will pass between them and the water. As a result there will be no shadows. The only way you can get shadows here is for someone to fall overboard, which interestingly enough happens often enough in spite of pier safety railings. In addition to these lights extending out from the pier, others can be located beneath the pier decking if the pier is rather high off the water. Pier overhead lights should be placed on standards high enough so that people walking back and forth will not cause moving shadows to fall on the water.

Generally there is no predictable one area where the fishing is likely to be best on the well-lighted pier, other than to point out that on normal and high tides, the action can be good anywhere along the pier, while on extreme low tides, the fishing will invariably be the best at the deep end of the structure. It is easier to predict where the action is likely to occur on the unlighted pier. The extreme low tide, of course, always means fishing the deep end. There is just no other way, for you can't fish where there isn't sufficient water. With normal and high tides one must take the darkness of the night into consideration. On a moonless, black night fish often forage in shallow water, often so shallow that their dorsal fins stick above the surface. I do most of my fishing on the Texas coast, and in night fishing I have caught twenty- to thirty-pound channel bass, black drum, and jack crevalle in water only two to three feet deep. These same fish don't come in nearly so shallow during daylight hours. I have also caught a good many fair-size sharks night-fishing in waters only slightly deeper.

On the dark, moonless night when the tide is normal or high, the pier fisherman should concentrate his fishing near the shallow water end of the pier. But as soon as the tide turns and begins to fall, he should then move toward the deep end. If there is a bright moon, skip the shallow water zone and fish from midpier to .the deep water end. Some rather long shadows can be cast across the water if the pier is a high one and the bright moon is low to the horizon. These shadows will be far less pronounced than those cast on a day with a bright sun in the sky, nevertheless these shadows from the moon are usually sufficient enough to cause fish near the surface or in real shallow water to spook. Therefore in this situation it behooves the fisherman to stay away from the shadow side of the pier. He will do far better fishing *toward* the moon and not back in the shadows. The same holds true in daytime fishing when the sun is low in the sky.

The fish species most active at night are those that feed by smell or sound. Although those which forage mostly by sight are far more active during the daylight hours, this does not mean that they will not strike at night. They will be active to some degree if the water is gin clear, there is some moonlight, or they are in the immediate vicinity of lighted piers, similar structures, or boats.

Most species that feed by scent generally work close to the bottom, which dictates that in going for these species, the bait must be worked on the bottom or at least quite close to it. The sight-feeders on the other hand are usually species that roam near the surface of the water, and if the fisherman is to catch these species, he must keep his bait, whether it is natural or artificial, reasonably near the surface. In the case of artificial lures this means the retriever must be started just a second or two after the plug, spoon, or jig strikes the water.

To keep natural baits—live or dead—near the surface the fisherman must use the same retrieve method used with artificial lures or he must resort to using a float. The float method is the better of the two systems. Ironically the lure-type retrieve used on live bait is rather ineffective. Lures are manufactured so they perform like minnows, shrimp, eels, worms, etc., when retrieved. This same retrieve used with live natural baits often causes the baits to spin or act unnaturally. Live bait is at its best when suspended under a float and allowed to swim about naturally. Retrieving, even a dead slow retrieve, hampers the natural swimming action of live bait.

Use of a float is an extremely deadly way to fish live bait at night from a well-lighted pier. The method here is to place the float three or four feet above the hook. Cast to where light floods over the surface of the water. The live shrimp, minnow, or whatever is used for bait will work frantically in attempts to get out of the cone of light and into the surrounding protective shadows. If the bait is large and strong and the float is small, the float quite likely will be pulled into the shadows. Where saltwater fishing is concerned, the current will carry the float into the shadows.

If gamefish are lurking in the darkness outside of the shadows, the frantic action of the bait will not go unnoticed. The result is a strike, and if the fisherman is alert and working at his sport, a hooked fish. The same minnow or shrimp could be just as active in darkened waters, but the strikes would be less frequent since the baits would not be silhouetted. When live bait is used in darkened waters, the main means of attraction then are scent and sound. A lot of fishermen overlook the importance of sound in connection with live bait, and this is especially so with minnows and shrimp. A frantically wiggling minnow can set up vibrations that a fish can feel from many feet away. The noises are even more pronounced when using live shrimp. These creatures make a distinct "crackle" or "snap" noise as they dart about in the water. Crayfish, which are popular freshwater baits, make similar noises.

The big disadvantage in night fishing is the lack of visibility. This is no problem on the well-lighted pier, but it can become annoying when the only light available is that of a flashlight or a gas lantern. Nevertheless this disadvantage can be far outweighed by any of several distinct advantages.

Consider, for example, average summer fishing. Except in waters far to the north, daytime fishing can get mighty unpleasant because of high temperatures. The heat makes it uncomfortable all the way around. The fisherman gets sunburned and soaking wet with sweat. The fish in the heat of the day sulk off to cooler waters, which usually means they go out to deep water well beyond casting limits from the pier. The fisherman should always keep in mind that fish are just like people, only they are wetter. When the water gets warm, fish move to cooler waters, and vice versa when the water gets cold.

There is even a far more important advantage to night fishing over day fishing when it comes to pier fishing, and especially if the pier is an unlighted one. Most fishermen dislike fishing in the dark; so this means you will have little competition. You don't have to worry about ducking flying sinkers when fellow fishermen cast out or getting involved in tangled lines when you fight a big fish. Personally I like fishing competition when it comes from a skilled fisherman. This kind of competition can keep a school of fish in the area; it is the competition from tyros that spooks fish and frightens them to the horizon.

The fellow who fishes at night usually works at the sport harder than he would during the day. The reason stems from one of those curious things concerning our senses. When one sense, for example sight, is sharply limited, another sense becomes keener as a compensation. If you have some doubts, a simple little experiment will prove it out. On your next fishing trip, close your eyes and keep them closed for about five minutes. Your sense of hearing begins to compensate for the loss of sight, and you begin to hear sounds that went unregistered when your eyes were open. This is what happens when fishing at night. You hear a school of minnows scurrying on the surface of the water. Fishing experience tells you that something big had to frighten the minnows and quickly you cast toward the sound of the minnows.

These same sounds are made during the daylight hours, but they are frequently missed because the fisherman does not have his hearing tuned in. He depends entirely on sight and forgets to listen. It's just as simple as that. There are, of course, more covering noises during the day. Boat traffic, water skiers, motor cars, and airplanes overhead all add to the noise level.

The main nighttime marine noises are caused by the wind and water. If the wind is up enough, waves will form to cause a "wash" noise around the pier pilings. When waves cross an area where the water is shallower than the scope of the waves themselves, you get still another noise. In this case the waves curl over, break, and become surf. This presents a roaring sound with a decided crash as the surf strikes pier pilings.

Fortunately for the night fisherman, the water is usually less active at night than day simply because the wind has a strong tendency to lay after the sun sets. This is an advantage to the fisherman in that it allows him to hear fish noises like the rip noises of schools of minnows scurrying on the surface of the water or the distant pop of a big gamefish grabbing something off the surface.

Where pier fishing is concerned, noises of another nature must be considered. There are noises that originate on the pier. How these noises help or hinder fishermen depends upon the degree to which these noises are transmitted into the water. This transmission in turn depends upon the materials used in the construction of the pier.

Wooden piers are the quietest; steel piers are the noisiest. Steel is an excellent conductor of sound, and steel piers really telegraph deck noises into the water. Some piers are a wedding of two materials—wood and steel. The degree to which these piers transmit sounds into the water depends upon the location of the steel components. A lot of noise will be transmitted into the water if the pier pilings are made of steel. But if the decking is steel and the pilings are wood, there is considerably less sound transmission for the wood members act as a cushion. This can become very important where sharp noises are made.

Concrete is used in the construction of many modern piers. It makes for sturdy, lasting construction that will stand in the heaviest of seas. A metal and concrete pier can be a noisy one with a lot of "ping" and "clang" unless the metal pilings are encased in concrete.

20

Landing Fish on Piers

When it comes to landing big fish, the pier is the place where the men are separated from the boys. Anyone can hook a big fish but not everyone can bring it to rest on the pier deck, and especially if the deck is ten to twelve feet above the surface of the water. It takes an expert fisherman to consistently deck large fish.

The pier fisherman must use his wits to win the game of the big ones, for he doesn't have the advantage of mobility that the wade-fisherman, the surf angler, and the boatman have. The boat fisherman has a tremendous advantage in the fight with the big ones, for he can maneuver his boat to keep the fish clear of obstructions. He can have a reel with insufficient line and still whip the fish with boat movements. There is no reason for the fish stripping all the line off the reel, for the boatman can jockey his craft in the direction in which the fish is moving. In this game the fish is ganged up on two to one—the fisherman and the boat.

The wade-fisherman has the same advantage as the boatman, only to a lesser degree. The wader can tire his fish and prevent it from cleaning his reel of line by moving parallel to the shoreline. If he is fishing an inlet or cove, he can work to the narrow neck of water and head the fish off at the pass, so to speak. You might say the wader loses his advantage when the fish heads out to sea where the water is too deep for the wader. This is true but only up to a point, which can best be explained with an actual example.

In this case the fisherman was using a reel with two hundred yards of line and he had hooked a fifty-pound fish in waist-deep water. The angler found he could wade out another twenty yards before the water got too deep. As soon as the fish started working seaward and toward that deep water, the fisherman started moving parallel to the shoreline. This lateral move was at ninety degrees or at a right angle to the movement of the fish. Most large fish hooked from the shore or a pier rarely move more than a hundred yards without altering directions, and these changes will usually be at an angle toward the strain that is pulling on the fish. Now the wader moving at the right angle to the fish bent on going seaward managed to deflect the run enough so that in a short time the fish's surge was parallel to the beach rather than straight out to sea.

You might wonder and ask why not attempt to check the fish's seaward run by staying behind it and increasing drag tension? If you use heavy enough line, this is entirely possible. It is also quite likely the added strain will tear the hook out of the fish's mouth. The fish that is pulling straight away has the advantage on its side since it is struggling against only one force. But when the fish has a strain applied on it from an angle, it is battling not one but two forces. One force, of course, is the pull of the line. The other is angle tension that tends strongly to upset the fish's equilibrium; consequently the fish is fighting line pull at the same time that it is struggling to maintain its balance in the water. This double fight, so to speak, quickly saps a fish of its energy.

The pier fisherman has only limited mobility when it comes to maneuvering a large fish. His movements are limited to up and down the pier proper and from one end of the T-head to the other. I recall the time I landed a fifty-pound shark on twelve-pound test line. My reel contained about one hundred yards of line, but I managed to beat the shark by wading it parallel down the beach for approximately two hundred yards. Had I been fishing from a pier I never would have beaten that fish because of limited mobility and insufficient line on my reel.

The first thing the pier fisherman must keep in mind is to use the proper rod and reel for the species of fish predominant in the area at a given time. When the channel bass, black drum, striped bass, and cobia runs are on and pier anglers get into them fast and furious, heavy tackle with a reel filled with ample line is necessary. Ample line means not less than two hundred yards if the line tests thirty pounds and over. A fellow using lighter test like ten to fifteen pounds better consider a minimum of three hundred yards.

Sufficient line is just part of the game of beating the big fish. The line allows the fisherman to best his prey at long range and lead it toward the pier. Now another phase in pier fishing, and this is the phase where most big fish are lost. The fisherman's problem is one of keeping the fish from running under the pier and around the pilings. If this happens, the fish might as well be written off, for the odds favor the fish brushing the line against the barnacle-crusted pilings. The shells of live barnacles are razor-sharp and that means a cut line.

So the fisherman must be careful to keep the fish at length from the pier. He can do this best if he has a long rod, a seven to nine footer. If the fish swims in too close but still out of gaff reach, the fisherman with this long rod can reach far out to maneuver and turn the fish away from the pilings. This is almost impossible to do with stubby rods of six feet or less in length.

The tendency of most fishermen when they hook a big fish is to hurry up and get it aboard. You hear someone shout: "Land it quick before it gets away." This has got to be the worst advice ever in fishing. The faster you try to land the fish, the better the odds are for the fish to escape. What it amounts to is trying to horse in the fish when it still has a lot of fight left. Instead of this "hurry up" jazz, take it easy; play the fish and play it until it is dog tired. Learn to recognize when the fish is beat and when it has given up the fight. This is easy to do. As a fish tires, it works closer and closer to the surface, and when all the fight is gone, it turns either belly up or on its side. Then it is a simple matter to lead the fish in close for gaffing or netting.

The fisherman battling the large fish should make every effort to work the fish around in such a way that water currents will be to the advantage of the angler. Suppose a fellow is fishing from a pier T-head, and he hooks a big one that takes off in a direction against the current. This is to the fisherman's advantage, for the fish is fighting two forces—current and line pull. This is a combination that can quickly sap a fish's energy. But as the fish tires, the fisherman should make an effort to work it around so the current will carry it out from the pier. At first this sounds crazy—trying to get a fish by letting the current carry it away from the pier.

It's not so far out when all facets are brought to light. A strong current can carry the fish under the pier where the line is likely to foul on the pilings and piling braces. If there is a surf running, the combination of current and breaking waves may swirl the fish under the pier and against the pilings with such force that the line will be cut on the barnacles. On the other hand when the fish is worked up to the pier side and into the current there is no danger of it being swept into the pilings. The current will tend to stand the fish out from the pier for easy gaffing or netting. This point will be driven home vividly the first time you try to gaff or net a big fish that has been swept under the pier. Keep in mind that a large hooped drop net is frequently used to net big fish. It is lowered into the water and then swiftly retrieved when the fish is led over it. You want the current to carry this net out away from the pier where it will be free from obstructions.

Whether one is fishing from a pier, from a boat, or just wading, the angler must keep his wits when scrapping the big ones. He should remind himself, vocally if necessary, that hooks are torn from mouths and tackle is broken not by the fish themselves but by haste and fishing inexperience.

With large fish such items as long-handled gaffs, flying gaffs, long-handled landing nets, and big hooped drop nets are absolute musts in bringing the fish to the pier deck. There is another way, but it is time consuming and somewhat uncertain. This is to slowly lead the fish down the length of the pier toward shallow water, then get off the pier and bring the fish up on the beach. It is uncertain because every time you approach a piling on your walk toward the shore you bring the fish near a place where a sudden surge or run can result in the line being cut by the sharp barnacles. The uncertainty is magnified if there is a running surf with breaking waves.

Small fish can be reeled up out of the water and then swung aboard the pier with the rod being used as a boom. If the rod is too limber to allow this, then the fish can be brought up by grabbing the fishing line itself and hand-lining the fish aboard. These methods work if the fish are hard-mouthed and the fisherman is able to see that the hook is deep in the fish's mouth. Landing nets, long-handled gaffs, or drop nets are needed if the fish are soft-mouthed or only lip-hooked.

Reel drag setting is very important in pier fishing. To repeat a point made in the previous chapter, the drag setting must be tight enough to maintain a steady pressure on the fish, yet loose enough to act as a shock absorber if the fish makes a run. Limited mobility on a pier makes drag settings critical.

Few fishermen today go out with just one rig. The wader always carries a spare in the car. The boatman, too, has a spare and often uses it by baiting up and sticking it in a rod-holder. Many pier fishermen as well go with several rigs. Some do so only to have a spare in the event something malfunctions on their number one rig. Others fish as many rigs as is permissible on a pier. In fact, almost all charge piers now have a rule limiting the number of rigs a customer can fish at the same time. On most such piers the limit is two.

Piers, however, do not have rod-holders on the railings. Consequently, the fellow fishing two rigs holds one and leans the other against the railing. More often than fishermen care to admit rods and reels are lost because of this practice. Sometimes it is a case of the fisherman straying too far away from the rig. This usually happens when the fishing is slow, few anglers are on the pier, and the guy decides to stroll to the concession stand for a quick beer. I have seen times when that forty or fifty cents beer really cost something like forty or fifty dollars when an unattended rig was snatched overboard. If a fellow is going to stroll off for a quick one, the sensible thing to do is to get his lines out of the water. There are times when rigs are snatched overboard with the owner standing just a few feet away. I have also seen a few cases of rods and reels being jerked right out of the anglers' hands. Invariably these things happen because the reel drags were screwed down too tight.

A fantastic number of valuable articles take the deep six annually off piers. Big fish are responsible for most rod and reel losses. Fishermen themselves somethings have ten thumbs, knocking over tackle boxes, bait boxes, and allied fishing gear.

Jumping fish like this scrappy dolphin are a lot of fun, but one must play a jumping fish with care to keep from tearing the hook from its mouth. As long as the fish is jumping, it isn't ready to be gaffed or netted.

"Hurry up and get him in! Quick! Reel him in before he gets away. Pull him over here quick so I can get him in the landing net!"

You hear these expressions time and again on the fishing piers, the charter and partyboats, on the bank below the dam, and in fact wherever fishermen gather. The advice is meant to be helpful. It is—only it helps the fish instead of the fisherman. Every day fish thousands of times over are hooked but get away because the hooks bent or broke, the hooks pulled out of their mouths, lines popped, rods broke, etc.

So Joe Angler at the office the next day tells about the one that got away because it was so big it broke his tackle. This is going to come as a shock to Joe, and in knowing circles he is going to have egg on his face because ninety percent of the fish that escape do so because they were aided and abetted by the angler himself. There's that old saw that ten percent of the fishermen catch ninety percent of the fish. Now we see that the other ninety percent of the fishermen lose through fault or faults of their own ninety percent of the fish they hook. There are times when I wonder how some fishermen ever catch any fish at all. They try and they try hard, but they make so many, many mistakes. I think it may come from the fact that the popular conception is that fishing is a lazy sport, whereas it is really a lot of physical labor.

Hooking fish is one thing; landing them is something else again. It doesn't take a heck of a lot of skill to hook a fish since the majority of the fish hook themselves when they strike the bait or lure. On the other hand it takes all kinds of finesse to lead that fish to gaff or into the landing net, and in the case of landing the fish, skill is not to be confused with muscles. One of the best ways to lose a fish, especially a big one, is to put too much muscle in your handling of the creature. Always keep in mind that fishermen and not fish break tackle.

In order to play a fish properly, one must understand his tackle and what roles the various components play in the sport. The hook is what gives the fisherman a purchase on the fish, and the line in turn is what connects the fish to the angler. Now we come to the rod and reel, two of the most misused and abused accoutrements in the game.

The rod is a lever, a whip, and a shock absorber all rolled into one, and interestingly enough all these principles play equally important roles in casting, working the bait, setting the hook, and finally in landing the fish. Understand these roles and their functions, and you will add immeasurably to your fishing enjoyment. Let's look briefly at each of the roles, starting with casting.

The rod becomes a lever in casting. It enables the fisherman to get distance and accuracy. The whip action of the rod tip is what gives the angler the ability to cast a light object a considerable distance. If you need proof, just compare distances in casting a quarter-ounce lure with a rod and then throwing the same lure baseball style. The shock absorber action is what permits the fisherman to cast out a soft bait without snapping it off the hook.

Okay, so now our lure is cast well out from shore. What is the rod's role in fishing the lure? To begin with the lure won't catch fish resting motionless on the bottom. The fisherman must put motion into it to attract and to stir fish into action. The rod is again a lever in that it allows the angler to work the lure to one side or the other, or hold the rod high overhead to work the lure over snags. That whippy tip is again a shock absorber. It bends with the action in such a way that the lure can be worked in a lifelike manner, not jerky like a puppet on a string.

When a fish turns over on its side, its fight is gone and its ready to be landed. The fish pictured is a small black drum.

When you get a strike and then in landing the fish, the rod reverses order and becomes first a shock absorber, then a whip, and then finally a lever and shock absorber combined. Quite frequently the strike of the fish is both sudden and unexpected.

Like the fish that hits when you're lighting your pipe. Without some sort of shock absorber a taut line can be snapped on a sudden, hard strike. Then after the fish is hooked, the rod is both shock absorber and whip. Every time the fish makes a run or surge, the rod bends and acts as a cushion to keep the hook from ripping from the flesh of the fish's mouth or to prevent the line from breaking. When the fish turns and runs in toward the fisherman, the rod bend straightens to aid in taking up any slack line between the fisherman and the fish. The angler than uses the lever action of the rod in turning the direction in which the fish runs, in leading it around obstructions, and finally in working it into reach of the gaff or landing net.

A reel is nothing more than a line storage device. The line is laid on orderly to facilitate ease in casting and then to pay out line evenly to minimize line tangles. The role is the same in playing and landing the fish. As the fish is brought in, line is laid evenly on the reel in such a manner that it is completely free of tangles. If the fish makes a sudden seaward run, and it is necessary for the fisherman to surrender line, he can do so without fear of line tangles and knots.

Until the invention of drags any tension put on a reel was applied by the fisherman's thumb. Today even the cheapest of reels have some sort of mechanical drag devices. Unfortunately too many fishermen do not understand the role of the drag. It is not a device to bring a fish's run to an automobile tire "screeching halt." It is instead a device designed to tire and wear down a fish, but in order to perform this function properly, it must be used wisely.

A properly set drag is one that is tight enough for the fisherman to use his rod as a lever to turn the direction of the fish but at the same time light enough so that the fish can take out line if it makes a sudden and unusually strong run. A properly used drag is insurance against line or rod breakage. You don't just set the drag and let it go at that. Instead within the course of battling a big fish, the skilled fisherman will alter drag settings several times. Let me illustrate this with the typical battle with a big fish.

Let's say the fish is a husky channel bass, a thirty-five-pounder hooked in the surf. Your reel is filled with three hundred yards of line. Fifty yards of line was off the reel when the fish was hooked, and the creature's initial run stripped off another fifty yards. You realize that in the course of the fight the fish could take off another one hundred yards. Does this mean tightening down the drag to make it harder for the fish to take line? Not at all. In fact, this is the incorrect reaction. As line goes out the just have enough energy left for one supreme bid for freedom. A drag screwed down too tight is a fine way to bust up your tackle and lose the fish. Set the drag light so that you will have a good cushion to take care of any sudden surge the fish may make. In fact, experienced fishermen play fish at this stage on the assumption the critter has the vitality and reserve strength for a couple of hard runs. They tire big fish all the way down before they attempt to land them.

This is a fifty-pound amberjack turned over on its side and ready to be brought aboard.

diameter of the remaining line and reel spindle combined decreases and the more this diameter decreases, the greater the tension needed to pull off remaining line. It can reach a point of breaking the line or rod tip. Consequently the right action to take is to gentle ease off on the drag tension as the fish takes line, but it goes without saying not to slack it off all the way. How far one eases off and how much tension one keeps on the drag setting are things determined only by experience. You can't categorically say a half turn or a full turn of the drag because there can be differences in the friction on the drags of identical reels.

You want the drag tension to be strong enough to keep pressure on the fish to tire it out and yet be light enough so that if the creature makes an unexpected run, the hook won't be ripped from its mouth or the line or rod broken. As line is retrieved on to the reel, the drag tension should be slowly increased. How much is again determined by experience. Now your fish is in sight. It's just thirty feet from your gaff. What's the next move? Tighten the drag and quickly pull the fish into the beach? For heaven's sake don't try that! When you see the fish, remember it can see you too. The fish might

A gaff is necessary to bring aboard big fish. The fish being gaffed is a fifty-pound amberjack.

Actually fish don't pull as hard as they seem. Results of laboratory studies reveal that the pulling strength of a fish is approximately half that of the fish's weight. This, then, means a twenty-pound fish will exert a pull of approximately ten pounds. But does this mean a twenty-pound fish can't exert a pull in excess of half its weight? Under certain circumstances any given fish species can exert a strain several times its weight. This becomes self evident to the fisherman tied onto a rainbow trout in a swift-running mountain stream. The experiments carried out in the labs were done with fish tethered and pulling on an already taut line. Give the fish a

The sure way to keep from losing a fish is to use a landing net.

running start and see what happens. That same twenty-pound fish can easily snap thirty-pound test line. Try this experiment. Tie a ten-pound weight on the end of ten-pound test line. You can pick up the weight if you do it slowly and very carefully. Try jerking it off the floor, and pop goes the line. Now take that same ten-pound test line, tie one end to a tree limb and suspend a two-pound weight from the other. Lift that weight up to the limb and then drop it. Again pop goes the line. This same thing happens with fish if the angler allows slack in his line.

And just look at what happens when there is line slack, the fish turns and heads out to sea, and the fisherman rears back on his rod. A five-pound fish can snap twenty-pound test line that way. The rod with the springy tip and the reel with the drag are devices designed to cushion such hard and sudden shocks. They are in effect devices that compensate for fisherman errors.

That same drag that can aid a skilled angler to land a huge fish can become a curse in the hands of an inexperienced fisherman, and it can happen with a run-of-the-mill fish. The crank handle on the conventional spool star drag reel can be turned with no corresponding revolution of the reel spindle. The spindle turns only when the drag is tightened or the fish lessens its pull. No sweat here. But try the same thing with a spinning reel or spin-cast reel. Here the spool is fixed with a bail circling the spool and turning when the reel crank is turned. The purpose of the bail is to lay line on the fixed reel spool in the same manner in which it was originally spooled. Every time this bail revolves but doesn't pick up line because of insufficient drag tension, a twist is put in

the line. A lot of turns on the crank can make fishing line as kinky as a wire spring.

The procedure here is to tighten down the drag enough so that line can be picked up. If that doesn't work, then dip the rod tip toward the fish and lift it up pulling in the fish that much. When the rod is again dipped toward the fish, reel rapidly to pick up line. It's a game of pump-reel, pump-reel, pump-reel.

A great many fish are lost just beyond reach of the gaff or the landing net, and again in many cases the blame must be attributed to fisherman inexperience. I've already mentioned how the fish is likely to make a new effort to escape when the creature sees the fisherman or the boat. The fisherman can prepare for this by loosening his drag a bit to cushion against any sudden surge.

Now we face another problem—that of actually getting the fish up on dry land or into the boat. If the fish is small and firmly hooked, it can be lifted and swung in with the rod used as a lever. Obviously if the fish is too big for this action, the fisherman has to turn to the gaff or landing net, but improperly used these landing devices can cost a fellow his big one.

The first rule to observe is never attempt to land a big fish that obviously still has fight left in it. Tire the fish and then go for it with gaff or landing net. The mark of a tired or whipped fish is when it swims on its side or shows signs of a loss of balance in its swimming. One that turns belly up at the surface is a completely whipped fish and actually one that is moribund. Let's go, however, back to the fish that is swimming erratically and go through the correct procedure of landing it with gaff or landing net.

Don't swat at a fish like trying to hit a tennis ball. Lead the fish head-first over the net and then scoop it up.

Let's view the gaffing method first. Don't try to gaff the fish at extreme distances. Instead use the rod as a lever and work the fish in close by swinging the rod from one side to the other. Often this rod swinging will cause the fish to swim a figure-eight pattern alongside the boat. Carefully slip the gaff into the water with the pointed hook at a level well below the fish. Coordinate your actions so that when the fish is led over the hook, you can bring the gaff up with a fast, strong sweeping motion. Often the momentum of the upward sweep is enough to swing the gaffed fish right into the boat. Never try to sink the gaff hook in the fish's mouth, under the gills or near the tail. Go for the middle part of the body, preferably the upper portion in the vicinity of the dorsal fin. The flesh is firm there and will not tear.

Use the same rod swinging to work the fish in close when a landing net is used. Also dip the landing net well below the surface, and when the fish's head appears just over the rim of the net, sweep the net upward and against the direction in which the fish is swimming. This will bring the fish head-first into the net. Never attempt to net a fish from behind. The fish will just jet out of reach when it is touched by the net. I've never seen a fellow yet who could sweep a landing net through the water as fast as a fish can swim, even a hooked and tired fish.

Whether gaff or landing net is used, the important thing is to prevent any slack line between the rod and fish. The fish can use it to advantage by jerking hard enough to tear out the hook or pop the line. Or if the fight has been a long one, the hook may have worn a hole in the flesh and then just drop out when slack line is allowed.

I lost an unusually large cobia just like that. The fish appeared to be about a fifty-pounder, and I had battled it for almost a half hour before I worked it close to the boat. There it was like a log alongside the boat. I slipped the gaff over the side, but as I reached out to bring the hook below the fish, I allowed slack line. It was then that the silver spoon just fell out of the fish's mouth, and it was all so close that I could see the hole that had been worn into the flesh. Then I panicked. The gaff just wasn't in position, but I tried to gaff the fish anyway. The gaff struck the fish a glancing blow, scratching the flesh rather than penetrating. It was just enough to spur the fish to make a couple of thrusts with its tail to move out of reach and vanish into the depths. Even with the spoon out of the fish's mouth, I still could have gotten the critter had I kept my wits and taken time with the gaff.

The landing of fish varies according to where the angler happens to be fishing. You do it one way from a pier, another from a boat, another from a pier, and still another wade-fishing.

22

Matched Tackle

Matched tackle is very important to successful and enjoyable fishing. Unfortunately too many fishermen fail to carry the "matched tackle" theme to what has to be the obvious conclusion. It could be that the obvious is overlooked because it is just that—too obvious.

There is far more to matched tackle than the perfect marriage of reel to rod and then rod and reel to style of fishing and species of fish sought. The line must be taken into consideration, and then there is the conclusion—the business end of the tackle. This business end is covered by the term *terminal tackle* and it takes into consideration hooks, sinkers, floats, snaps, and swivels. If the terminal tackle is wrong, fishing results will be skimpy regardless of how perfect the rod-reel-line union may be.

LINES

Most fishing lines are rated in pounds test, which is the maximum weight the line will lift without breaking. Some lines are designated by the number of threads in a braid and some by the line diameter in cross section. Lines come in as many colors as there are in a rainbow, and line color today is pretty much a case of fisherman's choice. The line least visible to fish is monofilament. The following is a description of popular fishing lines, other than fly lines.

MONOFILAMENT (round). This line requires little care and is good for spinning, casting, and trolling. It has good knot strength, low drag in wind and water, and has low visibility to fish. This is a hard line, however, that will cause heavy wear on guides and rod tiptops. Except for light test monofilament, this line tends to be stiff. It is a very dry line to cast with on revolving spool reels since the line does not absorb water.

MONOFILAMENT (oval or ribbon). This line is suitable for squidding and bait casting. It has good know strength and low visibility to fish. This line is not suitable for spinning or spin-cast reels because it will twist easily. It has a tendency to slip under the flanges on reel spools and is very stiff in tests in excess of about thirty pounds.

BRAIDED DACRON. This is very good line for bait casting, trolling, and stiff-fishing. It is very small in diameter and has low drag in water. Its knot strength is lower than that of nylon or silk. This line is water repellent and very dry, and as a result it is hot on one's thumb in casting.

BRAIDED NYLON. This line requires little care and is fine for squidding and casting. It has a smooth finish, small diameter, high knot strength, and is resistent to rot. The line, however, has comparatively high drag in water and has excessive stretch, which can cause problems in hook setting. The line also has some tendency to fray.

BRAIDED SILK. This line makes excellent bait-casting line because of low stretch and excellent spooling. It has a very smooth finish and high knot strength, but it requires a great deal of care because it is very subject to rot. It has comparatively large diameter for pound test.

Fishing is best enjoyed when the tackle matches the fish sought. These two-to four-pound spotted weakfish were caught on lures on baitcasting tackle.

TWISTED LINEN (Cuttyhunk). This is very good line for trolling and is used extensively for offshore saltwater trolling. It has low stretch, good knot strength, and is stronger wet than dry. The line is water absorbent and very wet and as a result casts poorly. This line is extremely subject to mildew and rot and requires very much care to maintain reasonable life.

WIRE, LEAD-CORED BRAIDS. These are specialized lines for trolling, and they are fast sinking without having to resort to using sinkers. These lines readily kink and are hard to pay off a reel without backlashing.

Regardless what kinds of lines are used, reels should always be filled to capacity so that the line in use will perform at its highest efficiency. When line is not in use for long periods, it should be stored on a large-diameter spool in a dry place at room temperature. Long periods in direct sunlight can cause synthetic lines to lose strength. Monofilament line stored tightly on a reel for a period of several months can develop an annoying coil that can hamper casting. The coil can be reduced by soaking the line in water for several hours before using it. Another method of removing the coil is to peel the line off the reel and stretch it.

LEADERS

Whether a leader is used depends upon the basic fishing line the fisherman employs, the style of fishing, and the species of fish sought. If he uses braided, silk, or linen line, he must use a leader, which in turn can be monofilament, wire, or cable. The leader material in turn depends upon style of

A bay popping rod with a float is a perfect tool for bay fishing. These small channel bass and spotted weakfish were taken wade-fishing.

But what good are these strikes if the bright objects are hookless?

HOOKS

The business end of the terminal tackle is the hook. This little piece of steel is the dividing line between success and failure. The hook is to fishing what the bullet is to the rifle, and like the bullet, the hook can be the least expensive but most important piece of metal in the sportsman's tackle box. Good fishermen are always cognizant of the fact that the hook is what keeps them connected with the fish. Consequently they are discriminating when they purchase hooks, and when it comes to certain species of fish, they are as finicky about hook selection as a mother is about her daughter's bridal gown.

Consider first the matching of the hook to the tackle. It should be self-evident that light rod and reel combinations require small, light hooks, while

fishing and fish species sought. Where trolling is involved, one must almost always use either wire or cable. The exception is when the fish sought are small ones without sharp teeth.

In still-fishing, surf fishing, and bait-casting, the most popular leader material is monofilament for fish that don't have sharp teeth. If the teeth are razorlike as in the case of lake trout, northern pike, mackerel bonito, and the sharks, wire or cable leaders are required.

The use of live bait such as shrimp, small minnows, or worms dictates using a monofilament leader. This material is light and supple, and it will permit the bait a lot of freedom of movement, which is the main reason for using live bait in the first place. Wire leaders can be used when the live baits are large, and again where sharp-toothed fish are involved.

The monofilament line on the fisherman's reel can become the leader itself when small fish or fish without sharp teeth are sought. This is in itself an advantage since it eliminates connecting links that often detract from the bait or lure. Fish frequently strike at bright objects such as swivels and snaps.

This is the mouth of a ten-pound flounder. Fishermen often make the mistake of assuming a fish with a large mouth dictates using a big hook. Big hooks are a handicap when live bait is used because the hook weight and size hampers the bait.

Here's proof that light spinning gear can be used successfully in wade-fishing in the surf.

heavy trolling and offshore gear demands stout, forged steel hooks.

Bait plays a role in hook selection, too. Always go with small hooks when live bait is used. The point here is to tax the strength of the bait as little as possible. The hook is important, too, even when dead or cut bait is used. If the bait is soft, use a "bait-holder hook" that has small barbs on its shank. This same hook is an excellent choice when plastic worms are used for largemouth bass fishing, since the barbs will aid in keeping the worm from slipping off the hook. Equally important where dead or cut bait is concerned, the hook should be small enough so that it can be covered by the bait.

Other than size, hooks come in various shapes, and there are advantages and disadvantages that must be taken into consideration. The following lists pros and cons on popular hook designs.

A short point-of-hook to point-of-barb hook will bed deep and fast in a hard mouth. Its disadvantage is that it can be thrown easily and is likely to slip out of torn flesh.

A long point-of-hook to point-of-barb hook holds well in torn flesh and is hard for the fish to throw. This same type hook is slow to drive home and needs deep penetration for the barb to catch.

A hook with direction-of-point directly in line of eye-to-point will penetrate easily. If the direction-of-point is tangent to the line of eye-to-point, considerable force is necessary to bed the hook. The great advantage of this hook is its holding ability since it digs deeper into the flesh and up to an angle of as much as forty-five degrees from eye-to-point.

The distance from hook point to shank is called the gap. If it is small, the hook takes a small bite into the flesh and is less likely to back out. If the gap is large, the hook will bite deep but it will also come out easily.

Then there is the distance from the point of the hook to the bend. If it is short, the bite into the flesh will be shallow and the hook can be thrown easily. A hook with a long bend gives deeper penetration and greater purchase on the flesh.

A long shank hook is ideal for fish with sharp teeth, but it has the disadvantage of not going deep into the fish's throat. The short shank hook will turn easily in a fish's mouth, but it will hook a fish much deeper in the throat.

The offset angle of the hook point to the shank is called straight, reversed, or kirbed. The straight hook will penetrate easily since the point is in line with the pull. The disadvantage of this hook is that it can be held in the fish's mouth without the point catching. Reversed or kirbed hooks are harder to penetrate in a tough mouth because the point angles away from straight line pull. These hooks bed easily in soft flesh and when flat in a fish's mouth, this hook is less likely to be pulled out. The reversed or kirbed hooks are not suited for trolling because the offset will cause the bait to spin and put twist in the line.

Hook sizes range from No. 32 to 22/0, with the No. 32 hook for the smallest of fish. The No. 20 hook is about the smallest size for practical sports fishing. From eye to bend this hook is $5/32$ of an inch. In general sports fishing, hooks are called small when they fall in the range from No. 20 to No. 4. Medium hook sizes range from No. 2 through 5/0. Large hooks are in the 6/0 to 13/0 range, and any hooks above that are considered as extra large.

The system of measuring and designating hooks by sizes originated in England. Unfortunately a lot of liberties have been taken with measures, and today a 5/0 hook manufactured by one company may well vary in size from a 5/0 hook made by another company. In addition you run into designations such as 5/0-S, 5/0-2xS, and 5/0-2xL. These additional codes refer to length of shank. The S is obviously for standard; the 2xS stands for extra short and the 2xL stands for extra long.

The following are popular hook styles for sports fishing.

ABERDEEN. This is a very popular live-bait hook for freshwater fishing. The hook is made of thin wire and is light in weight. It has a round bend and a wide gap.

CARLISLE. This hook is commonly used for large baits. It has a round bend, long shank, and kirbed point, which means that the point is offset to the left when the hook is held shank down with the point toward the fisherman.

EAGLE CLAW. This is a very popular hook. It has a round bend and a point that strongly resembles an "eagle claw."

GANG. This term is applied to any hook that has more than one tine. Common gang styles are double hooks and treble hooks. Double hooks are mainly for use with soft baits. Most artificial lures, especially plugs, come equipped with treble hooks.

KIRBY. This hook has a round bend and kirbed point, which means the point is offset to the shank and line of pull. The offset is to speed hooking.

LIMERICK. This is a hook of Irish origin. It is made of heavy wire and usually has a straight point and an almost round bend. It is quite similar to an American design called Cincinnati Bass, a hook that has a round bend and kirbed point.

O'SHAUGHNESSY. This is an extremely popular style for both salt- and freshwater fishing. It is made of heavy wire and forged for extra strength. It has a round bend with the point turned in. This is a favorite hook for big game fishing.

SHEEPSHEAD. This is a short shanked hook made of heavy wire. It is designed for sharp-toothed fish.

SIWASH. This hook has almost no shank. Its extra long point is for deep, fast penetration in tough months.

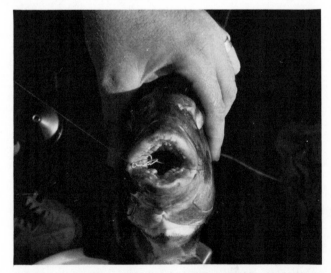

Hooks should be matched to the fish species sought. This is what happens when a strong-jawed, heavy-toothed fish like s sheepshead clamps down on a treble hook suitable for trout fishing. The result is a bent hook.

SNECK. This book has nearly right-angle bends from point to bend to shank. Hooks with this style of bend tend to break easier than hooks with a round bend. This hook is not nearly as popular as it used to be.

SPROAT. This is a popular saltwater hook. It has a round bend and is quite similar to the kirby, except that the point is straight instead of offset. This hook is sometimes forged for extra strength.

Some of the hooks listed above can be obtained with various point and eye styles, such as spear point, rolled-in or turned-in point, and hollow point; turned-up eye, turned-down eye, ball eye, or looped eye.

SINKERS

The difference between a full stringer and a waterhaul can often be traced to the type and size of sinker the fisherman used. When live bait is used, the sinker must be light so as not to interfere with the action of the bait. In areas where the water is calm, the rule of thumb is to go with as little weight as possible. Those big golfball size sinkers may be helpful in making long casts, but they make an awful splash when they hit the water. Since water is many times denser than the air above, the splash makes a lot of noise. Such splashes don't seem to bother the pesky bait-stealing fish, but all that noise can put down gamefish.

The sinkers sold at the tackle store are usually bright since they have yet to be exposed to oxidation that results from use. Particularly in trolling, one often has fish strike at these bright sinkers. By all means "weather" your sinkers to get rid of the shine. Put new sinkers out in the weather and in the space of a couple days they will turn dull gray.

Sinkers fall into three categories—bottom-fishing, still-fishing, and trolling.

BOTTOM-FISHING. These are heavy sinkers with the common shapes being round, diamond, and pyramid. Some are designed to dig into the sand or shaped so that they will not roll along the bottom.

STILL-FISHING. These sinkers are streamlined to make for easy casting. They are attached to the line by means of rings at each end, dog ears that are bent around the line, or by grooves that are crimped tight so as to bind on the line. These sinkers are generally used beneath a float.

TROLLING. These sinkers are designed to hold a bait at a desired depth when trolling at a particular speed. They are streamlined and so designed so that they will ride on an even keel to prevent the line from twisting.

BOBBERS

Bobbers, which are also called floats, are used in still-fishing to keep the bait off the bottom and at a specific depth and to indicate when a fish is biting. A form of bobber, usually just a round cork ball, is sometimes used in bottom fishing as a means of keeping the baited hook off the bottom. In such a case the bobber is rigged on the leader or line between the sinker and the hook.

Bobbers can be made of cork, balsa wood, or plastic and are usually brightly colored so that they are easy to see. Some have a concaved or dished top so that when the rod is manipulated the float will "chug" the water, making a sound much like that of a fish feeding at the surface. This type of bobber is called a "popping cork," and it is an extremely popular device in saltwater bay fishing. Bobbers come in many shapes, including round, oval, cone, and quill.

SWIVELS, SNAPS

Many top fishermen refrain from using either swivels or snaps if at all possible. They don't want to put anything on the line that may detract from the bait. There are times, however, when snaps and swivels are necessary.

SWIVELS. These are devices that will permit a bait or lure to revolve without twisting the line. They are considered a must in trolling. They are least used in still-fishing. Swivels come in many sizes and range from inexpensive ones that consist of two loops of wire with their ends tucked inside of a brass barrel to offshore big game fish models that are carefully machined and rotate freely on stainless-steel ball bearings.

SNAPS. These are wide devices that provide a quick way to change hooks or lures. They operate on the safety pin principle and lock when closed. Snaps should not be used next to lures unless so advised by the lure manufacturer. Snaps should not be used with small live bait because the extra weight will impede the action of the bait. Snaps and swivels are often made into a single unit that is called a snap swivel, an item used mainly in trolling.

The sketches are popular terminal rigs. The rigs with bottom fishing-type sinkers are for salt water. The bay fish-finder rig with the egg sinker that slips up and down the line can be used in both fresh and

PARTS OF A HOOK

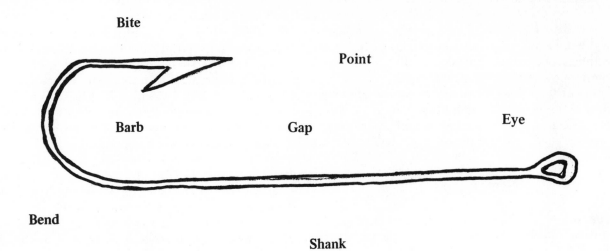

TYPE OF POINTS

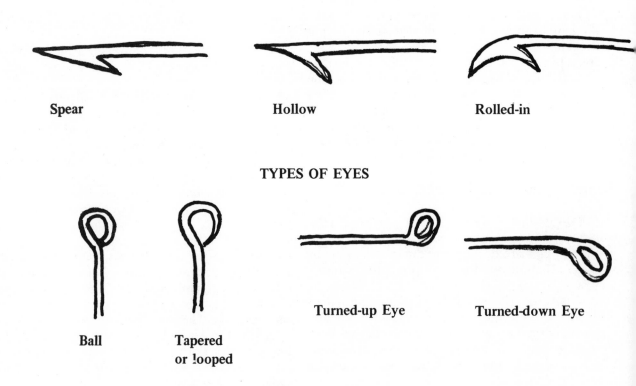

Spear   Hollow   Rolled-in

TYPES OF EYES

Turned-up Eye   Turned-down Eye

Ball   Tapered
or looped

TYPES OF SINKERS

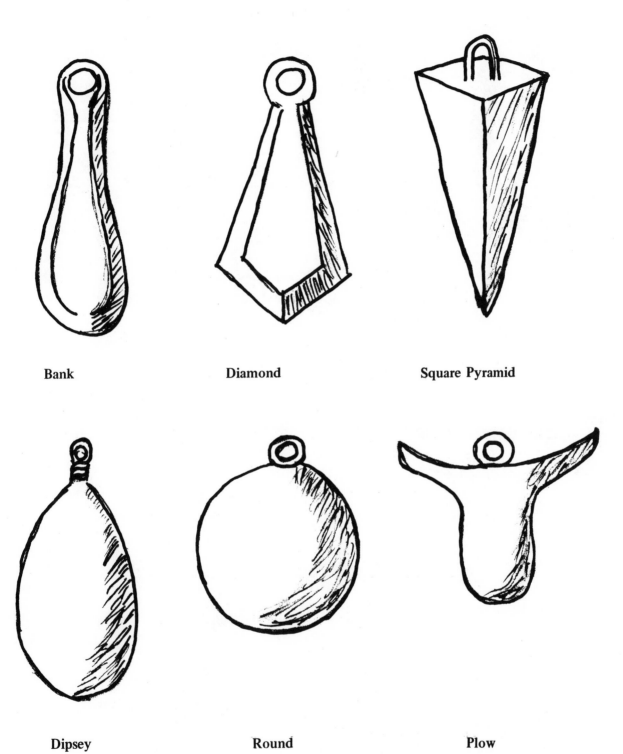

Bank   Diamond   Square Pyramid

Dipsey   Round   Plow

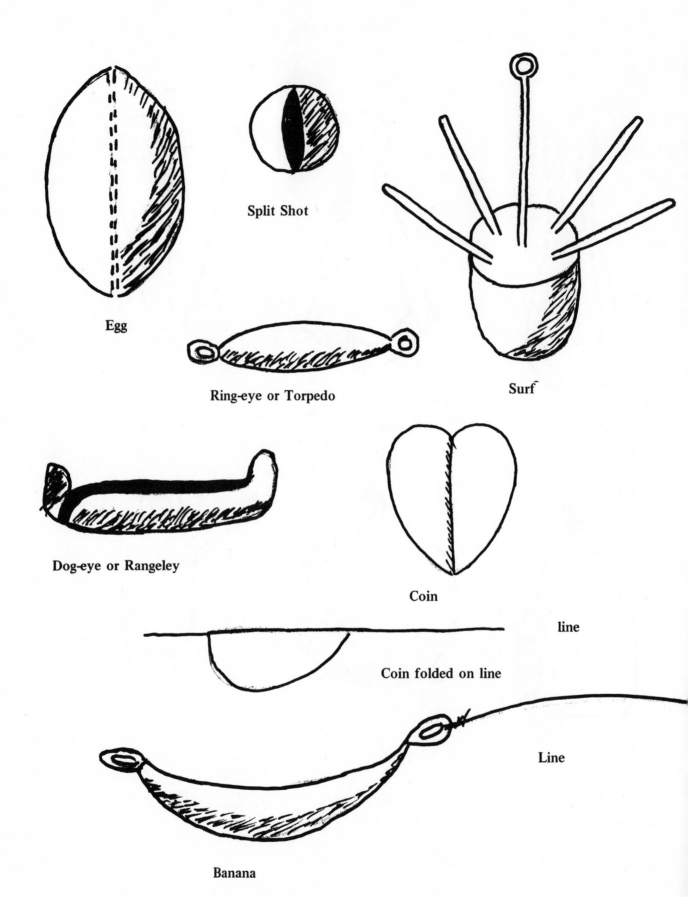

Egg

Split Shot

Surf

Ring-eye or Torpedo

Dog-eye or Rangeley

Coin

line

Coin folded on line

Line

Banana

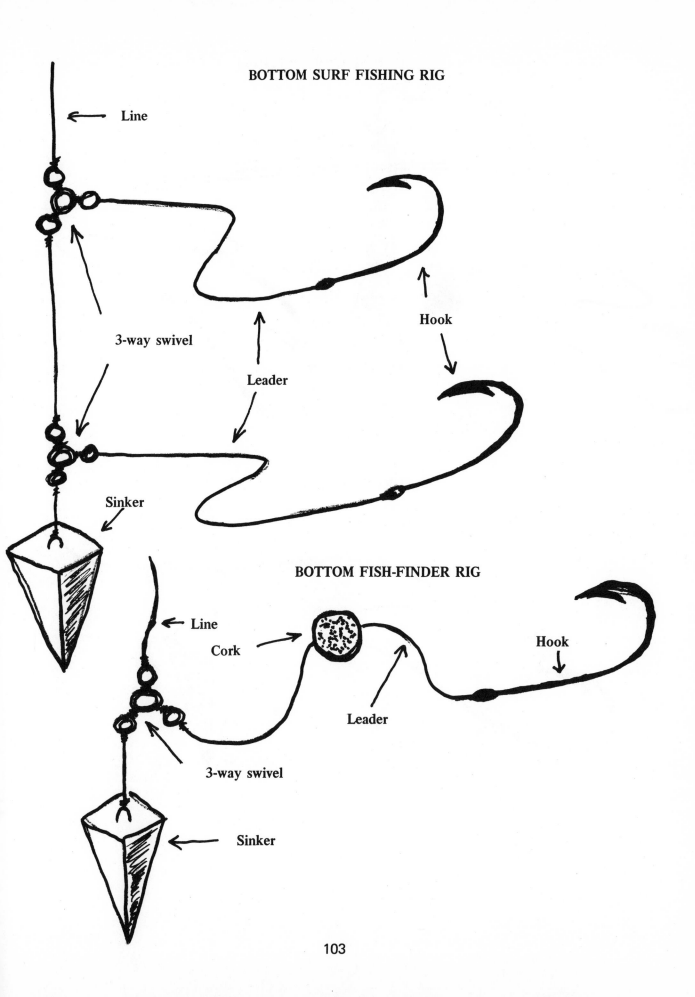

BOTTOM SURF FISHING RIG

Line

3-way swivel

Hook

Leader

Sinker

BOTTOM FISH-FINDER RIG

Line

Cork

Hook

Leader

3-way swivel

Sinker

103

BOTTOM SPREADER RIG

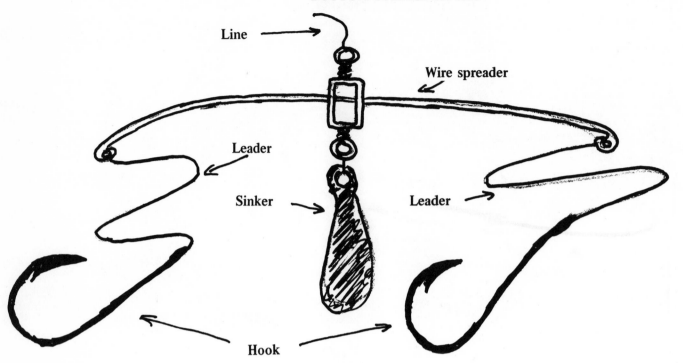

Line

Wire spreader

Leader

Sinker

Leader

Hook

SURF FISH-FINDER RIG

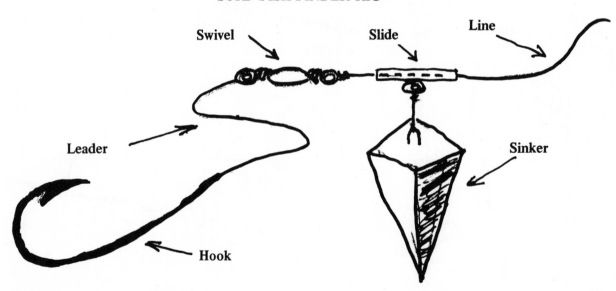

Swivel

Slide

Line

Leader

Sinker

Hook

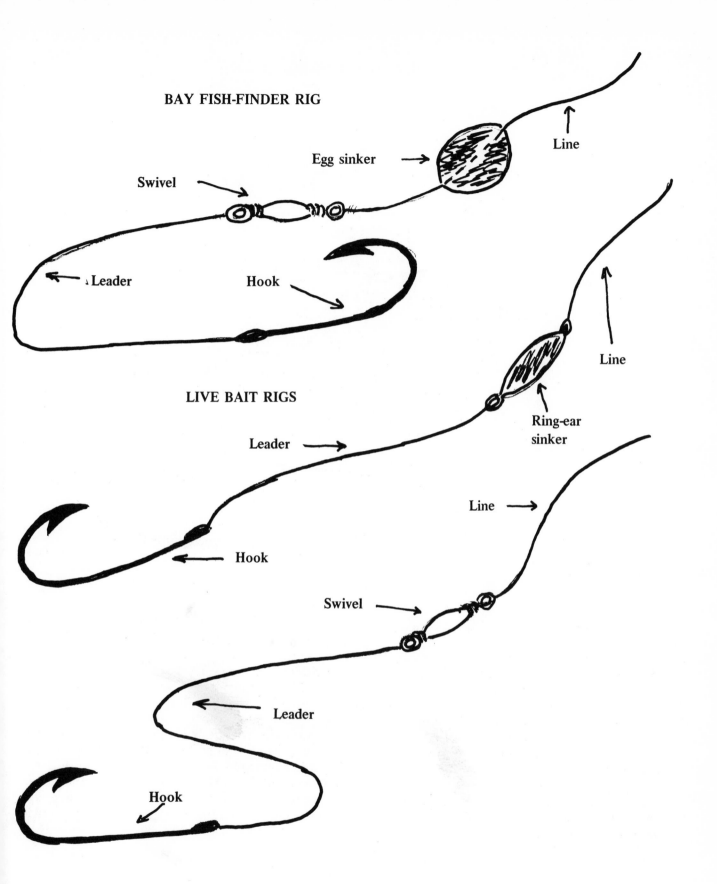

BAY FISH-FINDER RIG

Line

Egg sinker

Swivel

Leader

Hook

LIVE BAIT RIGS

Ring-ear
sinker

Line

Leader

Line

Hook

Swivel

Leader

Hook

salt water, as can the live bait rigs and the live bait float rig.

The length of leaders used on various rigs varies with the style of fishing. Where double drops are used, the leaders should be long enough so the hooks can swing free of the sinker, yet short enough so that when casting the stages will not twist around each other. Leader length on bottom fish-finder rigs can vary from twelve to twenty-four inches in length. The leaders on the wire spreader rig are usually twelve inches long. Leader length on live bait rigs should not be less than eighteen inches long, and leaders in excess of thirty-six inches usually make for difficult casting.

Leader length on live bait float rigs should be no less than twenty-four inches in length. This is necessary so that live bait can work over a considerable area. This working range can be extended by rigging the float several feet above the sinker, which should be either a ring-eye or dog-ear style. The depth can be extended even more by using a slip cork (the line runs through a small diameter rod through the center of the cork) and tying a knot in the line at any desired distance above the sinker. The cork slips down against the sinker when casting. When in the water the weight of the sinker and bait pulls the line through the cork until it jams against the knot in the line.

23

Fishing Knots

A knot is more than just a knot. The finest fishing equipment in the world is reduced to less than mediocrity if the fisherman insists on using incorrect or poorly tied knots. The point that must always be kept in mind is that somewhere between the fisherman and fish there must be a knot. Most frequently the knot is tied to the eye of the hook or lure. The next most frequent spot is at the snap or snap swivel, the hardware pieces that in turn attach to either the hook or the lure.

There are literally hundreds of knots in use by fishermen today, and perhaps because there are so many knots, the subject becomes a frightening one for the average fisherman. Actually if a fisherman learns just four knots, he can go through life wholly enjoying his sport.

We so often hear about the fish that got away because it broke the line. In more than a few places in this book I make a point of stating that fishermen, not fish, break lines. This is something in which I firmly believe and a point that I feel registers only if repeated time and time again.

When a line parts and you lose a good fish, the first thing you should do is give thought to how you battled the fish and how you employed use of the drag. You can do this in the time that it takes to reel in the loose end of the line. Then when you get in the line, check it to see where the break occurred. Most often it will be at the point of the knot. The logical thought that comes to mind is "I should have used heavier test line," but the logical thought is not always the correct thought, especially where fishing knots are concerned.

The wrong knot or the improperly tied knot can reduce line strength by as much as fifty percent. That twenty-pound test line then is reduced automatically to ten-pound test line at point of knot. So what we come up with here is not a case of lure failure but a case of knot failure. The square knot offers a good example. This knot has been around since string was invented, and while it is fine for tying Christmas gifts, it is totally unsuited for fishing. This knot when drawn up tight bites deep into the standing part of the line and reduces its strength by approximately fifty percent. The square knot is easy to tie, and I suspect that every person who ever wet a line used it way back when.

Down through the years I have had the privilege of fishing with a number of top fishermen and guides. All of them had heard of knots and knots and knots. One in particular demonstrated how to tie about four dozen different knots as the boat we were on traveled toward an offshore fishing spot. The same fellow told me he only used a half dozen knots, and he said all of the knots he had demonstrated were good but were not really necessary. I asked him what was the point of knowing all the knots if he used so few. His answer was thought provoking.

"Guiding is my business," he said. "I get a lot of customers who would feel my fishing knowledge was lacking if I couldn't tie dozens and dozens of knots. What I have shown you this morning is just part of my business pitch. You have no idea what some people use as a basis to rate the worth of a fishing guide."

Select the most practical knots and learn to tie them by practice. Select fifteen- to twenty-pound test line for practice, as such line is large enough to see without having to strain your eyes, yet it is light and supple enough to take bends and twists. Practice the knots until tying them becomes second nature.

Mastering the turns and bends are just the starter. Now we come to how to draw the knot up correctly, and this is the place where so many knots fail, for if a knot is to hold it must be seated properly. A knot functions because there is a jam that prohibits line from slipping, and unless this jam is uniform, the knot can "back off" or bite too deep into the line.

Before you begin to draw a knot up tight, you should make sure that the line is lubricated. Some fishermen do this by dipping the loosely formed knot in water for a few seconds. I consider saliva a better lubricant. This bit of wetting makes the line supple and will allow loops and twists to slip over the standing part of the line without abrasive scraping.

Now comes the part of tightening the knot. Do it with a continuous, steady pull and don't stop the pull until the knot is completely seated. The exception is the blood knot, which can be seated properly only with a sharp jerk. If you try to seat this knot with a steady pull, the coils in the knot will not tighten uniformly.

If a knot is seated properly it will not slip and consequently it can be trimmed closely. Trim with nail clippers, cutting pliers, scissors, or sharp knife. Under no circumstances burn the end of the knot with either a cigarette or a match. This sort of thing came into style when monofilament became popular, and unfortunately the practice has persisted to become a monster today. Heat, even that from a cigarette, can weaken synthetic line and reduce breaking strength seriously.

Before going into the tying of knots it is important to know the various parts of a knot. They are as follows:

(1) Standing part—The main part of the line that goes to the reel or the longer end of the line if working with leader material.

(2) Tag end—The part of the line in which the knot is tied. It is also called the short end of the line.

(3) Loop—This is a closed curve of line, formed by bringing the tag end of the line back and alongside of the standing part of the line; also by tying a knot that creates a loop.

(4) Turns—A turn is also called a wrap, and it is a complete resolution of line around another. It is usually made by passing the tag end of the line around the standing part or a standing loop.

You can get through a lifetime of fishing by learning to tie the following knots.

IMPROVED CLINCH. This knot is for joining the line to the lure of hook. Run the tag end of the line through the lure or hook eye and double back against the standing line. Make five turns with the loose end around the standing part of the line, then pass the tag between the eye of the lure and first coil. Next slip the tag end back through the loop that has been formed and slowly pull the knot tight.

IMPROVED BLOOD. This knot is for tying line to line or leader to line. Lap the ends of the lines to be joined and twist one around the other five times and bring the tag end back between the strands. Repeat at the opposite end, making five twists in the same direction and bring the tag end through the center of the lap but in the opposite direction of the first tag. Pull slowly allowing the turns to gather together, and then seat the knot with a sharp jerk.

DROP LOOP. This knot is used for tying line to a lure that must be allowed to wiggle freely. Tie a simple knot in the line about five inches from the end and draw it tight. Pass the line through the eye of the lure and bring it back parallel to the standing part of the line. Bend the tag down and around to form a circle below the parallel strands. Pass the tag around and through the circle in the line twice. Draw it tight slowly. Then pull on the lure and the jam knot will slide down to the simple knot. This will leave the lure attached with a loose loop that will permit the lure to wiggle freely.

DOUBLE O LOOP. This is another knot where a loose loop is necessary so that a lure may wiggle freely. Tie a simple knot in the line about three inches from the tag, but do not draw the knot up tight. Run the tag of the line through the lure eye and double back against the standing line, passing the tag through the loose simple knot. Take the tag and tie another simple knot, this time around the standing line. Draw the knots tight and slowly draw them together so that they jam against each other.

JAM. This knot is used for attaching a leader to the line. Turn the tag end of leader to form a loop and tie jam knot on standing part of leader. Tie simple knot in tag end of line. Loop the tag of line through the loop in the leader. Pull slowly to tighten.

I mentioned earlier in this chapter that the square know reduces line strength at point of knot by approximately fifty percent. The knots described above also reduce line strength at point of knot but not nearly so drastically. In relation to line strength, the knots described will test as follows: improved clinch (ninety-five percent), improved blood (ninety to ninety-five percent), drop loop (seventy-five percent), double O loop (seventy-five percent), and jam (seventy percent).

PARTS OF A KNOT

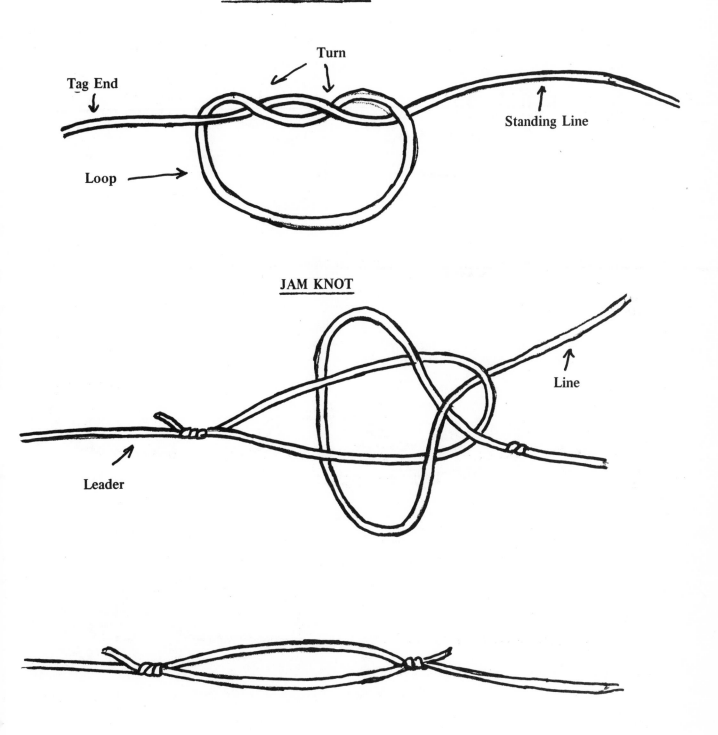

JAM KNOT

IMPROVED BLOOD KNOT

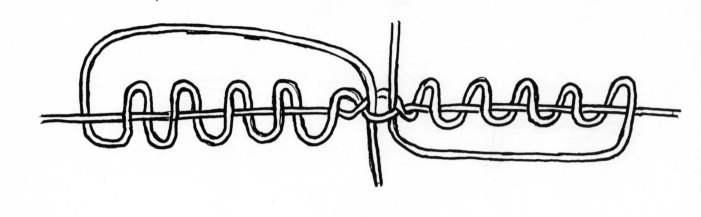

IMPROVED CLINCH KNOT

DROP LOOP KNOT

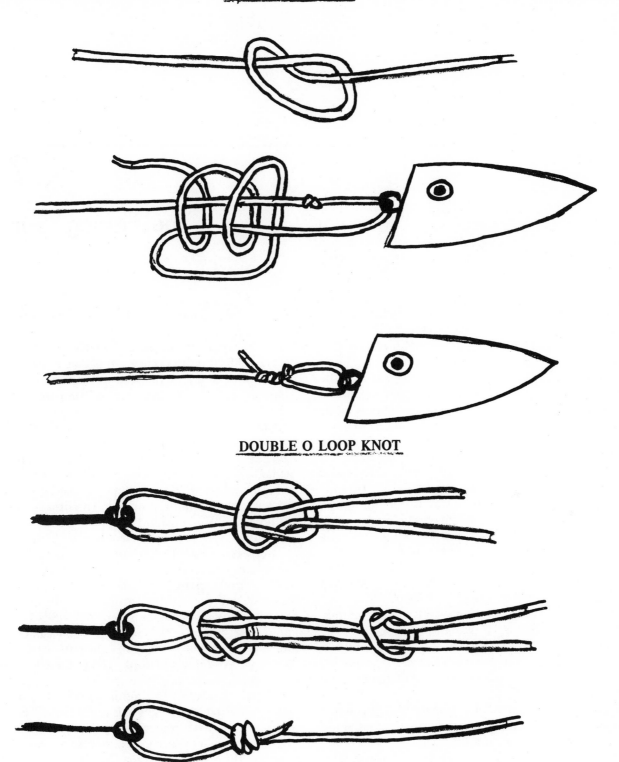

DOUBLE O LOOP KNOT

111

24

The Fishing Guide

"You mean you paid that fellow thirty dollars to show you where to fish? That's ridiculous! Why couldn't you just find the fish yourself? We could've used that money better on so many other things!"

The year was 1948 and the scene was on the Colorado River just below Roy Inks Lake in Central Texas. My wife was right about the money being needed for other things. I was just a couple of years out of the Army, faced with more than a few notes on a second hand '40 Ford coupe and trying to raise a young daughter to boot. Thirty bucks then was a heck of a lot of money, and especially so when my newspaper salary at the time was forty-eight dollars a week. Yes, I had some misgivings about spending the money, even though the guide put me into the finest bass fishing I had ever experienced up to that time. I don't recall the number of fish taken, other than I did bring in the limit and had even released a number of other fish.

Now I can say the money was well spent. Not only that, I would also say it was a necessary expense.

Obviously, the question in this chapter is whether or not to hire a guide. Are guide prices reasonable? When is a guide necessary? What is to be expected from a guide?

Quite obviously a guide is unnecessary if you fish from a pier, jetty, the bank, or for that matter wade the flats or shoreline. A guide can't give you much help here, unless you want him to catch the fish for you. In the type of fishing mentioned, the nearest tackle store or bait stand can give you all the information necessary about the place you plan to fish.

We have a whole new ball game, however, when a boat is involved and especially so where new waters are concerned.

Let me quickly dispense with charter boat and partyboat fishing by pointing out that in each case the skipper and the deckhands are your guides. They are included in the price of the trip.

In saltwater fishing and even when using your own boat, the hiring of a guide will be determined by your familiarity with the waters, your ability to navigate, and your knowledge of the fish. If you navigate the way people drive in West Texas—they just aim and let 'er rip—then you'll need a guide to put you on the fishing grounds. The other case for guides in saltwater fishing is where special species are sought, like bonefish, tarpon, etc.

There is still another time when the saltwater fisherman could use a guide to his advantage. Suppose the angler is a skilled boatman who can put his craft on the fishing grounds with unerring accuracy, but when it comes to fishing skills and fish knowledge, he is a rank tyro. This fellow can get his money's worth out of a guide if he just listens and observes the guide's actions. He is then in effect absorbing knowledge of the game.

When freshwater fishing is involved and the waters are expansive, a guide is a must if (1) it is your first time after a particular fish species and/or (2) it is your first time in the area. In either case a guide will save you time, and time in reality is more valuable than money. After all, you can lose a twenty dollar bill but regain it by working a little extra the next week. You can't ever make back time. Each minute that slips past is gone, kaput, forever. You can't save time for a rainy day.

The modern guide is practically a guarantee of fish. The guide I used back in 1948 put me in fish because he knew where they lurked from past trips and experiences. Today's guide not only has the knowledge of where they were hitting yesterday and the day before, he also has that blipping light on the magic black box—the electronic device that scans the waters beneath the boat. That electronic box is so sensitive that it can pinpoint schools of fish, even a single fish if it is of appreciable size. A guide in the space of a few months through the use of electronic gear and topographic maps can come to know the lake floor as intimately as his own home, and where largemouth bass are concerned, knowledge of the lake bottom is the name of the game.

For a great many years the largemouth bass was thought to be a shallow-water fish. Studies have proved otherwise. They frequent the shallows, yes, to feed, but in general they spend most of their lives in deep water in the immediate vicinity of lake bottom landmarks—landmarks like sunken logs, rock beds, brush piles, cuts, channels, etc. The guides call it structure; find the structure and you find the bass.

Finding the fish, however, is just part of the game. After that, you've got to entice the fish to take the bait. Here again is where it pays off to use a guide. Fish react to baits in different ways during the course of a year, or we should say according to the seasons. Guides through experience know that bass in a particular lake are prone to take certain types of baits in the summer and other kinds in the fall. A good guide, a talkative one, can give you hundreds of dollars worth of information if you just listen and remember.

On relatively small lakes you may only need to hire a guide for a trip or two; larger lakes will require correspondingly more. How many times, however, depends upon your ability to remember how to get to the payoff spots the guide visited. Don't ask him to draw you a map and expect to get anything near an accurate picture. Your request alone will alert him to the fact that his services are about to be dispensed with. He is likely to consider the situation as getting "fired," and he certainly won't cotton to passing out valuable information for free. Just make mental notes and go from there.

Personally I love the way bass fishing guides get you to structures that payoff. It's never forthwith; it's always devious and meandering. They run to a cove here for a half-hour try, then to a point on the other side of the lake, then to an island, and back to a timber stand on the other side of the lake. A couple of hours have gone by and perhaps not more than a couple of medium size bass are in the boat. Then the fellow sort of suggests: "We could run over to Alligator Head. Think we might be able to get a big one or two there."

This is the tipoff. It's the hot spot the guide has been saving. He needs only a nod from you to wind up the motor and head full bore for Alligator Head, which by the way is not likely to appear on any maps of the lake. The reason is because that is the name the guide gave it. He calls it that because he saw an alligator there once. Had he seen a coon at the water's edge, he might have named it "Coon Point." It's one of his prime fishing spots, and he's going to be darned sure it isn't printed on any maps of the lake.

Okay, so we reach Alligator Head, Coon Point, or whatever the guide chooses to call it. We get into some real tackle-busting bass and inside of an hour limit out. We land another dozen that are thrown back, and finally with no more time to go, it's crank up and head for the dock.

It always amazes me that while it took a half-hour at full speed to reach the payoff structure, it only took ten minutes at full bore to return to the dock. Now, this is where the customer has got to do some tall remembering. Remember the landmarks on the return journey, and when you get back to the cabin, reverse order and put them down on paper. Not every guide, but I'd say four out of five I've used employs the meandering route to reach the dividend structures. They are not stupid. They want to keep you direction-confused as long as possible, for as long as you're unsure of the way, the fellows know they have your return business.

And since when is this little game any different from the New York taxi ploy? If I went into guiding, I'd probably do the same thing. In fact, I've done it with a few acquaintances who have the habit of blabber-mouthing directions on how to get to choice fishing holes. I would say it has something to do with that instinct of self-preservation.

Note that I mentioned earlier that use of a guide is "practically a guarantee of fish." There are times when even the best of the professionals are unable to get fish. It's just part of the game, and something that has to be accepted.

Guide rates vary according to the part of the country, time of the year, and whether the services are for half or full day. I've seen them range from as low as twenty dollars for a half-day to sixty dollars for a full day in freshwater fishing and from a low of twenty-five dollars to a high of one hundred dollars in salt water.

What constitutes half day and full day? Here again it varies. Most half-day trips, except where charter and partyboats are involved, are of four to five hours duration. Full-day trips may range from eight to as much as twelve hours, with most of the twelve hour ones involving saltwater fishing. Trip duration, whether half or full day, includes boat running time out and return. For example, a half-day five-hour trip doesn't mean a full five hours of fishing. More likely it will include about four hours of actual fishing with the other time used in running out and back.

Without exception the guides I have used have always been liberal with their time. I have been on trips when the fishing was poor and the guides insisted on extending the fishing time an hour or two at no extra charge. Their best advertisements are satisfied customers, and without exception they aim to please. Any time they start shorting a customer you can pretty well figure the customer was abusive, obnoxious, overly demanding, or all three. I know this breed of fisherman; I've been in their company, and if the practice wasn't expressedly prohibited by law, I do believe I would have shoved some of them overboard. Not every person in the world is the north end of a horse heading north.

What are the usual services furnished by a guide?

A few at some of the ultraexclusive fishing resorts I've visited furnished fishing know-how and companionship only. Most, however, include in their fee the boat fuel, bait, and often tackle. You know, of course, that you'll have to pay extra for any gear you lose or break. Most guides will also rough dress the catch, although in all fairness you ought to pay a little extra if the catch is larger than usual. Don't expect the guide to fillet the catch for free.

Most of the guides I know are extremely conscientious fellows. They work hard to satisfy their customers. And do you know what many of them do when they don't have customers? They go fishing; they go looking for new and better payoff spots. They are always boning and honing to stay a step ahead of the other guides down the lake.

Guides who rest on their laurels are retired guides.

Now back for a final quickie on that fee that you may feel is rather exhorbitant. When you take out what the guide spends for fuel, bait, and ice plus the capital outlay for tackle, boat, and motor plus such other necessities like advertising, liability insurance, and taxes, the charge sounds more reasonable. The sixty dollars you paid him for a day on the lake doesn't all stay in his pocket; a good chunk of it goes into operating expenses. Sure these sixty-dollar-a-day guides have expensive, well-appointed fishing rigs. This is necessary as an aid in getting customers, for most fishermen hiring a guide expect to go first class. But while the guide's boat and motor may be this year's model, you'll probably find him driving a four- or five-year-old car with a couple of dented fenders. Even the best of guides don't get customers every day. Counting time out for the weather, necessary downtown business, and sickness, a top guide may average 250 trips a year. At sixty dollars each that will total fifteen thousand dollars for the year. Knock off ten dollars a trip for fuel and bait, and that's twenty-five hunred dollars off the top right there. Boat and motor repairs, insurance, tackle replacement, and such all take a bit out of the gross. And, of course, there's the biggest bite of all—income tax for the perpetuation of governmental waste and inefficiency.

By now you should see that the sixty-dollar-a-trip guide is really only another member of the nation's "affluent poor."

25

The Fishing Boat

You don't need a boat to get into good fishing, either in fresh water or in salt water, but having a boat sure enables a fellow to get to some productive waters that would otherwise be unreachable. Not only does a boat give the fisherman mobility to get around to many places in a minimum of time, it also gives him maneuverability when it comes to fighting a big fish, and finally it allows a fellow to fish in comfort.

Now to the hard part of the fishing boat issue. What is the right boat?

There is no such thing as the "right" boat. The boat that might be "right" for lake fishing may be totally unsuitable for offshore saltwater fishing, and the boat that might be "right" for white-water fishing on a fast-rushing river may be just as unsuitable for use on a placid pond.

There are too many variables involved to simply designate a boat or type of boat as the "right" one for fishing. Every boat is "right" for some phase of fishing, but as far as universal fishing is concerned, there is no single craft that is the "right" one.

So what does the fisherman do who wants a boat do? How should he go about selecting a fishing boat?

The first thing to do is to consider how often you go fishing. If you go fishing less than once a month, a boat is a waste of money unless someone makes you an offer you "just can't refuse."

Once you establish your frequency of fishing, check next on where you do most of your fishing. If you do ninety percent of your fishing in saltwater bays and in waters beyond the surf, then the "bass boat" that is so popular in freshwater fishing would be a poor choice. By the same token if ninety percent of your fishing is on the lake, then an offshore cruiser with its forest of outriggers would be an ungainly choice.

Next to be considered is size. Don't base size strictly on your eyes. Take into consideration your wallet, how long you plan to keep the rig, and how many people fish with you. Since a well-make boat that is given reasonable care will give good service for many years, it's to your advantage to be liberal in your thinking when it comes to the basic purchase price.

It pays to test ride in various types of boats and hulls before making your final choice. What looks good on paper or to your eye may not give you the performance expected when the craft is on the water. This extends right down to the material used in the construction of the boat.

In forty years of saltwater fishing, I have owned seven boats. My first boat was a cypress skiff. The boat I own at this writing is aluminum. In between I owned five plywood boats, four that I built myself. Each boat I owned served its purpose, and if it weren't for the fact that I enjoyed building boats, I certainly would not have owned as many. I sold each of the four boats I built. Someone would see the boat and offer to buy it. I always sold because I could always build another one.

Plywood is a fine boat material, but in this modern age it really isn't a match for either fiberglass or aluminum. Boats made of the last two mentioned materials require far less upkeep than plywood. My preference today is toward aluminum because of the weight factor. I like a good foredeck and windshield to keep spray out of the cockpit when running into seas or heavy weather.

Most fishermen I know modify their boats as soon as they buy them. I did just that. I removed the twin upholstered seats that folded down into recliners and replaced them with two swivel seats mounted on storage box pedestals. This gave me additional working room in the cockpit, and if there is any one thing really necessary in a fishing boat, it's fishing room.

Power is the next thing to consider. You can get into trouble by going too far either way—too much power or too little power. Get sufficient power so you can run reasonably fast without having to operate the motor always at full speed. Full speed should be the reserve to get you home ahead of the weather when threatening skies get serious.

Next consider what you plan to use in outfitting the boat. Remember that every item added takes up space and adds weight. I have a friend who bought a fourteen-foot outboard runabout. When he finished adding everything he figured he needed for fishing, he discovered he had added well over three hundred pounds in weight and took up so much space that the cockpit was too cramped for fishing two people. After two years of frustration, he got rid of the boat, bought a sixteen-footer of the same manufacture and found it to be perfect for his kind of fishing.

We are today living in an electronic age. There's a gadget for just about everything these days, and fishing certainly has its share. Are all these electronic marvels really necessary?

The answer to that is "yes" and "no." It's "yes" if you know how to use the gadgets and then how to apply that knowledge to fishing. But adding those gadgets because Joe down the street has them on his rig is just cause for saying "no."

There is at least one "must" item for the fishing boat, whether its a canoe or a twin-screw offshore cabin cruiser. That item is a compass. In fact, if I had a voice in marine legislation, I would make it mandatory that a compass be installed on every boat powered by a motor, regardless of how little the horsepower. Down through the years and over and over again, I've seen fellows venture many miles from the dock simply because they had mechanical power hanging over the stern of the boat. I've also seen some get into trouble—several times with disastrous results—when an unexpected fog or haze hid all landmarks.

A good fishing boat needs to be one of unusual stability. Its primary purpose is that of offering a good fishing platform. Some fishermen only confuse themselves by considering the primary purpose of the fishing boat is to get them to fishing waters. That's just partly right because far more time is spent in the boat when it serves as a fishing platform than time spent running to and from fishing spots.

You shouldn't stand up in a small boat. Still I want one with sufficient stability to allow me to stand up if necessary. There are times when you have to stand on the bow or even on the gunwale. This dictates a boat with considerable beam in relation to its length. You can stand on the gunwale of an eighteen-foot fishing boat designed for saltwater use without tipping it over, but you won't be able to do the same thing in a eighteen-foot canoe. The beam makes the difference.

PART II
The Fishes

In the description of the fishes that follows, the ranges cover those waters where the species listed are commonly found. The ranges, however, are by no means the absolute limits, for fish species have been known to stray far from their beaten paths.

The majority of the fish species in this section are treated individually. There are a few that are lumped under a common grouping and treated collectively (1) because of similarity of habits, range, and methods of fishing and/or (2) because all members of the group are not prized highly either as gamefish or important food fish. The groupers, snappers, salmon, trout, pinfish, and porgies are treated as groups. In the case of groupers, snappers, salmon, and trout, the reason for the lump treatment is the similarity of range, habits, and fishing methods for the species within the group. The pinfish and porgies, too, have almost identical range and habits, and in addition they are neither gamefish nor food fish. These fish, however, must be included because they are so abundant and because of their appeal to youngsters. These fish are easy to catch, and a parent interested in turning his children to fishing should start the youngsters on these fish. Sports fishermen generally regard the piggies and porgies as pesky bait-stealers or as species that make good baits for the large gamefish.

World-record sizes are omitted because the records change so frequently. Since records are kept for all-tackle, line test, spinning, and fly-fishing, it is not at all uncommon for dozens of changes to be recorded each year.

Up-to-date world or national record information can be obtained from the following:

International Game Fish Association, Alfred I. DuPont Building, Miami, Florida 33131.

National Spin Fishing Association, P. O. Box 81, Downey, California 90240.

Salt Water Fly Rodders of America, Inc., Box 304, Old Court House, Cape May, New Jersey 08210.

Each of the associations listed records claims in a number of classes according to line test. In addition to these groups, many states have records systems within their borders. Information for filing for state records can be obtained by writing the game and fish departments of the individual states.

Considerable information is required in filing for a claim. For example, in the case of the International Game Fish Association, the fish must be weighed and measured at an authorized station when IGFA affidavits are available. The completed affidavit along with a clear photograph of the fish and a ten-yard sample of the line used to make the catch must be sent to the IGFA headquarters in Miami.

The section that follows is divided into two parts, one for saltwater fish and the other for freshwater species. Neither part lists all the fish species that can be found in the waters within and waters around the North American continent. The lists have been streamlined down to those that are most popular with sports fishermen, plus some species that are caught quite frequently when the fisherman may be seeking more desirable species.

These are three of the Gulf Coast's most popular game-fish. Top to bottom are spotted weakfish, Spanish mackerel, and bluefish.

ATLANTIC BLACKFIN TUNA
(Parathunnus atlanticus)

Range—In the Atlantic but generally south of Hatteras.

Description—Fish is deep blue on its back and silvery on the lower sides and belly. It may or may not have a yellow flush down the sides. These fish travel in small, compact schools often in the company of other tuna and bonito. In some circles this fish is called albacore; the British refer to it as the little tunny. It is an offshore fish that is very rarely taken near the coast.

Fishing methods—Trolling. This fish is seldom specifically sought. It is usually caught incidentally while trolling for more desirable members of the tuna family. It strikes hard and wages a strong determined fight that can be most exciting on light tackle. However, the waters from which it is taken contain gamefish of sizable proportions, and as a result the tackle used is much too heavy to give the Atlantic Blackfin Tuna much leeway to display its wares.

Food value—Fair.

Average size—Six to eight pounds; any over fifteen pounds are considered big.

27

Popular Saltwater Species

ATLANTIC BONITO
(Sarda sarda)

Range—Through the Gulf of Mexico, Caribbean, and up the Atlantic to Long Island.

Description—Fish is entirely scaled. It has a dark blue back, overlaid with narrow black markings extending forward and downward. It is brightly silver on the lower sides and belly. This is a blue water migratory fish that comes to the surface to feed. These fish travel in dense, compact schools and when feeding on the surface churn the water white. The fish is heavy at the shoulders and slims to almost nothing at its forked tail. This fish is a fast swimmer that feeds on small fish such as menhaden, alewives, and herring.

Fishing methods—Trolling and to a lesser degree casting into schools when they are milling at the surface. Bonito take feather jigs, big spoons, lead-head jigs, and underwater plugs trolled at a considerable speed, six to ten miles per hour. The fish is also taken near offshore banks and drilling platforms still-fishing and drift-fishing. Most effective of all baits is strip bait made from a bonito's belly. Bonito strike savagely and make long, hard runs that are hard to stop. The fish offers excellent sport on light tackle.

Food value—Poor. The meat is very bloody and oily and is very seldom used for food. It is sought, however, as bait for larger gamefish in that bonito belly strips make very enticing baits. Bonito cut in half or into large chunks make excellent bait for

Atlantic Bonito

shark fishing. Because of the blood and oil content, the fish is often ground up for chum.

Average size—Five pounds. Anything over ten pounds is big.

ATLANTIC CROAKER
(Micropogon undulatus)

Range—Over the Atlantic and Gulf Coasts in surf, inlets, bays, cuts, and passes.

Description—fish is a member of the drum family and gets its name from the croaking sound made by both male and female. The fish is brassy in color; in the spring the fish are iridescent with upper fins dusky and spotted and low fins yellow to reddish. Croakers are bottom feeders and prefer to range over hard sand or shell bottoms. They feed on all types of small marine life, including some vegetation. They make mass migrations to deep water in the fall, and frequently these fall runs result in huge catches of these fish.

Fishing methods—The fish is taken strictly bottom fishing in the surf, bays, from piers, boats, or wade-fishing on shallow, hard sand flats. During the fall runs the fish are caught in deep water along the edges of cuts, passes, and channels. Shrimp, squid, and small cut bait, including belly flesh of croakers, make ideal baits. The fish is taken only incidentally on lures, usually very small spoons, spinners, and jigs. Although the fish strikes hard, its fight is not long, since it gives up quickly. Its croaking sound is clearly audible when the fish is hooked or placed on a stringer. What the fish lacks in individual fighting ability is made up for by numbers of fish. The biggest

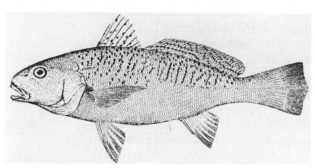

Atlantic Croaker

runs occur in September and October when schools head for deep water. This fish can best be enjoyed on light tackle.

Food values—Excellent, although the fish may be strong with an iodine scent when dressed. The flesh is firm, white, and sweet. It can be frozen and kept for long periods.

Average size—Three-fourths of a pound, although croakers to three pounds are not uncommon.

ATLANTIC MACKEREL
(Scomber scombrus)

Range—From Hatteras on the New England coast up to the Bay of St. Lawrence.

Description—Fish is metallic blue on the back, overlaid with black, wavy markings. The sides are faintly green along the lateral line; the belly is silvery. It is one of the most beautifully marked of all the mackerels. Formerly call the "common mackerel" this is a small member of the mackerel family. It has a tail more deeply forked than most mackerels. Atlantic mackerel appear from offshore in Hatteras waters generally in late March and slowly work northward to the Bay of St. Lawrence. The fish feed mainly on menhaden, pilchard, and free-swimming crustaceans. These fish reserve the route in their return migration that usually starts in October. In some New England areas these fish move in so close that they can be caught from shore and piers.

Fishing methods—Casting from piers, surf-fishing to a lesser degree, and trolling with spoons, plugs, and feather jigs. Once schools are located, many fishermen stop boats, drift with the fish, and cast plugs, jigs, and small spinners. The fish are small and their fight can best be enjoyed on light tackle.

Food value—Very good and very rich.

Average size—Two pounds, with three pounders not uncommon.

ATLANTIC SAILFISH
(Istiophorus americanus)

Range—Gulf of Mexico, in the Gulf Stream to the West Indies and to the Virginia Capes.

Description—Most striking feature of this fish is the extremely large, blue-purple dorsal find commonly called the sail. When this fin is lowered it is sheathed in a cavity in the back. The sail when extended is faintly marked with vertical rows of small, black dots. The fish's back is bluish, lower sides silvery, and belly white. When excited or hooked, vertical rows of light blue spots appear on its sides. It bill or spear is slender and dark in color,

Atlantic Sailfish

the tail black and deeply forked, and ventral fins long, reedlike and black. As a result of its slim, rakish body, the fish is a fast swimmer. Sailfish feed on small fish, especially balao and flying fish. It is a frequent jumper and has the ability to cross considerable surface "walking on its tail." The fish often reveals its presence by showing its dorsal fin extended above the surface. Sailfish have an unusual way of feeding. They tap or strike their prey with their bill (upper jaw) to stun it, and then they circle back to ingest it.

Fishing methods—Almost all sailfish are taken trolling offshore with balao or other prepared baits. The method is to have the line rigged so that at the tap, the line is released and the bait begins to sink slowly. The fisherman engages his reel and strikes when the fish returns and picks up the bait. The angler must strike hard to bed the hook in the fish's mouth. The fish makes long runs, frequent jumps, and does spectacular tail-walking. Sailfish are most plentiful in Florida waters and around the West Indies from January to May. They are found from June through August off the Gulf Coast states and in Mexican waters. Atlantic sailfish travel in schools in January and July, but tend to be loners at other times of the year.

Food value—Fair. The flesh is oily and strongly flavored and is seldom used fresh. It is most delicious when smoked. Unless the sailfish is of trophy size or desired for mounting, it should be released back into the sea as quickly as possible.

Average size—Forty to forty-five pounds with fish in excess of seventy pounds considered rare trophies. The Atlantic sailfish is smaller than its West Coast cousin, the Pacific sailfish.

ATLANTIC YELLOWFIN TUNA
(Neothunnus argentivitatus)

Range—The Atlantic from below the West Indies to the Carolinas.

Description—Fish is dark blue on its back with bright silver on sides and underparts. The breast is suffused with yellow. The bright yellow dorsal and anal fins are elongated and reach almost to the base of the tail. This is a migratory school fish found most abundant around the Florida Keys, Great Bahama Bank, and Little Bahama Bank. It feeds on small fish, mainly menhaden, mullet, small mackerel, and herring. It is a very swift swimmer.

Fishing methods—Trolling natural baits or with artificials such as feather jigs and spoons accounts for most Atlantic yellowfin tuna. The fish is usually caught around the outer reefs and quite often on sailfish rigs. It strikes hard and runs fast and strong, and although it does not grow to the size of the bluefin tuna, its fight is considered to be more than outstanding. The fish is most plentiful January through May, and it is frequently referred to as Allison tuna in Florida waters. It responds to fast-trolled baits and lures dragged almost in the propwash of the boat.

Food value—Good, although quite oily.

Average size—Fifty to sixty pounds with fish over one hundred pounds occasional.

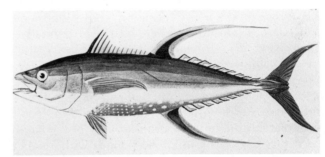

Atlantic Yellowfin Tuna

AMBERJACK
(Seriola islandi)

Range—Gulf of Mexico, Caribbean, and in waters around Florida and West Indies, and up the Atlantic to the Carolinas.

Description—Fish is grayish purple on the back, golden on the sides, and lighter beneath. A noticeable dark band runs from the mouth through the eye to the beginning of the first dorsal fin. This is an offshore reef fish that frequents coral reefs, wrecks, and since the advent of offshore petroleum developments, the offshore oil rig platforms. These fish travel in pods rather than schools. The big trophy specimens are almost always loners. It is a member of the crevalle family and it prefers deep water, although pods are often chummed almost up to the surface. It often goes into deep water harbors in Florida and the West Indies. Amberjacks normally feed on small fish.

Fishing methods—Trolling and still-fishing. This

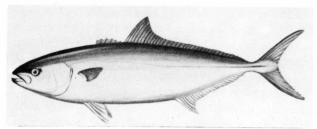
Amberjack

fish is often taken trolling strip baits, spoons, feather jigs, and plugs fished deep around the edges of reefs, banks, offshore structures, and wrecks. In still-fishing the popular method is to anchor near the banks and reefs or slowly drift over them. Small fish are the best baits for this kind of fishing. The fishing is fairly deep, fifteen to thirty feet or more down, but where pods of jacks are concerned, the fish can often be brought much nearer the surface by chumming. The amberjack hits hard and then has the habit of diving for a hole in the reef or wreck in much the same manner as do groupers. The amberjack was once considered a heavy tackle fish, but fishermen today are conquering it on light gear, which greatly enhances its gamefish and sporting qualities.

Food value—Excellent, although many frown on it because of its relation to the common jackfish or jack crevalle, a species quite oily and bloody. If an amberjack is to be used for food, it should be bled immediately to eliminate a musky taste.

Average size—Ten to fifteen pounds with loners commonly going in excess of fifty pounds.

BLACK SEA BASS
(Stereolepis gigas)

Range—Worldwide.
Description—Fish is grayish-black overall with belly shading to gray or "dirty white." This is a fish that grows to huge size. It is a bottom feeder that takes small fish, crabs, crustaceans, mullet, etc. It is nonmigratory in nature, although it moves out to deep water in the winter. The fish is most active in summer months and is found around jetties, deep water docks, bridges, coral banks, and kelp beds. The black sea bass has a huge, cavelike mouth and large gills. It does not have to move through the water to breathe, and it can remain motionless in one place for hours. The fish inhales its food rather than strike. The fish has a squarish tail, not rounded like that found on the Atlantic jewfish and the groupers. It is also known as the giant sea bass.
Fishing methods—Still-fishing on the bottom with dead or live bait. A fisherman's first knowledge of a black sea bass on the line is when line begins to pay out. A characteristic of the fish is to inhale the bait and then slowly swim off with it. The fish is sluggish and slow, but it can put up a good fight with a strong, steady pull. The fisherman must always be on the alert to pull the fish away from holes or caverns on the bottom, for once inside of these hideouts the fish will be lost to the fisherman. Baits must be large, three to five pounds in size.

Food value—Good. The meat from the fish's throat and cheeks make excellent eating, and when fried taste a lot like fried chicken.

Average size—Upwards of one hundred pounds with fish to two hundred pounds not uncommon.

BLUEFISH
(Pomatomus saltatrix)

Range—Along the Atlantic Coast, Gulf Coast through the West Indies to South America. Most plentiful off New Jersey.
Description—The bluefish has a greenish-blue back, fading to silver on its sides and nearly white on the belly. The fish is streamlined and a fast swimmer. Bluefish are pelagic, travel in dense schools, and often go on wild feeding binges on the surface. Schools appear off the South Atlantic Coast in late March and reach New York waters by late May. Bluefish frequently go into bays and inlets and are often caught in the surf. Milling and screaming gulls almost without fail pinpoint feeding schools of bluefish. These fish feed on menhaden, herring, shedder crabs, shrimp, and squid.
Fishing methods—Trolling, surf-casting, and casting from piers are the most popular methods. Best results are usually enjoyed in July-September. Fish the bays and inlets on the incoming tides. Chumming is a very popular method of luring fish to an area and holding them in the vicinity of the fishing boat. This is a sharp-tooth fish that requires use of a wire leader. Bluefish readily strike spoons, plugs, bait-tail jigs, and feather jigs.

Food value—Excellent. Fry small one, broil or bake those of five pounds or more.

Average size—Three to four pounds. Specimens over five pounds are considered large.

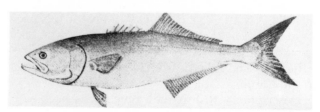
Bluefish

Bluefin Tuna

BLUEFIN TUNA
(Thunnus thynnus)

Range—A cosmopolitan fish and one of importance in world fisheries for centuries.

Description—The bluefin tuna has a deep blue back, silver sides and nearly white belly. It may or may not have a brown flush down the sides. The bluefin is the largest of the tunas, and it is a schooling, migratory fish with young fish ten to one hundred pounds considered school fish. Adults are those fish in excess of one hundred pounds. Tuna feed on small fish such as mullet, sardines, herring, flying fish, menhadden, etc. These are offshore, deep-water fish that stray close to the coast only when pursuing schools of baitfish. In U. S. waters the bluefin is sought mostly in the vicinity of the Bahamas and off Nova Scotia. The fish move along the edge of the Gulf Stream and appear in the Bahamas in late April and off Nova Scotia by mid-June.

Fishing methods—These fish are fast swimmers and most are taken trolling. The accepted method is to troll ahead of the schools with natural baits such as whole mullet, small mackerel, and menhaden or artificial lures such as big spoons and feather jigs. A popular method off the Jersey coast is to moor or drift with the currents, fishing natural baits. Where trolling is involved, tuna, especially school-size fish, frequently strike almost in the prop wash of the boat. The strike is a hard jolt with the first run a long and fast one. The fight of the fish is long and determined. Wedgeport, Nova Scotia, is world famous for its sports bluefin tuna fishing. Wherever bluefin tuna are caught, they are often located by surface signs or by trolling "blind" over known feeding grounds. The bluefin tuna is highly prized as a blue-water gamefish.

Food value—Good. The flesh of fresh tuna is rather oily since these fish feed on herring, bonito, mackerel, and menhaden, all species that are heavy in oil content.

Average size—School bluefin tuna run ten to one hundred pounds with fifty pounds being about the average. Adults are those fish over one hundred pounds in size, with the average here going three hundred fifty to four hundred pounds.

BOCACCIO
(Sebastodes paucispinis)

Range—This is a Pacific Coast fish that is most abundant along the California coast. It is sometimes called the rock cod or salmon grouper.

Description—The back of this fish is olive to dusky brown on its back. This shades to dull orange and reddish on the sides, and then from pale pink to white below. It is flushed throughout with red and sometimes has black splotches on its body. The fish has a prominent projecting lower jaw. An important aid in identifying the species is the broad convex space between the eyes.

Fishing methods—This is a coastal fish found mostly around rocky areas, and because of this it is called a rockfish in some areas. These fish are caught mainly on natural baits fished on bottom rigs. The fish puts up a dogged fight and it ranks as an important fish on the California coast.

Food value—Very good.

Average size—School bocaccio run around three pounds in size. Ten-pounders are considered large, but fish to twenty pounds in size have occasionally been taken.

Bocaccio

BONEFISH
(Albula vulpes)

Range—This fish is known worldwide and it is found on the sandy coasts of most tropical oceans and seas. In the Northern Hemisphere bonefish are most plentiful around Florida and the Bahamas. Over on the Pacific Coast it ranges from Panama as far north as San Francisco. It is most plentiful in waters touching the United States from the month of May until early in the fall.

Description—The bonefish varies considerably in coloration and markings. Usually the back is olivaceous, sides silver, and belly nearly white. Scales are iridescent. Another phase registers pronounced longitudinal stripes extending well down the sides. The body is firm, head large and

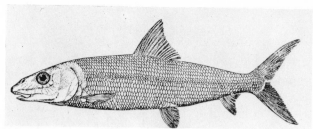

Bonefish

bare of scales, with the mouth under the rounded nose. The tail is deeply forked. The bonefish is exclusively a bottom feeder, and a fish that is extremely easy to spook. It is a warm-water fish and is generally most active on shallow flats. The fish feeds by standing on its head and in water so shallow that its tail sticks above the surface. In addition to sand flats where it roots for sand fleas, bottom crustaceans, and worms, the fish frequents the shallow waters around banks and small islands. It is an extremely fast-swimming fish.

Fishing methods—Most bonefishing is done from shallow draft boats quietly poled over the flats. These fish are taken to a lesser degree by still-fishing from a drifting boat or by wading the flats. In wade-fishing for bonefish, the fisherman must be most careful not to make sudden moves or noises or create any waves. The fish readily takes natural baits such as small shrimp, hermit crabs, conch meat, small crawfish, and sand fleas. They are also taken on flies and small spinners, occasionally on small diving plugs. The fish strikes hard and makes fast runs that easily sizzle a hundred yards or so of line off a fisherman's reel. The fish is one of the most highly prized of gamefish in that it requires patience, superb fishing ability, and know-how to catch. It pays to fish with a guide familiar with area waters and one skilled in knowing how to look for bonefish. Tailing bonefish, fish feeding with their tails sticking out of the water, are relatively easy to spot. It takes experience to pick up the shadow of one that does not show any of its body above the surface. The fish gets its name because of so many bones in its body. Unless the bonefish is a record fish or one desired for mounting purposes, it should be returned to the water.

Food value—Poor, although this is a debatable matter in some island circles. The fish's true values stem from its gamefish and sporting qualities.

Average size—Three to five pounds; specimens over eight pounds are considered trophies.

BROADBILL SWORDFISH
(Xiphias gladus)

Range—Atlantic Coast of the United States from the West Indies to Cape Breton, and on the Pacific Coast from Chile to California.

Description—The coloration of this fish varies with the size of the fish. Large fish are very dark or bronze with silvery reflections and are light or silvery on the belly. Small specimens are usually deep blue on back with dark fins. The swordfish has a huge blue eye. The fish usually feeds deep on bottom fish and comes to the surface to rest and bask in the sun. This is a true ocean or blue-water fish that travels singly or in pairs. The fish's habit of basking on the surface allows commercial fishermen to approach close enough to use harpoons.

Fishing methods—Trolling with cut bait or whole squid, mackerel, small bonita, or flying fish. Swordfishing is highly specialized and practiced by only a small group of sports fishermen. These fish are most plentiful in the Atlantic in July and August and in the Pacific from May through October.

Food value—Excellent and in great demand commercially.

Average size—Three hundred pounds with fish to five hundred pounds occasional.

CALIFORNIA BARRACUDA
(Sphyraena argentea)

Range—Pacific Coast, Gulf of California from Cape San Lucas to Puget Sound.

Description—Dark brown on back with bluish reflections. Sides and belly silvery. The fish is long and slim and has large canine teeth, but it is considerably smaller than its Atlantic cousin. These fish are found the year around off the Mexican Coast but appear off the United States coast mainly in the summer. The schools begin appearing in California waters in March.

Fishing methods—This fish readily hits live bait as well as spoons and metal jigs. During the early fall, many of these fish are caught trolling when they move out to deeper water.

Food value—Considered good, although not in much demand.

Average size—Six pounds. Fish in excess of ten pounds are considered large specimens.

California Barracuda

CALIFORNIA CORBINA
(Menticirrhus undulatus)

Range—This is a Pacific Coast fish that is native to the California coast.

Description—The back of this fish ranges from dirty gray to steel-blue in color. Its sides are gray and belly is white. The fins are dusky. The fish has large pectoral fins. The tip of its snout extends beyond the tip of the lower jaw, and it has short, fleshy barbels at the tip of the lower jaw.

Fishing methods—This is a very popular gamefish that ranges almost entirely in the surf. It feeds mainly on small fish and sand crabs. It is a bottom feeder that is found most frequently on sandy beaches.

Food value—Fair to good depending upon the size of the fish. Large specimens may have a gamy taste.

Average size—Two pounds with fish to ten pounds not uncommon. Some as large as twenty pounds have been reported caught.

CALIFORNIA HALIBUT
(Paralichthys californicus)

Range—This is one of several halibut and sole species found on the Pacific Coast, and in general is considered to be the most important. Other important species include the Pacific halibut (*Hippoglossus stenolepis*) and the English sole (*Parophyrs vetulus*).

Description—The California halibut is greenish to grayish-brown and is sometimes mottled with darker or lighter spots. It can be either a left or right-sider flounder. It has large jaws with sharp teeth. The eyes are small with a flat area between them. The Pacific halibut is uniform dark brown with defined paler spots. It is a right-sided flounder, although some left-sided specimens have been taken. The English sole is brown with dark-tipped dorsal fins. It has smooth scales and pointed jaws.

California Halibut

Fishing methods—These are bottom feeders that are inclined to lie on the bottom and grab food as it drifts. past. They feed on all varieties of marine life. These fish are important to sports fishermen as well as commercially. They are sometimes taken by bouncing jigs along the bottom.

Food value—The Pacific halibut is considered a food delicacy. The California halibut is rated as excellent food, while the English sole is regarded as good to fine.

Average size—Sixteen pounds for the California halibut, with occasional fish to fifty pounds taken. The average size for the Pacific halibut is twenty pounds. Specimens to one hundred and one hundred fifty pounds occasionally caught, while the largest on record weighed five hundred pounds. About three-fourths of a pound is average for the English sole, which is the most plentiful of the soles in the Pacific.

CALIFORNIA WHITE SEA BASS
(Cynoscion nobilis)

Range—This fish is found in goodly numbers along the Pacific Coast from lower California to Vancouver Island. It is quite abundant around Santa Barbara and along the lower California coast. This fish is considered a close cousin of the weakfish, common and spotted, found on the Atlantic Coast.

Description—The fish is bluish on its back and shades from silver-blue on its upper sides into gray with dark speckling. The belly is silvery. Young specimens have several dark vertical bars. The fish has a row of small teeth in the roof of its mouth. Although this fish is designated as a bass, it is more in the weakfish family. It is considered the Pacific Coast version of the sea trout found on the Atlantic and Gulf Coasts. These fish are found close to shore and around kelp beds where they feed on herring, sardines, smelt, shrimp, and squid. In addition to the Pacific Coast this fish is also found in many other parts of the world.

Fishing methods—Surf-casting, still-fishing with live bait around kelp beds, and trolling spoons, underwater plugs and jigs around the edges of kelp beds. The fish has the barracudalike tendency to lie hidden in the edge of a kelp bed, and then dart out to viciously hit a bait as it passes. The California white sea bass has a strong determined fight and ranks high on the list of gamefish. It ranges as far as Juneau, Alaska, but is more usually found on the California coast from May to September and is most plentiful around the channel islands in April and August.

Food value—Excellent.

Average size—Twenty to twenty-five pounds; fish over forty pounds are considered large.

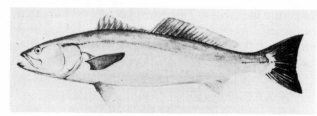

California White Seabass

CERO MACKEREL
(Scomberomorus regalis)

Range—Warm waters of the western world.

Description—Light blue on back with sides and belly brightly silver. Markings on sides may be absent or differ considerably. Usually there are four or five narrow, dull gold to deep brown horizontal strips that extend from the gill cover to the tail. The middle strips is solid, while the others are broken and appear as elongated dashes. The markings are nearly uniform in adult fish. The fish has small scales and the teeth are needlelike. The fish is often mistaken for the Spanish mackerel, which has no solid stripe and whose gold spots are oval rather than rectangular. The cero mackerel is one of the migratory mackerels that travels in small rather than dense schools. It feeds on small fish and shrimp and frequents the outer reefs and banks.

Fishing methods—Almost all are caught trolling with the same type lures used for the other mackerel. The cero mackerel is not often caught by design but more by accident when fishing for other mackerel species.

Food value—Excellent. The meat is the whitest of all the mackerels.

Average size—Three pounds. Fish over ten pounds are considered large.

Cero Mackerel

CHANNEL BASS
(Sciaenops ocellata)

Range—From the mid-Mexican coast over the Gulf Coast of the United States and up the Atlantic Coast to New Jersey.

Description—The coloration of this fish varies with size and locality. Small specimens are nearly white. Usually fish under fifteen pounds are coppery-red. Specimens in excess of fifteen pounds are likely to be brassy colored, although at times some will be overall silver. The black spot at the base of the tail is reliable identification. Two to three such spots are not uncommon. Small channel bass are found in bays, inlets, and along the surf. When fish reach maturity in three to four years they move into deep water, and as adults their migration is one of deep water to surf and return rather than north to south. The fish feed on shrimp, squid, mullet, menhaden, and crabs. Large channel bass make two surf runs each year—a minor one in the spring and a major run in the fall. The fish takes food slowly and often mouths it before swallowing. The fish is a very popular gamefish.

Fishing methods—Small channel bass are caught from bays and tidal flats still-fishing with bait or casting small spoons or jigs. Large specimens are taken still-fishing from bait, piers, or in the surf using whole small fish or cut bait. Large specimens are only occasionally taken on artificial lures.

Food value—Excellent from fish under five pounds; good from fish up to fifteen pounds. Fish over fifteen pounds have course, stringy meat that is best when used in chowders.

Average size—Six to eight pounds for fish taken from bays and tidal flats; twenty-five to thirty pounds for those taken from surf and deep offshore waters. Channel bass in excess of forty pounds are considered trophies.

CHUB MACKEREL
(Pneumatophorus grex)

Range—Plentiful in the Pacific Ocean and Mediterrean Sea but appear only erratically in the Atlantic.

Description—Same as the Atlantic mackerel with these notable differences: black wavy lines on the chub are more open and broken and extend farther down the sides, and there are dusky spots on the silvery lower sides and belly. The chub is a school fish and feeds on small pilchard, menhaden, and free-swimming crustaceans. Its habits are much the same as those of the Atlantic mackerel.

Fishing methods—Trolling and casting. Chub mackerel readily take spoons, jigs, and bucktail lures. They are often caught drifting with the school and by casting small lures on spinning gear. Their fight is neither strong nor sustained.

Food value—This is an excellent table fish when prepared fresh. It can be salted and brined for later use.

Average size—Less than two pounds.

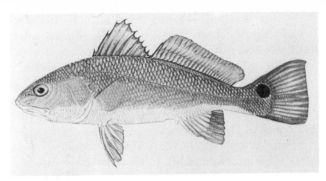
Channel Bass

CODFISH

ATLANTIC COD
(Gadus morhua)

PACIFIC COD
(Gadus macrocephalus)

Range—Respective species are found in the Atlantic and Pacific temperate zones to as far north as the Arctic Circle.

Description—Atlantic cod: dark brown on back shading to lighter brown on sides with white belly; dark brown spots over back and sides; whitish lateral line; distinct chin barbel. Pacific cod: gray to brown on back and upper sides; belly whitish; brown spots on back and upper sides; distinct chin barbel longer than diameter of the eye. These are deep-water fish and bottom feeders that move inshore in the fall and winter. They are voracious feeders that thrive on any bottom marine life small enough to eat.

Fishing methods—Still-fishing on the bottom from partyboats is the most popular method. This fish takes all kinds of natural baits but is rarely caught on lures. Since these fish hit so readily, big catches are quite common. The fish is a bottom feeder and deep-water species, consequently heavy sinkers are necessary to get the baited hook to the bottom. A cod's fight is one of a lot of sharp tugs and jerks. It is often taken on handlines when fishing in extremely deep water.

Food value—Excellent.

Average size—Five to ten pounds with specimens to twenty pounds not uncommon.

COMMON WEAKFISH
(Cynoscion regalis)

Range—Found on the entire coast of the Gulf of Mexico and up the Atlantic Coast north almost to the Bay of Fundy.

Description—Olivaceous back with light blue and brassy scale reflections that may appear as wavy lines; sides and belly are silver; upper fins dusky; lower fins yellow. In the fall large specimens may have a yellow flush overall except on belly. This is basically a bay and surf fish, although it is taken from deep water immediately adjacent to coastal waters. It ranks as one of the most popular small sports fish on the Gulf and Atlantic coasts. The fish has soft mouth membranes that tear easily, hence the name "weakfish." It feeds on small fish, mullet, shrimp, sea worms, squid, and small crustaceans. The fish is most abundant on the North Atlantic Coast from July to October and along the South Atlantic Coast from January to June. It is found the year around on the Gulf Coast. The fish is found most frequently in cuts, passes, the surf, and around jetties, but rarely goes into very shallow water as does the spotted weakfish. It is a wary fish that is easily spooked by noises and undue commotion.

Fishing methods—Surf-casting, bait-casting, still-fishing, fishing with float, and slow trolling. The most popular bait is shrimp. The fish also take spoons, plugs, and jigs. The fish strike hard and make short but fast runs. The fish should be played skillfully because of their tender mouths, and unless they are hooked in their gullets, they should never be lifted from the water by the fishing line alone. A landing net is a must on all fish that are just lip hooked. This weakfish is a top choice species with Atlantic Coast bay fishermen.

Food value—Very good, although the texture of the flesh is not suitable for long periods frozen.

Average size—One to one and a half pounds; fish over five pounds are big.

DOLPHIN
(Coryphaena hippurus)

Range—Worldwide in warm seas and oceans.

Description—The dolphin is one of the most beautiful of all gamefish. The males and females differ in colors and shape of head. The male dolphin has a high forehead that comes down to the lower jaw in almost a straight line. The female's head curves down to snout in an arc. The male has an iridescent bluish-gold back that merges to blue-black. Back and sides are covered with small purple spots, while the fins and tail are golden yellow. The female is greenish-gold instead of bluish gold. When hooked these fish change colors and color patterns, but within minutes after death, they fade to gray. The dolphin is one of the fastest swimming fish in the sea and it frequently jumps out of the water, especially when chasing flyingfish.

Fishing methods—Trolling, drift-fishing, fly-casting, and bait-casting. This fish readily takes all

Dolphin

types of lures, especially those that run just a foot or so beneath the surface and often break the surface as they skip from wave to wave. Dolphin hang out around patches of seaweed, driftwood, or whatever is floating on the water. It is a common practice to always keep one hooked dolphin in the water as it seems to excite the others in the school and the result is that these fish will strike at any and everything in the water.

Food value—Excellent.

Average size—Three to five pounds. Dolphin twenty to thirty pounds are not uncommon but they travel in small pods rather than in large schools as is the case with smaller dolphin.

GAFFTOPSAIL CATFISH
(Bagre marinus)

Range—The Atlantic Coast south from Hatteras and over the entire coast of the Gulf of Mexico.

Description—Olivaceous to grayish back, paler on upper sides, and yellowish to whitish on belly. Fish has four barbels, two on upper jaw and two on lower; deeply forked tail, and dorsal and pectoral fins with saillike filaments. Fish gets its name from its fins, which resemble the gafftopsails on sailboats. These are migratory fish that appear with warm weather and then move back to more tropical waters in the winter. The fish's deeply forked tail gives it a lot of power. These fish frequent the surf, deep waters around jetties, channels, buts, and bays. Gafftops feed on small fish, shrimp and crustaceans at all levels, although they are basically bottom feeders.

Gafftopsail Catfish

Fishing methods—Still-fishing with bait. Occasionally these fish are taken on small, atificial lures, but this occurs more often by accident than design. The fish in recent years has become extremely popular with visitors to the Gulf Coast because it is easy to catch and appears in big schools. Its popularity and appeal to tourist has earned it the nickname of "tourist trout."

Food value—Good. Years ago its reputation was spoiled by its relationship to the lowly sea catfish, a true saltwater scavanger.

Average size—One and a half pounds with fish running to six and seven pounds not uncommon.

GREAT BARRACUDA
(Sphyraena barracuda)

Range—Tropical waters of the world, most plentiful around Florida, the Bahamas, and throughout the Gulf of Mexico and Caribbean.

Description—Light green to nearly black on back; silvery sides with nearly white belly; fins dusky. Irregularly shaped black dots may or may not be present on lower sides and belly. In its silver phase the fish is overall iridescent silver, including the fins but without the dots on lower sides and belly. This is a mean and dangerous gamefish that feeds on all kinds of marine life. It has strong, caninelike teeth, slightly curved inward. The fish is torpedo-shaped and very fast. The barracuda has a habit of lying in the shade of piers, boats, bridges, or seaweed patches waiting to pounce on victims that stray nearby. The fish is able to start very fast, but it does not make long runs. Barracuda are most plentiful around banks and outer reefs and is found in both shallow and deep water. The fish is often a pest in slashing up hooked fish as they are being hauled in.

Great Barracuda

Fishing methods—Trolling around reefs and cays, still-fishing at offshore banks or from bridges, docks, and piers. The fish will strike at just about any object that moves, including boat propellers. It readily takes all kinds of artificial lures that are bright or light colored. The fish's strike is sudden, hard, and with a jolt. It fights savagely at first with hard but short runs, but it gives up after a short fight. This, however, does not mean the fish is finished, since many tyro fishermen have been severely bitten and lacerated in trying to unhook a boated barracuda seemingly near dead. The fish should be killed or thoroughly immobilized before attempting to remove the hook, and even then it should be done with long-handled degouger or pliers. The fish has a rather disgusting odor.

Food value—Poor. The flesh can be poisonous when taken from fish caught around coral reefs in tropical waters.

Average size—Ten pounds with fish in excess of thirty pounds considered large specimens.

GROUPERS

Because of the similarity of the many popular groupers, the species that follow will be treated as a group as to range, fishing methods, food value and average size. The various species will be given more detailed and individual treatment in their descriptions. In general many grouper species have unusual colorations that can best be appreciated with live specimens. The colors on these fish fade with death.

BLACK GROUPER
(*Mycteroperca bonaci*)

BLACK JEWFISH
(*Garrupa nigrita*)

CONEY
(*Cephalopholis fulvus*)

GAG
(*Mycteroperca microlepis*)

NASSAU GROUPER
(*Ephinephelus striatus*)

RED GROUPER
(*Epinephelus morio*)

RED HIND
(*Epinephelus guttatus*)

ROCK HIND
(*Epinephelus adscenionis*)

SCAMP
(*Mycteroperca phenax*)

SPOTTED JEWFISH
(*Promicrops itaiara*)

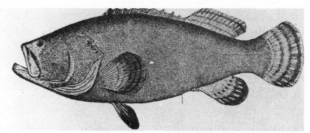
Jewfish

YELLOWFIN GROUPER
(*Mycteroperca venenosa*)

Range—Generally worldwide for many species. In North America on the Atlantic Coast from Virginia, through the West Indies to South America, throughout the Gulf of Mexico and Caribbean Sea. On Pacific Coast southward from Cape San Lucas.

Description—Black grouper: grayish with all fins but first dorsal barred with black; sides and back flushed with soft blue-green elliptical markings that give appearance of both vertical and horizontal markings. Black jewfish: overall gray with grayish-black back. Coney: overall dark reddish with yellowish spots: fins may or may not be tinged with blue and/or yellow. Gag: brownish-gray with greenish tint but sometimes brown overall; dorsal fin dusky green edged in white; black tail fin has bright blue patches with white outline. Nassau grouper: color varies from nearly solid white to solid gray-brown; four irregular dark vertical bands on sides each enclosing small white spots; stripe runs from snout through eye to base of dorsal fin. Red grouper: brownish-red with salmon cast over body; sides darkly mottled; inside of mouth bright orange. Red hind: reddish-brown on back and spotted with small scarlet dots; fins are olive-lemon and spotted. Rock hind: reddish-brown with olive blotches on sides and back; whitish blotches with pinkish cast over entire body; orange spots on head and lower part of body. Scamp: brownish-gray; overall spotted with darkish blotches on upper sides. Spotted jewfish: overall brown with markings and spots

Nassau Grouper

129

faded or absent on large specimens; small fish light drab with mottlings on sides and numerous small, black spots. Yellowfin grouper: one of most beautiful of all the groupers; usual color is grayish to olivaceous on back and sides with belly white; has innumerable small spots, those on tail and back dark or black, those on head and belly bright red. All of the groupers are reef and banks fish and bottom feeders. All have bucketlike mouths whether the fish is large or small. They are slow swimmers that take up residence in holes and under overhangs of reefs, banks, wrecks, and jetties. All feed on small fish and crustaceans. Large species inhale food rather than outright strike.

Fishing methods—Still-fishing over reefs, banks, jetties and wrecks with heavy tackle. Fish are caught on natural baits on or near the bottom. There is some trolling for big groupers in the Bahamas using small mackerel or barracuda as bait. The trolling is always deep with heavy trolling sinkers and often monel line. Fish do o not run fast when hooked but bore deep seeking to get into holes, caverns, and under ledges. Fight is one of tug-of-war with fisherman winning only if he can keep the fish free of bottom obstructions. Fish usually give up halfway to surface when changing pressure causes stomachs or swim bladders to pop out of mouths.

Food value—Excellent as fillets or as base for fish chowder. The flesh from cheeks and throats of big specimens are a delicacy.

Average size—Black jewfish also called warsaw (sixty-eighty pounds); Nassau grouper (forth-fifty pounds); spotted jewfish (one hundred pounds); coney (two pounds); black grouper (five pounds); red grouper (five pounds); gag (three pounds); rock hind (two pounds); yellowfin grouper (four pounds); scamp (five pounds); red hind (two pounds).

JACK CREVALLE
(Caranx hippos)

Range—Through the Atlantic Ocean and Gulf of Mexico.

Description—This fish has a light olive back that shades to grayish-gold on the sides and yellowish on the belly. The fish has a broad, forked tail and a distinct black spot on the gill covers. These fish travel in schools and may be found in the surf as well as many miles offshore. They move toward northerly waters in the summer and retreat back to southern waters in the winter.

Fishing methods—Trolling, bait-casting, jigging, surf fishing, and bottom fishing. These fish take all kinds of natural baits with a preference for shrimp, squid, and cut mullet. They readily strike artificial

lures. The fish strikes hard and is a savage fighter. Pound for pound it is considered to be one of the toughest fighting fish found in the sea. The fish has amazing stamina, and it is not at all uncommon for just a fair-sized jack to put up a half-hour battle. In spite of its fighting qualities, the fish is seldom specifically sought, and it is usually caught while fishing for some other fish species.

Food value—Poor. The meat is very bloody and oily. It makes good bait for shark fishermen.

Average size—Five to seven pounds with thirty- to forty-pounders quite common.

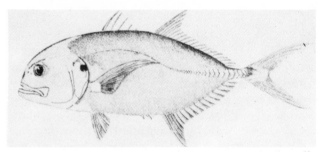

Jack Crevalle

Kelp Bass

KELP BASS
(Paralabrax clathratus)

Range—Throughout the Pacific Coast. The kelp bass is considered to be the equivalent of the Atlantic sea bass.

Description—The fish has a mottled bluish-black back that shades off to white on the belly. It has the typical square tail of the sea bass but without the soft appendage found on the Atlantic Sea Bass.

Fishing methods—Still-fishing and surf-casting. This fish spends its time in kelp and seaweed beds, feeding on the marine life within. Small fish and small shellfish make excellent baits. They are only occasionally taken on artificial lures.

Food value—Excellent.

Average size—One pound. Five-pounders are considered huge.

Kingfish (Northern Whiting)

KINGFISH

NORTHERN KINGFISH
(Menticirrhus saxatilis)

SOUTHERN KINGFISH
(Menticirrhus americanus)

Range—Atlantic and Gulf Coasts, with the Northern kingfish found only occasionally in the Gulf.

Description—Both species are overall grayish-silver with irregular dark bars running obliquely forward and down. The bars on the northern species are quite dark, while those on the southern species are sometimes barely visible. These are bottom feeders that dine on very small fish and crustaceans.

Fishing methods—Still-fishing and surf-casting. Use small fish or shrimp for bait and fish on the bottom. Small hooks must be used because of the fish's small, underslung mouth. It's a scrappy fighter on light tackle

Food value—Good.

Average size—One pound, with two- and three-pounders not uncommon.

KING MACKEREL
(Scomberomorus cavalla)

Range—In the Atlantic from Cape Cod south to Brazil; abundant throughout the Caribbean and Gulf of Mexico.

Description—Greenish-blue back, sides dusky silver, and belly whitish; elongated, dull yellow spots may be present on sides of specimens less than six pounds. The king mackerel, also called kingfish, is a migratory species that feeds near the surface, although at times some unusually large specimens are caught deep. The fish tend strongly to school according to size with the small to average size fish congregating around offshore banks and in the Gulf of Mexico around offshore oil platforms. The larger, trophy-size fish tend to travel in pods and run deep. King mackerel feed on all kinds of small fish and tend

to follow working shrimp boats in huge schools. They are fast swimmers and occasionally jump. This member of the mackerel family is most abundant in the Gulf of Mexico and around Florida northward up the Atlantic from June through September. These fish very rarely even stray to inside waters.

King Mackerel

Fishing methods—Trolling, still-fishing, drift-fishing, and casting, with trolling by far the most popular. Baits include natural baits such as mullet, balao, flying fish, or ribbon fish. These fish readily take artificial lures with feather jigs, big lead-head jigs, spoons, and diving plugs the favorites for trolling. In still-fishing around offshore banks and oil platforms and in drift-fishing, the popular rig is to use a float with the bait suspended three to five feet beneath the surface. Baits include mullet, balao, and small panfish. Spoons, diving plugs, and big jigs are used for casting. The fish's fight is strong and determined with a lot of fast runs. It occasionally jumps when hooked. A wire leader must be used because of the fish's razor-sharp teeth, which means exercising care when removing hooks.

Food value—This is a controversial matter with opinions ranging from fair to excellent. The flavor is best when smoked. The meat is oily and does not keep well unless salted.

Average size—Eight to ten pounds with fish to thirty pounds not uncommon.

LADYFISH
(Elops saurus)

Range—Warm waters of the Atlantic, Pacific, and Gulf Coasts.

Description—Light green to blue-green back, bright silver sides, with nearly white belly. This fish is often mistaken with the bonefish. The ladyfish has small, thin scales, a pointed head with large mouth and jaws that extend beyond a vertical line from back of the eye. None of these are found on the bonefish. The ladyfish is a migratory fish that moves along sandy beaches, into inlets, passes, and bays with the coming of warm weather. It feeds on a wide variety of marine matter and is a fish species that is very active at night. These fish school along channel

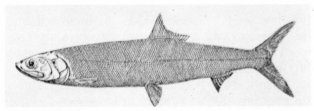
Ladyfish

banks, bars, bridge pilings, etc. The ladyfish is also known as a horse mackerel and ten-pounder.

Fishing methods—This fish is caught casting, trolling, and still-fishing and usually when the fisherman is seeking more desirable species. The ladyfish hits all kinds of natural baits and artificial lures on the bottom, midwater or surface. The strike is sudden and very hard and is usually followed by wild jumps and cartwheels. Although the runs are not long, they are strong and determined. On light tackle the fish is a sporting fighter supreme.

Food value—The meat has a fine flavor but is seldom eaten because the fish is a mass of tiny bones.

Average size—Three-fourths of a pound. Any specimens over three or four pounds are considered large.

LITTLE TUNA
(Euthynnus alletteratus)

Range—Gulf of Mexico and up the Atlantic to waters off New Jersey.

Description—Deep blue back with wavy black markings from middle of first dorsal fin to the tail; undersides silvery with several small black dots beneath the pectoral fins. This is a small tuna that travels in closely packed schools. It is found in the Gulf of Mexico in June; around Florida from April through the summer; and up the Atlantic Coast during the summer. It is often caught in considerable numbers off the Carolinas in midwinter. These tuna feed on menhaden, herring, and other small fish. The schools travel so deep that often commercial fishermen travel right over the schools without disturbing them. The fish is commonly called the "false albacore" in some regions.

Fishing methods—Trolling. The fish is caught incidentally when fishing for more desirable tunas. It strikes hard and fights well.

Food value—Excellent, although meat does not store well, even overnight, unless brined.

Average size—Five pounds; rarely over ten to twelve pounds.

BONITO

OCEANIC BONITO
(Katsuwonus vagans)

PACIFIC BONITO
(Sarda chiliensis)

Range—Oceanic bonito throughout tropical and semitropical oceans and seas; Pacific bonito in Pacific from Chile to Gulf of Alaska.

Description—Oceanic bonito: bluish black with wavy dark markings on back from dorsal to tail; dark stripes from breast upward and backward to tail; rosy flush to underparts. Pacific bonito: dark blue back and silvery below; dark oblique lines on back; large teeth, widely spaced. The Oceanic bonito is one of the most beautifully marked of all the tunas. These are dense schooling fish that travel deep except when coming to the surface to feed. They are fast swimmers that feed on menhaden, herring, sardines, and other small fish.

Fishing methods—Trolling. These fish take feather jigs, spoons, and plugs trolled deep and fast. They also readily take bonito belly strips. Bonito strike savagely and fight very strong.

Food value—Poor; meat is very bloody and oily. Makes excellent chum and bait for shark fishing.

Average size—Five pounds. Fish over ten pounds are considered large.

PACIFIC AMBERJACK
(Seriola colburni)

Range—In the Pacific from Peru, including the Galapagos Islands, through the Gulf of California to Cape San Lucas.

Description—Bronze to reddish-brown back and yellowish to reddish underparts. All fins blackish except pelvic. This is a pelagic, inshore fish. This species of amberjack became known to marine biologists in 1938. The fish is distinguished from the yellowtail (Seriola dorsalis) by its bronze color and the absence of the yellow stripe down each side. The Pacific amberjack is a bottom feeder that takes small fish, crabs, shrimp, and crustaceans. The fish is usually most plentiful in North American waters April through June.

Fishing methods—Still-fishing or drift-fishing with cut bait, and trolling jigs and spoons deep and slow.

Food value—Good.

Average size—Twenty-five to thirty pounds with occasional specimens to one hundred pounds.

132

Oceanic Bonito

PACIFIC SAILFISH
(Istiophorus platypterus)

Range—Throughout the tropical Pacific and in the eastern Pacific from Chile to Monterey, California. Cape San Lucas seems to be a rallying point in the Eastern Pacific.

Description—Dark blue back with silver underparts. This fish is epipelagic. It feeds on small fish, squid, mackerel, and sardines. It often basks on the surface with its sail extended. The fish is a very fast swimmer and an excellent jumper. It differs from the Atlantic sailfish in having a more slender body, two dorsal fins closer together, most subdued coloration and generally larger size. It first strikes its prey with its bill to stun and then returns to ingest.

Fishing methods—Trolling with baits rigged to stop and sink slowly when tapped by the fish. Fisherman must strike hard to bed the hook. The fish makes long runs, spectacular leaps and does a lot of tail-walking. It is found in temperate waters from April to October and in more tropical waters in winter months.

Food value—Fair; best when smoked. Unless desired for mounting or a trophy speciman, the fish should be returned to the water.

Average size—Sixty to seventy-five pounds with specimens over one hundred pounds not uncommon.

PINFISH AND PORGIES

BERMUDA CHUB
(Kyphosus sectatrix)

GRASS PORGY
(Calamus artifrons)

JOLTHEAD PORGY
(Calamus bajonado)

LITTLEHEAD PORGY
(Calamus proridens)

PIGFISH
(Orthopristis chrysopterus)

PINFISH
(Lagodon rhomboides)

PORKFISH
(Anisotremus virginicus)

SAILOR'S CHOICE
(Haemulon parrai)

SAUCEREYE PORGY
(Calamus calamus)

SCUP
(Stenotomus chrysops)

SOUTHERN PORGY
(Stenotomus aculeadus)

Range—Tropical and temperate waters with numerous subspecies and relatives the world over.

Description—Bermuda club: generally dark with faint stripes on sides and checkered in a pattern of white or gray; fish has ability to change color rapidly. Grass porgy: silvery with bluish reflections; central and base portions of each scale is goldish that form horizontal stripes; has darkish vertical bars from back to lower sides. Jolthead porgy: darkish back with lavender-purple stripe that follows the line of the fish's deep slanting profile. Little head porgy: overall silvery with bright reflections; upper scales have spot of blue at base that forms longitudinal stripes; orange spots on underparts. Pigfish: dorsal fin spotted with bronze; tail yellow and dusky tipped; blue streak on side of upper lip; light blue and silver striped nose with brown spots on snout. Pinfish: pale blue and yellow alternating longitudinal bars; distinctive black spot behind gill cover. Porkfish: bright yellow with black stripes. Sailor's choice: his single dark spot; other markings changeable. Saucereye porgy: same coloration as grass porgy except for presence of very large eye. Scup: brownish on back to silver sides to white belly; fins mottled with dark markings. Southern porgy: cheek bright yellow, fins marked with black; distinctive band runs from forepart of cheek to the tail. All of these fish are basically coastal, bay, and tide water fish best described as "panfish" because of their generally small size. These fish migrate to deep water in winter rather than move north and south. They feed on small shrimp, crustaceans, and marine vegetation and are usually found in schools.

Fishing methods—Still-fishing with natural baits on or near the bottom; occasionally caught on small wet flies, spinners, and tiny jigs. These fish are favorites with youngsters because of their willingness to bite and great numbers. Sports fishermen often refer to them as "trash fish" because they so often steal baits. All of these fish make excellent baits for larger gamefish such as tarpon, yellowtails, striped bass, channel bass, and the mackerels.

Food value—Good to excellent, although few bother to eat them because of the many small bones and the fact that a lot of fish are necessary to make a meal.

Average size—Bermuda club (one pound); grass porgy (one-half pound); jolthead porgy (two pounds); littlehead porgy (one-half pound); pigfish (one-half pound); pinfish (one-half pound); porkfish (one pound); sailor's choice (one-half pound); saucereye porgy (one-half pounds); scup (three-fourths pound); southern porgy (three-fourths pound).

POLLOCK
(Pollachius virens)

Range—North Atlantic.

Description—Dark greenish-blue back shading to greenish sides with a silvery cast; light-colored or white lateral line extending from head to tail. Pollock travel in big, sometimes dense, schools. For many years the fish was thought to be a deep-water species, but fishing over the years has revealed that the fish often feeds near the surface. It is most plentiful in the North Atlantic from May to October. The fish feeds mainly on the bottom on small fish and crustaceans.

Fishing methods—Still-fishing with natural baits in deep water was long the accepted method. Now pollock are taken trolling metal squid, feather jigs, and prepared strip baits. The fish strikes very hard and is quite quick to take artificial lures. For a species generally not considered a gamefish, the pollock puts up a good fight.

Food value—Good, although fish can not be stored long because the flesh becomes quite soft.

Average size—Five pounds with fish to ten pounds not uncommon. Specimens over fifteen pounds considered very big.

SHAD
(Alosa sapidissima)

Range—Found in the Atlantic from Florida to the Gulf of St. Lawrence. Introduced from the Atlantic into the Pacific and now found from Baja California to Alaska and Kamchatka.

Description—Bluish black with silvery sides; dark spot behind opercle; dark spots on back. This fish is anadromous. These fish spend most of their lives at sea but make annual runs up and down the coast. Shad move into fresh water to spawn and then return to the ocean. In these spawn runs the males enter the freshwater streams first and then the females follow. The fish seldom eat until the eggs are dropped, but after that they strike at anything resembling insects. Their migration is one of from deep to shallow water and return rather than north and south. Shad feed on small marine life.

Fishing methods—Fly-casting in fresh water. Spinning and spin-cast tackle is usually used in tidal waters. The fish will readily strike flies and any lures that resemble insects. Spinners are very effective lures.

Food value—Excellent, especially the roe.

Average size—Three pounds with anything over five pounds considered a large fish.

SHEEPSHEAD
(Archosargus probatocephalus)

Range—From the Delaware Cape to Texas and into northern Mexican waters.

Description—Deeply olivaceous to black black back with black vertical bars alternating with light or nearly white bars. The colors are contrasting and deep-hued in young fish, but fade and often are only faintly visible on old fish. Sheepshead are schooling in habit and frequent dock areas, piers, jetties, bridge pilings, wrecks, and shell reefs. The fish is able to break shellfish with its strong jaws and teeth. Sheepshead are bottom feeders that dine on shrimp, fiddler crabs, barnacles, and small crustacea. The fish is quite wary.

Fishing methods—The fish is caught still-fishing. The fish nibbles at the bait and because of its sheeplike teeth, long shanked hooks are necessary. When hooked the fish's fight is one of swimming

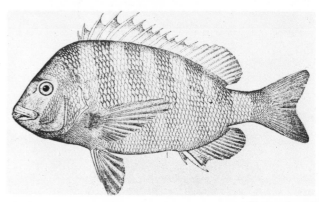

Sheepshead

134

around in circles with numerous dives for the bottom.

Food value—Excellent, although some people object to the oysterlike odor of its flesh.

Average size—One to two pounds with fish over ten pounds considered extremely large.

SNAPPERS

DOG SNAPPER
(Lutjanus jocu)

LANE SNAPPER
(Lutjanus aya)

MANGROVE SNAPPER
(Lutjanus griseus)

MUTTON SNAPPER
(Lutjanus analis)

RED SNAPPER
(Lutjanus aya)

SCHOOLMASTER
(Lutjanus apodus)

YELLOWTAIL SNAPPER
(Ocyurus chrysurus)

Range—Tropical waters of the world. In the New World snappers are most plentiful in Gulf of Mexico, Caribbean Sea, all around Florida, and in the Atlantic Ocean from Bermuda to Brazil.

Description—Dog snapper: olive back, reddish sides and light belly; coppery overall with faint vertical bars. Lane snapper: rose color shading to silvery with olive cast; golden stripes along the sides. Mangrove snapper: bronze-green back with brassy red sides and gray belly; dark streak from nose across eye to the dorsal fin. Mutton snapper: orange-red to salmon-colored back; black spot on each side near juncture of the hard and soft dorsal fins; blue streak from nose to eye. Red snapper: overall brick red shading lighter on the belly. Schoolmaster: red-brown back with orange cast sides; greenish-white vertical bars from back to lower sides. Yellowtail snapper: gray-blue with yellow spots and lines; broad yellow stripe from nose to tail; fins are yellow. All of the snapper are bottom feeding reef and banks fish that dine mainly on small fish, shrimp, and squid. They are nonmigratory and are found the year round in their respective ranges. All are schooling in nature, and some like the red

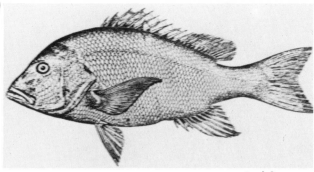

Red Snapper

snapper and yellowtail snapper are beautifully colored. The red snapper is the most important and ranks high as a commercial fish.

Fishing methods—Still-fishing with bait on or near the bottom around reefs, banks, wrecks, and offshore oil rigs. All snapper readily hit natural baits but only occasionally take artificials, usually slow-moving jigs. They are sometimes taken by accident when trolling near the bottom. The fish strike hard and put up a fight of sharp jerks and tugs, always bent on regaining the bottom and the safety of holes and caverns. The fish give up quickly when hauled about halfway to the surface because changing water pressure sometimes causes stomachs to pop out of their mouths. The fish can be lured to near the surface by persistent chumming.

Food value—Excellent; flesh is firm and will keep well in frozen state.

Average size—Dog snapper (ten pounds with specimens to twenty-five not uncommon), red snapper (five pounds, frequently to fifteen), lane snapper and mutton snapper (four pounds), mangrove snapper and schoolmaster (two pounds), yellowtail snapper (one pound).

SNOOK
(Centropomus undecimalis)

Range—Florida south through the West Indies and along the Mexican coast. Six species of this fish are found on the Pacific Coast.

Description—Color varies from light to dark, depending upon the water in which it lives. It has a dark brown back with yellowish sides when found in brackish waters. Sea-run snook have straw-colored backs, silver sides, and near-white bellies. The lateral line is prominent and black. This fish shows a preference for sand shores and often moves well into tidal rivers. It eats shrimp and small fish. It is a pikelike fish that often lies waiting in the shadows to pounce on smaller creatures that may venture nearby.

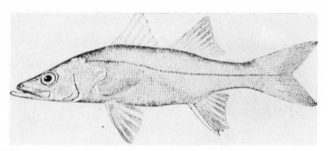

Snook

Fishing methods—Still-fishing, baitcasting, and trolling. Snook take natural baits such as shrimp and small fish and readily strike plugs, spoons, and spinner baits. It is often taken in Florida tidal canals on flies. Although the fish is a relatively fast swimmer, when trolling for it, the troll must be very slow. Snook are most active from spring until early fall. The fish is a tackle buster and one that readily takes top-water baits.

Food value—Fair. The meat is quite flakey and with large specimens is somewhat tasteless.

Average size—Five pounds; fish in excess of fifteen pounds are considered large.

SPANISH MACKEREL
(*Scomberomorus maculatus*)

Range—Atlantic Ocean from Cape Ann to Brazil and throughout the Gulf of Mexico and Caribbean Sea. In the Pacific the fish has a close relative in the sierra mackerel that ranges from California southward to Panama.

Description—Greenish-blue back, silvery sides and belly and bright gold round spots on the sides. The cero mackerel is often confused with the Spanish mackerel. The cero has elongated dull yellow broken lines that appear as oblong dots down its side. One line is solid. Spanish mackerel are migratory, schooling fish that travel near the coast, often going into inlets, channels, cuts, and occasionally bays. It often moves close enough to shore to be caught by surf-casters. The fish feeds on shrimp, menhaden, and other small fish. It has razor-sharp

Spanish Mackerel

teeth and will often hit anything moving in the water.

Fishing methods—Casting, still-fishing, and trolling with trolling being the most popular method. Spoons, drones, jigs, spinner baits, and hooties are trolled about seventy-five feet behind the boat. Mackerel strike as hard they hook themselves. They make fast runs and occasionally jump when hooked. Care must be taken in removing the fish from the hook because of the sharp teeth. In still-fishing the method is to use natural bait, preferably peeled shrimp, suspended about three or four feet beneath a float. The baitcaster can use spoons, jigs, and plugs.

Food value—Excellent. Tastiest when baked or broiled. The flesh is oily and will not keep frozen. If mackerel are to be stored for a long period, they should be brine salted.

Average size—Two pounds with six-pounders not unusual. Cero mackerel average about six pounds with some occasionally going to ten.

SPOTTED WEAKFISH
(*Cynoscion nebulosus*)

Range—Gulf of Mexico and up the Atlantic Coast to Long Island. The numbers of these fish in northern Atlantic Coast waters seem to be decreasing. This fish is more popularly known as the speckled trout and spotted seatrout, although it is a member of the croaker family.

Description—Color of back varies from dark or nearly black to grayish, with considerable iridescence or powder-blue reflections; lower sides and belly are silvery; round, black spots mark the back above the median line. The spots extend from over the second dorsal fin and tail. This is a much-sought after game and food fish that frequents bays, cuts, and channels connecting bays with the open seas and along the surf. The fish gets the name weakfish because of the soft membranes around the mouth. Although the fish does most of its feeding near the bottom, the fish sometimes feeds at or on the surface in shallow water, particularly at night. It is found over bay flats, in channels and inlets and ranges in the surf when the water is clear. The fish is wary and can be easily spooked by commotion. The fish feeds on shrimp, small fish, and small crustacea. It frequents the bays and bay flats in the spring, moves into the cuts and channels and the surf in the summer, and then goes into deep holes in bays and channels in the winter.

Fishing methods—Bait-casting, still-fishing, and occasionally slow trolling in deep water holes in winter. Fish hit best on live shrimp as bait, but the

Spotted Weakfish

Striped Bass

biggest ones are usually taken on small live mullet. These fish readily take spoons, jigs, and bottom-bumping plugs. Fish must be played with care to prevent tearing hook from its soft mouth. Small fish travel in big schools, but big lunkers are often loners. Use of live bait suspended beneath a popping cork is an extremely deadly way of attracting this fish.

Food value—Excellent. Flesh is firmer than that of other weakfish species and will keep for a longer time.

Average size—Two pounds with fish to six pounds fairly common. Specimens over eight pounds are considered big.

STRIPED BASS
(*Roccus saxatilis*)

Range—Original range on the Atlantic Coast was from mouth of the St. Lawrence River south to Florida. Introduced in Pacific waters in 1879 and 1882, and now ranges from California north to Oregon. It is most plentiful now in the Pacific in the vicinity of San Francisco Bay. Best fishing on the Atlantic Coast is from Cape Cod south through Georgia. The fish has been successfully planted in freshwater impoundments.

Description—Olive-greenish on the back, shading is greenish silver on the sides with a brassy cast; belly is light silver; dark horizontal stripes of a greenish cast run from head to tail just below the lateral line. Fish twelve to fifteen pounds frequent bays, while larger specimens frequent the surf and offshore waters. Although stripers are often caught near the surface, they are basically bottom feeders that take small fish, shellfish, sand eels, blood worms, shrimp, and squid. Large stripers are most plentiful in the surf on both the Atlantic and Pacific coasts in a period from May to November. The fish ascend rivers to spawn and become semidormant in midwinter. Schools generally move mortherly in April and May, although actually they have more of a deepwater to shallow-water migration and vice versa rather than a true north and south migration.

Fishing methods—The striped bass is highly prized by surf-casters. Other fishing methods include still-fishing and trolling along the coast and around jetties. In back bays, small stripers are taken on flyrods. Stripers readily take natural baits and strike spoons, metal squids, plugs, and bait-tail jigs.

Food value—Excellent. Fry small ones, broil or bake the large fish.

Average size—Two to fifteen pounds in bays and inlets; twenty to forty pounds offshore and in the surf.

FLOUNDER

SUMMER FLOUNDER
(*Paralichthys dentatus*)

WINTER FLOUNDER
(*Pseudopleuronectes americanas*)

Range—The winter flounder is nonmigratory and is found on the Atlantic Coast from Maine to Georgia. It is replaced by the summer flounder from Florida through the Gulf Coast states and into Mexican waters.

Description—Summer flounder: dark olivaceous; swings on its right side. Winter flounder: olivaceous but may be brown in some waters; underside is white. Like all flounders both species are normal swimming when hatched but as they grow older one eye "migrates" to one side of the head. The left eye

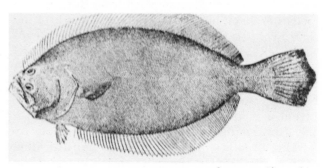

Summer Flounder

A gourmet's delight is the flounder exhibited by the author's daughter, Laura.

moves to the right side of the head on the winter flounder. All flounders can change colors to some degree, and in the case of some species the coloration conforms with that of the bottom on which the fish rests. All flounders are bottom feeders that lie on sandy bottoms and are lightly covered with sand with only eyes protruding. Flounders feed on shrimp, squid, small fish, and small crustacea. Flounders are scattered over bays but usually are found in concentration around rock jetties, bulkheads, piers, and bridges. Summer flounders are frequently caught in the surf. The winter flounder is distinguished from the summer species in that it has its eyes on the right side of the body, whereas the summer flounder has both eyes on the left side. Right and left sides are determined by looking at the fish in the direction in which it is facing and noting where the throat is located. Flounders school and move to deep water with the advent of cold weather.

Fishing methods—Strictly bottom fishing by working all areas within casting range or drift-fishing with a float keeping the bait a few inches off the bottom. Stirring up the both with a long pole will

sometimes bring in nearby flounders to feed on matter freed from the bottom. Numerous baits including shrimp, squid, clams, small minnows, bloodworms, and fiddler crabs are used. Flounders have an uncommon manner of striking. Usually they will grab a bait and hold it in their teeth for a few seconds before taking it well into their mouths. Consequently fishermen must allow the fish to take the bait well into its mouth before attempting to set the hook. A flounder on the line often feels like a snag until the bite of the hook causes it to react. Its fight is in circular runs near the bottom, and it uses its footballish shape to advantage in putting up stubborn resistance.

Food value—Excellent. Fry small fish; stuff and bake or broil large ones.

Average size—One and a half to two pounds; five- and six-pounders occasional.

MARLIN

BLUE MARLIN
(Makaira nigricans ampla)

STRIPED MARLIN
(Makaira audux)

WHITE MARLIN
(Makaira albida)

Range—These fish are indigenous to the warm waters of the world. Striped marlin are more abundant in Pacific waters than in the Atlantic.

Description—Blue marlin: the back and dorsal fin are deep blue with lower sides and belly silvery; fish has a pronounced shoulder hump. Striped marlin: purplish-blue back with silvery underparts; back is crossed with fifteen vertical light blue strips. White marlin: deep blue back shading to silvery lower sides and belly; light blue vertical stripes may or may not be present but are more evident on specimens caught from southerly waters; fish has a huge eye. These are ocean and blue-water fish that feed on flying fish, mackerel, bonito, smelt, etc. They first stun prey by tapping it with their bill (upper jaw) and

Blue Marlin

White Marlin

then returning to ingest. These fish are migratory and do most of their feeding near the surface.

Fishing methods—Trolling. Lines are rigged so that they will release when the bait is tapped. Fisherman has to sock it to the fish to bed the hook when the fish makes the pickup. Sometimes long slices of strip bait are used, but more usually mackerel or bonito are sewed on the hooks for trolling baits. These fish make long, determined runs and do a lot of jumping. All are highly prized gamefish.

Food value—Fair. Flavor can be improved by smoking.

Average size—Blue marlin (275 pounds with specimens to 500 pounds not uncommon); striped marlin (150 pounds with some going to 250); white marlin (60 pounds, this marlin rarely exceeds 100 pounds).

Sports fishermen unload one of the blue-water prizes, a blue marlin.

TARPON
(Tarpon atlanticus)

Range—From the South Atlantic off Brazil, through the Caribbean and Gulf of Mexico, up the Atlantic to Long Island. This fish is most abundant in Mexican waters, around Florida, and in the Florida Keys.

Description—Olivaceous to black back with silvery sides; scales are edged in gold; fish has no teeth but a mouth of hard cone. Tarpon are fast swimmers and ready jumpers. They feed on mullet, menhaden, crabs, and small fish. The fish travel in schools, frequently making their presence known by "rolling" at the surface. This is not a true roll but rather a brief surfacing of the fish as the fish breaks the surface with its dorsal fin and back. Tarpon move into the mouths of rivers, channels, around islets, and into open bays.

Fishing methods—The popular method depends upon where one is fishing. The methods include trolling, baitcasting, still-fishing, and fly-casting. In trolling the lures are out 100 to 150 feet behind the boat. Popular trolling baits include natural baits sewed on the hook so the action in the water is that of swimming fish. Trolling lures include spoons, feathered jigs, and big lead-head jigs. Plugs and spoons are used mainly in baitcasting. Fly-fishing for tarpon is usually done in shallow bays and up secluded rivers, with the flies large in size. The still-fishing method is done from piers, docks, and drifting boats, and in this method of fishing a live natural bait is suspended about four feet beneath a float. Although tarpon strike hard, they are difficult to hook because of their hard, bony mouths. The fisherman must strike hard several times to bed the

Tarpon

hook. The fish makes long runs, jumps, and does a lot of tail-walking, all plus items that make the tarpon a highly prized gamefish. These fish are migratory and are found in considerable numbers in the Gulf of Mexico and Florida waters from June through September.

Food value—Poor. Dedicated sportsmen release the fish unless it is a prize or record specimen.

Average size—Fifty to sixty pounds with fish to one hundred pounds occasional.

TAUTOG
(Tautoga onitis)

Range—Atlantic Coast from New Jersey to New Brunswick.

Description—Deeply olivaceous but sometimes brown; overall mottled or irregularly barred with black. This fish is armed with heavy, strong teeth for breaking shellfish. It also has extra teeth or "grinders" in its throat. Tautog feed on lobsters, crabs, mussels, and clams. The fish is a member of the wrasse family. It is a bottom feeder that hangs around rocky shores, wrecks, piers, and over hard sand bottoms. The fish moves back and forth between deep water and close to shore in the winter and when waters are rough. The fish sometimes moves into bays and harbors.

Fishing methods—Still-fishing on the bottom. Fishermen must be skilled in striking as soon as they feel a nibble, or they will miss hooking the fish. Tautog taken on lures are caught by accident only. Tautog are popular with partyboat fishermen and are most plentiful from May through November.

Food value—Excellent. The meat is tastiest when the fish is skinned.

Average size—Two to three pounds with occasional five-pounders.

WAHOO
(Acanthocybium solandri)

Range—Throughout tropical oceans. In U. S. waters wahoo are found mainly around the Florida Keys. They are also found in some numbers around Bermuda, the Bahamas, and West Indies.

Description—Grayish blue back fading to lavender and silvery on the lower sides and belly. Vertical markings are present in small wahoo. The vertical markings are pronounced in large fighting fish but they fade and vanish quickly in death. Quick loss of color with death is true with many migratory fish species. The fish has large, numerous teeth and has an elongated front dorsal fin of nearly even height over its entire length. This fish has tremendous speed, and some authorities credit it as being the fastest swimming of all fish. The wahoo is a blue water species, although it is often caught in the vicinity of offshore banks and reefs. The fish are migratory and surface feeders. They travel in small pods rather than large schools.

Fishing methods—Trolling. Prepared natural baits, whole and strip, as well as spoons, drones, jigs, and feathered jigs are used. The fish hits very hard, makes tremendously fast runs, and does a lot

Wahoo

of jumping. Catching a wahoo is considered a real fishing accomplishment, and as a result all wahoo caught are regarded as trophies. Wahoo catches by methods other than trolling are extremely rare.

Food value—Excellent, although the meat is somewhat oily as is the case with most of the members of the mackerel family.

Average size—ten to twenty pounds with occasional catches over forty.

WHITE PERCH
(Morone americana)

Range—Atlantic Coast from Virginia to Maine.

Description—Coloration varies considerably from light to olivaceous green on back and silvery on lower sides and belly to dark brown or black on the back with yellowish sides and belly. This fish is actually a bass and "perch" is a misnomer. It is a close relative of the striped bass. It is an anadromous saltwater fish that goes into fresh water to spawn. Even when it takes permanent residence in fresh water, it appears to prefer brackish waters. It is usually found in bays and in the lower reaches of large rivers. It feeds on small fish, marine worms, and invertebrates. The white perch is a game fighter, but it is often considered a nuisance when it becomes plentiful in fresh water. These fish are taken the year round but are most active in early morning and late evenings.

Fishing methods—Still-fishing on the bottom with grass shrimp, tiny bits of crab, pilchards, and bloodworms. Where waters are shallow, the fish will readily take wet flies and small spinners. These fish appear in dense schools and often will take baits until schools are decimated. It is a light-tackle fish.

Food value—Excellent. It is best prepared as a panfish. Some New Englanders prefer the flesh of white perch over that of the brown trout.

Average size—One-half pound, occasionally to one pound.

YELLOWFIN TUNA
(Neothunnus albacora)

Range—Gulf of California south to the Galapagos,

around Hawaii, Japan, and India. Yellowfin tuna found in the Atlantic is *Neothunnus argentivitatus*, and differs from the Pacific species in length of dorsal and anal fins.

Description—Metallic dark blue back with silver gray below; when caught usually has a golden iridescent band along its sides. This is a migratory, deep-water, and ocean fish that feeds on shrimp, small fish, and octopi. These fish travel in schools of considerable size.

Fishing methods—This is a highly prized gamefish that is usually taken on swiftly trolled lures such as metal squids, feathered jigs, and big spoons. The trolling speed is generally around eight to ten miles per hour. This trolling speed, however, is slowed a bit when strip bait, small fish like herring and sardines, and othe natural baits are used because water pressure is likely to tear these baits off the hook. The trolling method is to drag the lure or bait fairly close behind the boat, for yellowfin tuna often strike right in the prop wash. These fish are also taken drift-fishing when the water is chummed with herring and sardines. The fish strikes hard and wages a strong, determined fight. Yellowfin tuna are found in good numbers off California from August to October, in the Gulf of California from June through August, and off Mexico and Central America from September through May.

Food value—Excellent. The flesh is considered to be superior to that of bluefin tuna.

Average size—Eighty pounds with specimens over one hundred occasional.

YELLOWTAIL
(*Seriola dorsalis*)

Range—Pacific waters from Cape San Lucas north to Santa Barbara Islands and on both sides of the Gulf of California.

Description—Steel-blue back shading to bluish-silvery sides; irregular yellowish stripe extends along the sides from the eye to the tail. The yellowtail is one of the highest regarded members of the pompano family. It is migratory in nature, found in the Gulf of California and along the lower coast in fall and winter, and up to Los Angeles in summer. It

feeds on small fish, shrimp, squid, and small crustacea. These fish school, although unusually big specimens appear to be loners or pod-travelers at best.

Fishing methods—Trolling, dirft-fishing, and still-fishing. Yellowtails readily take trolled lures such as spoons, mental squids, and feathered jigs. The baits are often trolled fairly deep. Natural baits are usually used in drift and still-fishing, where it is also common to chum. The fish is a vicious striker and a very hard fighter. It rightfully ranks as a prize gamefish and is one of the Pacific coast's most popular sports fish.

Food value—Excellent as is the case with many members of the pompano family.

Average size—Eight to ten pounds with fish over fifteen pounds not uncommon. Specimens in excess of twenty-five pounds are considered very large.

Shark fishing is becoming increasingly popular on the Atlantic, Pacific, and Gulf Coasts.

California Yellowtail

141

Cabio

Giant Sea Bass

Pacific Mackerel

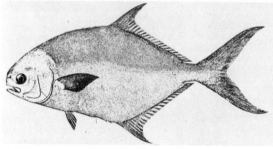

Pompano

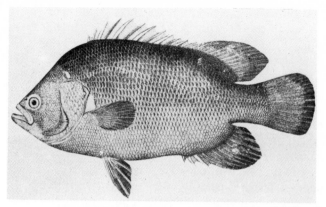

Tripletail

California Bonito

Black Drum

28

Popular Freshwater Species

ARCTIC GRAYLING
(Thymallus articus)

Range—Montana northward to Alaska and Northern Canada.

Description—Purplish-blue on back, lighter purple on sides and underparts. Small black dots on forward part of body. Dorsal fin is dusky green with brilliant orange and rose markings. The dorsal fin is large and saillike. The beauty of this fish makes it excellent for mounting, even nonrecord specimens. Although this fish is found in cold, clear lakes, it has a decided preference for cold, clear, and fast-running streams. Improved hatchery and stocking techniques are aiding the Arctic grayling in making a comeback in the United States. These fish are plentiful in streams in Alaska and Canadian provinces of Saskatchewan westward through the Canadian Rockies.

Fishing methods—Fly-fishing or casting small spinners or jigs, using light spinning or spin-casting tackle. These fish are rarely sought with natural baits. The arctic grayling ranks as a prized gamefish.

Food value—Excellent.

Average size—One pound; specimens in excess of three pounds are considered real trophies.

THE BASS

KENTUCKY SPOTTED BASS
(Micropterus punctulatus)

Range—The original range of this fish was south from Maryland on the Atlantic seaboard and west to Ohio and East Texas. It has been introduced in other states through planting.

Description—Greenish back shading to white belly. Spots are distinct on sides. This bass prefers cool water and is found in cool lakes and fast, clear streams and rivers. It feeds on small marine life, worms, and aquatic bugs. It frequents sand and gravel bars when the weather is cool but goes into deep holes and pools in warm weather.

Fishing methods—Bait-casting and fly-rod fishing are the favorite methods. The fish readily takes minnows, worms, flies, and popping bugs. It strikes hard and puts up a good fight on light tackle. Beginner fishermen often confuse the species with the smallmouth bass.

Food value—Good.

Average size—Three-fourths of a pound with occasional specimens to one and one-half pounds.

Arctic Grayling

Kentucky Spotted Bass

Largemouth Bass

LARGEMOUTH BASS
(*Micropterus salmoides*)

Range—This bass is found in every state in the United States as well as in Canada and Mexico. The largemouth bass is the most widespread and popular freshwater fish in North America. It has been transplanted successfully in many foreign countries.

Description—Popularly called the black back, which is one of dozens of provincial names, the largemouth bass varies in size and color according to the waters it inhabits. It grows largest in southern waters where it is generally active the year round. Its color is very dark green and at times almost black when it is found in muddy waters or where there are flooded cypress timber stands. Its color is a lighter green in clear lakes and streams. It prefers lakes to moving streams. It is also found in ponds, reservoirs, irrigation ditches, and lowland potholes filled by floods. The largemouth bass feeds on minnows, worms, insects, small sunfish, small rodents, snakes, and insects. It will grab just about anything that moves. It shows a decided tendency toward cannibalism. The fish is active the year round in southern waters, except in lakes and ponds where rotting vegetation may cause a water "turnover" in late July or August. The fish becomes inactive in northern waters during the winter and late in summer when rotting vegetation releases gases that cause lake "turnover." The fish is not migratory other than to move back and forth between shallow and deep water to feed and spawn or with the change of seasons. The largemouth bass was once thought to be a shallow-water fish. Research has shown the fish to reside in deep water as it grows older. Big bass tend to become loners and "homebodies" in that they remain mostly within a small area except when they move out to feed or spawn. School-size bass often move in dense packs as they herd and feed upon surface minnows. The fish can swim fast for short distances but generally is a slow swimmer. Big specimens are inclined to take up residence under docks and piers, around bridge pilings, in flooded brush and timber stands, around sunken logs, and under floating vegetation.

Fishing methods—This bass is taken casting, still-fishing, trolling, and fly-fishing, with casting ranking as the most popular style. Largemouth bass readily taken such natural baits as minnows and live worms. All types of artificial lures—spoons, plugs, jigs, and flies—are attractive to the fish. The bass is curious and often strikes because of temper as well as to secure food, but it often studies an object for many seconds, sometimes for minutes, before making any moves. Hence a proven way to catch the fish is to allow the bait or lure to lie motionless for a short time before imparting action. The fish hits with savage run and where surface lures are involved, it frequently goes completely out of the water on the strike. Unless hooked in shallow waters or over weed beds, the fish does little fighting on the surface. When it does fight on the surface it can shake its head like an angry bulldog and tail-walk across the water like a tarpon or sailfish. The fish has a tough mouth that requires a lot of sock on the part of the fisherman to bed the hook. More specialized tackle—rods, reels, lures, and even lines—has been developed for the largemouth bass than for any other single fish species in the northern hemisphere.

Food value—Excellent up to three or four pounds when taken from clear waters. Fish caught from muddy waters are likely to have a muddy taste. Lunker-size bass in excess of six or seven pounds are likely to be stringy and dry tasting.

Average size—School bass run three fourths of a pound to a pound. Three- to five-pound bass are fairly common, with eight- and nine-pounders not uncommon, especially in southern waters. Southern waters consistently yield the biggest bass.

SMALLMOUTH BASS
(*Micropterus dolomieu*)

Range—The original range of this fish was in the Atlantic seaboard states stretching from southern Canada to Georgia. Through widespread planting the smallmouth bass is now almost nationwide, except for those states bordering the Gulf of Mexico. The fish is found in limited areas of the northern portions of some of the Gulf Coast states.

Description—This fish is bronze-golden green but lighter than the largemouth bass. The darker bronze markings tend toward vertical patches. Easiest identification is made by noting the size of the mouth in relation to the eye. On the smallmouth bass the maxillary extends to a vertical line through the eye. On the largemouth bass the maxillary extends beyond a vertical line through the eye. The smallmouth bass has seventy-two rows of scales between the gill and tail, while the largemouth has never more than seventy, with the average being sixty-five. This fish shows a decided preference for fast, clear streaks and rivers and cool lakes. It cannot survive or propagate in waters where temperatures run high for any length of time. Smallmouth bass feed mainly around sand and gravel bars and along the shorelines. The fish feed on other small fish, small animals, flies, bugs, and aquatic worms. These fish are generally most active at night. The fish goes into deep water in warm weather and is usually found in deep holes and pools near banks and the bends in streams and rivers.

Fishing methods—Bait-casting and fly-fishing are the most popular methods. The fish takes natural baits as well as small underwater plugs, spoons, and jigs. The fish strikes hard and is a determined fighter. It puts on its best performance when taken on fly rod, and since it so readily hits flies and bugs, the smallmouth bass is a favorite with fly-rodders.

Food value—Good.

Average size—Most run three fourths of a pound to a pound in size. Smallmouth bass in excess of four pounds are considered large specimens.

WHITE BASS
(Roccus chrysops)

Range—Mainly in waters east of the Rocky Mountains. The fish is also referred to as the striped bass, and its range has been extended through transplantations.

Description—The fish is silvery with its under-parts slightly tinged with yellow. Longitudinal stripes mark its sides with the lower stripe usually intermittent. The fish's general habitat is still, deep water over sand and gravel bottoms. The fish move in large schools, and when herding and feeding on surface minnows, while bass churn the water white. They frequently gather in schools in the race waters at the foot of dams. White bass feed on small marine life.

Fishing methods—Bait-casting with light tackle is the popular fishing method. The fish hit small jigs, spoons, plugs, and especially spinners. When schools are feeding, huge catches of white bass are common.

Food value—Good.

Average size—One pound. Fish in excess of three pounds are considered trophies.

BOWFIN
(Amia calva)

Range—Throughout Gulf Coast states and tributary waters of the Mississippi River.

Description—Elongated in shape and mottled olive overall. The male in breeding season has a black spot rimmed with orange at the upper base of the tail fin. This is a typical mudfish that inhabits sluggish rivers and prefers weeds and mud in swamps, lakes, rivers, and bayous. The fish is often referred to as a grindle.

Fishing methods—Still-fishing and bait-casting. This fish is almost always taken incidentally while fishermen are seeking other species, usually bass. The bowfin readily hits lures and does so with a terrific jolt. The fish is usually included in sports-fishing guides because of its tenacious and long fight. It is an extremely ill-tempered fish that needs to be handled with care, even when boated.

Food value—Poor.

Average size—One to two pounds. Considered large in excess of five pounds.

Carp

CARP
(Cyprinus carpio)

Range—Widespread over the United States in rivers and lakes.

Description—Carp vary in coloration according to the waters in which they are found. Coloration ranges from yellowish or brassy silver to green or black. The species can be easily recognized by the

White Bass

145

chin barbels. This fish, also known as the German carp or European carp, was originally introduced in this country from Europe, where today it is a much sought-after fish. Although considered a nuisance in the United States, there is a growing number of sports anglers who seek these fish. Carp like muddy bottoms and somewhat stagnant water. They fish has no teeth in its mouth but does in its throat.

Fishing methods—Still-fishing with dough-baits, kernels of corn, or commercially prepared carp bait.

Food value—Poor.

Average size—Five pounds.

THE CATFISH

BLACK BULLHEAD
(Ictalurus melas)

BLUE CATFISH
(Ictalurus furcatus)

BROWN BULLHEAD
(Ictalurus nebulosus)

CHANNEL CATFISH
(Ictalurus punctalus)

FLAT BULLHEAD
(Ictalurus platycephalus)

FLATHEAD CATFISH
(Ictalurus olivaris)

YELLOW BULLHEAD
(Ictalurus natalis)

Range—Throughout the United States east of the Rocky Mountains.

Description—Black bullhead: brown-green to black on back and shading to green or gold; underparts dirty gray; light bar across base of tail. Blue catfish: slate or dull blue shading to whitish underparts; barbels usually color of body. Brown bullhead: dark yellowish-brown, sometimes mottled with darker brown; lighter brown on belly. Channel catfish: slate gray with bluish tint to silvery on underparts; speckled with black. Flat bullhead: olive-brown ranging to yellowish or greenish; dark horizontal bar at base of dorsal fin; fish is slender and nearly round and strictly herbivorous member of catfish family. Flathead catfish: Yellowish mottle with green and brown; lighter underparts; an overall repulsive looking fish. Yellow bullhead: yellowish mottled with dark brown; belly bright yellow; body short with very wide mouth. All catfish are

Blue Catfish

Channel Catfish

bottom-feeders that dine on all kinds of animal matter.

Fishing methods—Still-fishing, usually with a bobber that keeps the baited hook suspended a foot or so off the bottom. All catfish put up dogged, pulling fights that make for good sport on light tackle.

Food value—For the species listed the value ranges from fair on yellow bullheads to excellent on blue catfish, flat bullhead, and brown bullhead.

Average size—Black bullhead (half pound); blue catfish (three pounds with specimens to forty and fifty pounds not uncommon); brown bullhead (one pound with fish to five pounds common); flat bullhead (two pounds); channel catfish (four pounds with ten-pounders not uncommon); flathead catfish (five pounds); yellow bullhead (three-fourths pound).

CRAPPIE

BLACK CRAPPIE
(Pomoxis nigromaculatus)

WHITE CRAPPIE
(Pomoxis annularis)

Range—Widespread over the United States except in extreme north and mountainous regions.

Description—Black crappie: liberally sprinkled with black spots over a silvery background; spots form numerous patterns; distinguished from white crappie by seven to eight dorsal spines, whereas the white crappie has six. White crappie: same as black species except spots are lighter. Crappie are actually

146

Black Crappie

White Crappie

sunfish, but they are treated separately here because of their rank and importance to sports and recreational fishing. Crappie prefer reasonably clear water and cluster in schools around sunken brush, drowned timber, and boat docks. Both species are deep-bodied with flattened profiles. Both species feed on small fish, including their own, and insects.

Fishing methods—Still-fishing, fly-fishing, and spin-fishing. Crappie are readily taken on natural baits such as worms, crickets, grasshoppers, etc. Both species readily strike at popping bugs, flies, and small spinners. The fish are sport supreme on ultralight tackle.

Food value—Excellent.

Average size—Three-fourths of a pound; specimens to one and one-half pounds are not uncommon.

FRESH WATER DRUM
(Aplodinotus grunniens)

Range—Lakes and sluggish streams of Southern states; also in the Great Lakes.

Description—Grayish to dark on back; silvery sides and whitish belly. This fish strongly resembles the black drum found in salt water. The fish is a slow swimmer and a bottom feeder. It grubs the bottom for both marine and animal matter.

Fishing methods—Still-fishing with worms or cut bait. This fish is very rarely caught on artificial lures.

Food value—Poor.

Average size—Five pounds.

GARS

ALLIGATOR GAR
(Lepisosteus spatula)

SHORTNOSE GAR
(Lepisosteus platostomus)

LONGNOSE GAR
(Lepisosteus osseus)

Range—Lakes, rivers, and streams of Southern United States.

Description—Alligator gar: greenish brown on back; light brown sides; yellow belly; long, alligator-like jaws. Shortnose gar: solid greenish on back to yellowish on belly; has some spots on tail and a few along side of body. Longnose gar: greenish black on back to yellowish on belly with series of spots along the lateral line. The gar is a holdover from the Carboniferous age of many millions of years ago. Their heads and bodies are encased in armorlike scales. All gars are scavangers.

Fishing methods—Until recent years the gar was regarded as a nuisance, but since the mid-1950s the fish has won over a sizable following of sports anglers because of its fighting ability. It is caught mainly still-fishing using a bloody stink-bait, a mouse, or a dead bird. It is also taken casting colored and unraveled nylon rope. When the fish strikes the unraveled nylon, it is snagged by the many filaments that tangle in the fish's teeth and bony mouth. The fish are also taken with wire lasso rigs. A notable and legal sport in much of the South is to travel small rivers and bayous and take gars with harpoons or bow and arrows since gars have a habit of frequently rolling at the surface of the water.

Food value—Considered nonedible.

Average size—Alligator gar (twenty pounds with seventy-five pounds not uncommon); shortnose gar (two pounds); longnose gar (four pounds).

Alligator Gar

MOUNTAIN WHITEFISH
(Prosopium williamsonii)

Range—Rocky Mountains and Canadian Rockies.

Description—Light bluish-silver back with silver sides and whitish belly. Fish has a very small mouth. These fish are found in cold-water streams and lakes.

Fishing methods—Fly-casting and ultralight bait-casting. Small lures are necessary because of the fish's small mouth. These fish readily take small artificial lures but are not considered as gamy as any of the freshwater trout species.

Food value—Good.

Average size—One pound. Fish in excess of three pounds are considered quite large.

MUSKELLUNGE
(Esox masquinongy)

Range—Throughout Canada and the northern United States. This fish has been introduced into the northern parts of many Southern states and Gulf Coast states through planting.

Description—Darkish green back with yellowish sides and white underbelly. Fish has dark spots on its upper sides. A cross breed known as the tiger muskellunge has both spots and bars on its sides. This fish shows a preference to large spots and bars on its sides. This fish shows a preference to large lakes and northern rivers. The fish becomes solitary in habit after the late spring spawn. A considerable water area is needed to support a single fish, which reportedly eats about one-fifty to one-fourth its weight daily. The muskellunge, also called musky for short, tends strongly to go to the cool part of lakes and in rivers moves into quiet stretches. It often lurks in the shadow of lugs and boulders of hidden in flooded grass stands in wait for victims to pass near. The musky is known to range over wide areas, feeding on smaller fish, crayfish, frogs, waterfowl, small animals, and even its own kind.

Fishing methods—This fish is most commonly caught trolling the shorelines of lakes and in the quiet parts of rivers. The best lures are large spoons and plugs. Commotion lures fished near flooded grass stands and points are especially deadly. When it comes to using natural baits, live baits are the best, and then the bait must be put on the hook in a special manner—either hooked through the mouth or lips. The musky invariably takes live bait head first. The fisherman has to strike hard to bed the hook because of the fish's hard, bony mouth. Best fishing is early in the morning and late evening in the spring after the spawn and again in the fall prior to the advent of cold weather. The fish goes deep in the summer and becomes quit dormant in the winter. Wire leaders are required because of the fish's sharp teeth. The fish is sometimes called the "freshwater barracuda."

Food value—This is a matter subject to a lot of pros and cons. The fact that Canadian Indians feed these fish to their dogs may be the reason some people question eating the fish.

Average size—Ten to twelve pounds. Specimens over twenty-five pounds are considered large.

NORTHERN PIKE
(Esox lucius)

Range—Plentiful in Canada and the northern United States. Numerous transplants have been successful to extend the range of this fish into southerly states.

Description—The fish has a green back shading to greenish-yellow sides and belly; olive green blotches appear in chains or lines. The chain appearance leads to the fish erroneously being called chain pickerel. The pike prefers quiet lakes and ponds. When found in rivers or streams, the fish invariably gravitates to the deep holes in the backwashes. Northern pike are solitary in nature and stay in rather small areas. They feed over grass beds and along the edge of lily pads, always lingering in the protective shadows of stumps, logs, and rocks. The fish feeds voraciously on small fish, frogs, young waterfowl, and small animals. The fish reportedly consumes approximately one-fifth its weight daily.

Fishing methods—Trolling, casting, and still-fishing. Big spoons and plugs, preferably in red, white, yellow, and green combinations, are the best lures for general trolling and casting along the shorelines. Pike will also strike large flies and bugs worked over grass stands or around logs and stumps. The fish hits hard, fights hard, and often jumps. The most effective still-fishing is with live bait. Commotion plugs and spinners, jointed plugs, and wobbling spoons are the most productive artificial lures. The best northern pike fishing is generally found in the spring and fall. The fish goes deep in the summer. It can be caught through the ice in the winter by fishing live minnows.

Northern Pike

148

Food value—Good from fresh-caught fish. The pike's reputation as a food fish is probably damaged by the widespread use of its flesh as dog food in parts of Canada. The fish are plentiful and offer the Canadian Indians the easiest and cheapest way to feed their packs of dogs.

Average size—Four to five pounds with fifteen-pounders considered large.

King Salmon

SALMON

ATLANTIC SALMON
(Salmo salar)

CHINOOK SALMON
(Oncorhynchus tshawytscha)

CHUM SALMON
(Oncorhynchus keta)

COHO SALMON
(Oncorhynchus kisutch)

PINK SALMON
(Oncorhynchus gorbuscha)

SOCKEYE SALMON
(Oncorhynchus nerka)

Range—Atlantic as well as Pacific salmon species migrate to salt water to spend most of their lives and return to fresh water to spawn. The Atlantic salmon, unlike the Pacific species, does not die after spawning and returns to the sea. The range of the Atlantic salmon is rapidly dwindling and is now mainly in Newfoundland, Nova Scotia, and Canadian provinces fronting the Atlantic. Most Pacific species range from San Francisco northward to Alaska. The Coho salmon is thriving in some of the Great Lakes.

Description—Atlantic salmon: when fresh from the sea, the back is a beautiful steel blue, with silvery sides spotted above the lateral line. The bright colors fade in fresh water and take on a reddish tinge. Chinock salmon: dusky back with silvery sides and belly; black spots on back, dorsal fin, and tail. Chum salmon: coloration similar to that of the chinook abut without spots. Coho salmon: bluish-green back with silver sides; spots are obscure and fewer than on the chinook. Pink salmon: smallest of the Pacific salmon, with coloration similar to the chinook; body has a distinct humpback. Sockeye salmon: bluish back with silvery sides and belly; lacks spots. When in salt water all of the salmons feed on herring, anchovies, sardines, other small fish, shrimp and small shellfish. The Pacific species do not feed and rarely strike when they return to fresh water where they spawn and then die. Atlantic salmon feed heavily on insect life in fresh water and on shrimp and crustaceans in tidewaters. The Atlantic salmon is noted for its gamefish qualities.

Fishing methods—Fly fishing, still-fishing, and trolling. The Atlantic salmon is a light-tackle fish taken mostly on fly tackle. The fish puts up an excellent battle, including frequent jumps. The Pacific species are caught when they leave the open sea to start spawning migration into fresh water and are usually caught at river mouths and in the brackish waters immediately above the river mouths. They do not feed and rarely strike when they go into fresh water. Natural baits include anchovies, sardines, and small fish. Salmon also take spoons, plugs, and spinners.

Food value—Good to excellent, depending upon species and waters from which they are taken. The meat of the Atlantic salmon is excellent but only for a few weeks after leaving salt water.

Average size—Atlantic salmon (ten pounds), Chinook (twenty pounds), chum (five to seven pounds), Coho (ten pounds), pink (four to six pounds), sockeye (five to seven pounds).

SUNFISH

BLUEGILL
(Lepomis macrohirus)

GREEN SUNFISH
(Lepomis cyanellus)

LONGEAR SUNFISH
(Lepomis megalotis)

PUMPKINSEED
(Lepomis gibbosus)

REDBREAST SUNFISH
(Pelomis auritus)

Bluegill

ROCK BASS
(ambloplites rupestris)

WARMOUTH
(Chaenobrytthus gulosus)

Range—The sunfish family is very large, and only those members found in large numbers over considerable areas are listed. These fish are exclusively North American and are generally abundant over the United States east of the Rocky Mountains and north into Canada. So many of the species interbreed that species often blend in such a manner that only a trained biologist can tell them apart. Each species has a number of provincial names. As an example, the bluegill has more than fifty provincial names.

Description—Bluegill: coloration varies with water conditions; usually dark greenish on back with purple luster and chainlike transverse greenish bars; fins greenish and cheeks iridescent blue; belly often reddish-copper; noticeable marking on top of head resembles an old injury. Green sunfish: greenish back; black gill cover is only on bony part and not on the membrance back. Longear sunfish: dark-greenish with reddish belly; gill cover flap is darkish and unusually long. Pumpkinseed: greenish-olive back; purplish-blue upper sides spotted with orange; belly orange; cheeks orange with long wavy blue streaks; reddish-orange spot at edge of gill flap. Redbreast sunfish: back darkish and olivaceous overall with breast of male usually yellow or orange-red. Rock bass: olive-green back; sides tinged with yellow and dark mottling; belly yellow-white;red eye. Warmouth: dark olive-green back; upper portions mottled with dark colorings and often flecked with green or yellow; belly light yellow; at times red markings are present. All species have similar habits in preferring to hang around submerged brush piles, drowned timber

stands, boat docks, and lily pads. All feed on insects, worms, and any small fish they can catch.

Fishing methods—Still-fishing, fly-fishing, and spin-casting. Still-fishing is best with worms, crickets, grasshoppers, and small minnows. All sunfish take both wet and dry flies and frequently strike popping bugs. Spin-cast fishermen frequently catch them on tiny jigs and spinners.

Food value—Fair to excellent, depending upon waters from which they are taken.

Average size—Six to eight ounces for bluegills; rock bass in excess of a pound not uncommon. Any of the species in excess of two pounds is a trophy fish.

TROUT

BROOK TROUT
(Salvelinus fontinalis)

BROWN TROUT
(Salmo trutta)

LAKE TROUT
(Salvelinus namaycush)

CUTTHROAT TROUT
(Salmo clarkii)

RAINBOW TROUT
(Salmo gairdneri)

DOLLY VARDEN TROUT
(Salvelinus malma)

Range—All of the American trout are members of the salmon family and are widespread in the rivers, streams, and lakes of the United States and Canada. They range from the Atlantic to the Pacific. Planting has widely expanded the range of these fish and today they are found in all suitably cool waters in North America.

Description—Brook trout: colors vary greatly from black green or olivacous to a light, yellowish green black: lower sides and belly lighter to nearly white and flushed with pink. Brown trout: dark

Lake Trout

Rainbow Trout

Chain Pickerel

brown back blending into lighter brown sides: red and black spots mark the sides and back; introduced into U.S. waters in 1882. Lake trout: mostly dark gray and widely covered with pale spots that are usually tinged with pink. Cutthroat trout: color varies with water conditions; back is olivaceous silver with many rosy spots along the lateral line; pronounced red streaks on both sides of the lower jaws. Rainbow trout: color varies with the water and part of the country where the fish is found; bluish or olive green back with silvery sides and widely covered with small black spots; has wide lateral band that is purplish-red in color. Dolly Varden trout: olivaceous back with small red and orange spots that become larger as they extend to the sides; lower fins have pale stripe; when found in salt water the fish has darker colors with a silvery cast. All of the trout feed on flies, worms, insects, small fish, and minnows. Trout carry a number of provincial names, often names taken from the waters in which they are found. The lake trout is also called the Mackinaw and Togue; the rainbow is known as the McCloud River trout, salmon trout, and Pacific trout, to mention a few. All of the trout are cold-water fish.

Fishing methods—Fly-fishing and trolling. They readily take artificial flies, and large species such as lake trout hit plugs, spoons, and spinners. Trout are synonymous with fly-fishing and are considered to be the backbone of that form of fishing. All put up good fights with the rainbow trout considered to be the gamiest of all. The rainbow readily breaks water and jumps when hooked. Trout take natural baits such as flies, bugs, insects, worms and minnows, but in trout-fishing circles it is considered a mortal sin to catch them any way other than flies. The exception is the lake trout that often responds only to large lures trolled at considerable depths.

Food value—Excellent.

Average size—Brook trout (one pound), brown trout (one and a half pounds), lake trout (six to ten pounds with twenty-pounders not uncommon), cutthroat trout (two pounds), rainbow trout (one and a half pounds), Dolly Varden trout (two to three pounds with ten- and twelve-pound specimens not uncommon.)

Walleye

151

The following section includes a thumbnail description of fishing in each of the United States, Canada, and Mexico. In the case of inland states, figures are listed for square land miles and square miles of surface water within the states. The total water area within a state includes lakes, reservoirs, and ponds forty acres or more in size; streams, estuaries, and canals one-eighth mile or more in width, deeply indented embayments and sounds and other coastal waters behind or sheltered by headlands or islands separated by less than one nautical mile of water, and islands having less than forty acres of area. The figures do not include coastal surface waters or waters not defined as inland waters.

In addition to land area and inland water area listed for each coastal state, figures are included for general coastline and tidal coastline. The tidal coastline takes in the coastline of the outer coast, offshore islands, sounds, bays, rivers, bayous, and creeks to the head of tidewater or to a point where tidal waters narrow to a width of one hundred feet. A guideline to an area's coastal fishing can be taken from the tidal coastline. The longer the tidal coastline, the better the fishing for native fish species because of the vast nursing areas that tidal coastlines afford.

The fish species listed for each state, province, or nation are those that are in most abundance and those sought by the most fishermen, either for sport or food. All species found within a particular area are not listed because they are restricted to a very small portion, rare or available on a special fee basis. Transplanting in recent years has accounted for new species in many areas, and as a result of this work in years to come some species may be listed as common or in abundance in the states into which they have been introduced.

The range of saltwater fish, too, is subject to change. In some cases overharvesting by commercial interests and/or pollution have altered the ranges of some species. The most notable example in recent years is the Atlantic salmon.

ALABAMA

Land area: 50,851 square miles; water area: 758 square miles; coastline: 53 statute miles; tidal coastline: 607 statute miles.

There are no closed seasons in Alabama, a state noted for fine freshwater and good saltwater fishing. Alabama's saltwater fishing is on the Gulf of Mexico. Its coastal saltwater fishing offers spotted weakfish, channel bass, black drum, flounders, and croakers. The state's offshore salt waters offer fishing for tarpon, sailfish, cobia, Spanish mackerel, king mackerel, red snapper, and bluefish. Alabama's inland waters contain largemouth bass, smallmouth bass, spotted bass, striped bass, yellow bass, white bass, bluegills, crappie, catfish, and pickerel. Lake Eufaula rates as the state's best freshwater fishing impoundment. Another notable impoundment is Smith Lake.

ALASKA

Land area: 566,432 square miles; inland water area: 19,980 square miles; coastline: 5,580 statute miles; tidal coastline: 31,383 statute miles.

Alaska with three million lakes of twenty acres or more sports extraordinary fishing. It is one of the few remaining areas on the North American continent where one can find excellent roadside fishing. The state is laced with small lakes and its fly-in fishing is like much of Canada's—unbeatable. The great number of small lakes and fly-in aspects open virgin territories yet to be fished. Main fish species found in abundance in the state include lake trout, rainbow trout, Chinook salmon, coho, Arctic char, whitefish, Dolly Varden trout, grayling, and pike. Alaska has various fishing seasons that can sometimes be limited by the weather. The Inland Passage offers five kinds of salmon, sea-run varieties of trout, and halibut.

ARIZONA

Land area: 113,563 square miles; inland water area: 346 square miles.

Although Arizona ranks low in fishable waters, it is a state that has some fine fishing in parts. The state is divided as far as individual species are concerned. Lake Havasu, Lake Powell, Lake Mead, Big Lake, and waters along the Colorado River are major fishing areas. Good fishing for largemouth bass, yellow bass, and catfish is found in central Arizona along the Salt River. Trout fishermen favor the northern and eastern portions of the state.

ARKANSAS

Land area: 52,175 square miles; inland water area: 929 square miles.

Arkansas boasts some of the finest largemouth bass fishing to be found in America. Bull Shoals is the state's most renowned lake. Other major fish-producing waters include Lake Quachita, Beaver Lake, Lake Catherine, Lake Hamilton, Green's Ferry Lake, and the numerous small lakes in the foothills of the Ozark Mountains and those formed along the White River, which in itself is a major fishing attraction, especially in connection with float trips. Fish species in plentiful supply in the state include largemouth bass, smallmouth bass, Kentucky bass, bream, crappie, and rainbow trout, especially in Ozark Mountain streams, the White River, and Little Red River.

CALIFORNIA

Land area: 156,537 square miles; inland water area: 2,156 square miles; coastline: 840 statute miles; tidal coastline: 3,427 statute miles.

California is one of North America's most popular sports-fishing states, offering many fresh- and salt-water species. More than twenty species of game and panfish are found in the state's inland waters, while the state's salt waters harbor everything from huge billfish offshore to steelhead, salmon, and striped bass angling in coastal waters to the tiny grunion that makes spawn runs on California beaches. California has a wide variety of fishing regulations and seasons.

Rocky Mountain streams offer superb trout fishing as well as scenic splender as in this Colorado fishing scene.

COLORADO

Land area: 103,794 square miles; inland water area: 453 square miles.

Colorado has both cold-water and warm-water fish species. The warm-water species include largemouth bass, white bass, yellow perch, wall-eyes, and catfish in the eastern part of the state. The cold-water species, which include rainbow trout, brown trout, brook trout, cutthroat trout, konanee salmon, and whitefish, are found in the mountain streams and lakes in the central and western parts of the state. Overall the state's best fishing is in the mountain streams. Grand lake, the largest glacial lake in Colorado, is the source of the Colorado River, which offers fine trout fishing.

CONNECTICUT

Land area: 4,870 square miles; inland water area: 139 square miles; coastline and tidal coastal: 618 statute miles.

Connecticut is a small state, but nevertheless one renowned for fine saltwater fishing and good freshwater angling. Striped bass, bluefish, weakfish, flounders, and tautog abound in the state's salt waters. Its freshwater fishing includes warm-water species like large- and smallmouth bass, sunfish, and yellow perch and cold-water specimens such as rainbow trout, brown trout, brook trout, golden trout, and tiger trout. Excellent trout fishing is found on the Housatonic River and Farmington River in the northern part of the state.

Colorado's fighting trout really give anglers a run for their money. More than 2,000 lakes and 1,300 streams are stocked annually with 1,200,000 pounds of trout and are open to public fishing.

DELAWARE

Land area: 1,982 square miles; inland water area: 175 square miles; coastline: 28 statute miles; tidal coastline: 381 statute miles.

Delaware's inland water areas don't amount to much more than big ponds, but they do offer some creditable fishing for largemouth bass, sunfish, yellow and white perch, and chain pickerel. The state's coastline is extremely short, but with bay indentations, tidal creeks, etc., there is considerable tidal coastline, and in places it offers some fine saltwater fishing. Indian River and Rehoboth Bay are excellent for flounder fishing. Weakfish, croaker, and porgie fishing is good in Delaware Bay,

while offshore waters offer black sea bass, marlin, bluefish, and tuna action. There is some trout fishing within the state, but it is on a put-and-take basis with special license fees involved.

DISTRICT OF COLUMBIA

Land area: sixty-one square miles; inland water area: six square miles.

The seat of our government is not noted for fishing, but if a person persists in wetting a line within the District, white perch and shad can be caught in the Potomac River. Interestingly enough the District of Columbia is one of the few areas on the North American continent where no fishing license is required.

FLORIDA

Land area: 54,136 square miles; inland water area:

4,424 square miles; coastline: 770 statute miles; tidal coastline: 5,095 statute miles.

Whether it is in fresh water or salt water, Florida is truly a fisherman's paradise. Inland waters are alive with large-mouth bass, a strain that today is known as the Florida bass. These bass are bucketmouths with five- to ten-pound specimens being quite common. Florida has the usual other species of freshwater fish, but they are in effect mostly neglected because of the state's reputation for big largemouth bass. The best bass fishing is in the lakes in the northern part of the state. Notable bass fishing hot spots include Lake Kissimmee, St. John's River, and the Everglades. Florida's saltwater fishing is truly exciting with a great variety of fish species in the offering. Florida waters are renowned for fine tarpon, snook, bonefish, sailfish, barracuda, wahoo, and marlin fishing. Some of the most exciting saltwater fishing to be found in North America can be enjoyed in the Florida Keys. The state's climate and temperatures are such that fishing is good the year round.

GEORGIA

Land area: 58,197 square miles; inland water area: 679 square miles; coastline: 100 statute miles; tidal coastline: 2,344 statute miles.

Although this state hasn't received an abundance of fishing publicity, it is in reality one of the finer fishing states in the Union. Streams in northern Georgia have good trout fishing, while waters to the south offer good largemouth bass, smallmouth bass, bream, and catfish action. Some of the top fishing lakes in the state include Lake Seminole, Lake Lanier, and Lake Walter George. The largemouth bass is the state's most popular gamefish and specimens to ten pound are not uncommon. The larger impoundments have good crappie and white bass populations. Georgia's saltwater fishing is seasonal and offers good action for channel bass, spotted weakfish, tarpon, and members of the mackerel family.

HAWAII

Land area: 6,425 square miles; inland water area: 25 square miles; coastline: 750 statute miles; tidal coastline: 1,052 statute miles.

Completely surround by the blue Pacific, it goes without saying that Hawaii stands as a jewel in a setting of excellent saltwater fishing. Its ocean fishing boasting such species as dolphin, marlin, tuna, bonito, snapper, grouper, and jacks draws the prime interest. Oddly enough the islands offer some good, although limited, freshwater fishing for trout, largemouth and smallmouth bass, and bluegills.

IDAHO

Land area: 82,677 square miles; inland water area: 880 square miles.

Although Idaho boasts an almost unlimited variety of fishing waters and many species of fish, its fishing is seasonal, running from June to October. The Clearwater, Snake, and Boise Rivers are world famous for trout fishing. Priest Lake, the most primitive of the big lakes in Idaho's northern panhandle, is a snow-fed lake that is famous for big Mackinau trout running twenty pounds and over. Trout species such as Dolly Varden, rainbow, brook, lake, golden cutthroat, and brown make for some fabulous fishing in the high mountain lakes, some that can be reached only by hiking or horseback. Large lakes like Pend Oreille boast fine chinook and sockeye salmon, steelhead, and Kokanee. The state's mountainous streams, clear and cold, make excellent settings for the fly-rod fisherman.

ILLINOIS

Land area: 55,877 square miles; inland water area: 523 square miles.

Illinois has good largemouth bass fishing in the Mississippi River and lakes in the southern part of the state. The state's fishing for walleye, sauger, crappie, bluegill, and catfish is generally fair. Trout fishing includes rainbows and browns, but it is on a put-and-take basis. The state has a number of fish species, but in general Illinois fishing suffers from rather severe winters, and the lack of water runoff tends to make sports fishing something of a problem. Lake Shelbyville, 11,100 acres in size, is one of the state's notable fish-producing waters.

INDIANA

Land area: 36,189 square miles; inland water area: 102 square miles.

The Hoosier State's fishing headliners are largemouth bass, crappie, and bluegills. Lake Monroe, with its 150 statute miles of shoreline, is the state's most productive lake. The Tippecanoe River is famed for good smallmouth bass fishing, and Kankakee River yields good walleye, bass, pike, and catfish action. There is considerable trout fishing on a put-and-take basis in the state's northeastern lakes and streams, where holdover trout sometimes run to five pounds in size.

IOWA

Land area: 56,043 square miles; inland water area: 247 square miles. Iowa has fifty-two natural lakes covering forty-five thousand acres, plus some manmade reservoirs and thousands of farm ponds. Its standout fish are pike and walleyes. Other species found in the state include trout, white bass, yellow perch, largemouth bass, crappie, and catfish. The East Okoboji, West Okoboji, and Big Spirit Lakes in the northwestern part of the state are known as Iowa's Great Lakes.

KANSAS

Land area: 82,056 square miles; inland water area: 208 square miles.

The Neosho River has excellent fishing for channel catfish, flatheads, and bullheads, and the Fall River Reservoir is good for largemouth bass, white bass, and crappie. The Kansas Forestry, Fish and Game Commission has done much for sports fishing by creating manmade lakes and reservoirs.

KENTUCKY

Land area: 39,851 square miles; inland water area: 544 square miles.

The Blue Grass State is one of our richest states when it comes to sports fishing. With its thirty-five hundred statute miles of lake shoreline, there is no shortage of water in the state, and its streams, major impoundments, and farm ponds combine to offer excellent fishing. Dale-Hollow and Cumberland are top waters for smallmouth bass and white bass. Kentucky Lake is renowned for its crappie runs in the spring. Lake Barkley is another good fishing lake. All of the state's waters boast good to excellent fishing for largemouth bass, Kentucky bass, walleye, bluegill, and catfish. Trout fishing is becoming popular in the state, but it is on a put-and-take basis.

LOUISIANA

Land area: 45,155 square miles; inland water area: 3,368 square miles; coastline: 397 statute miles; tidal coastline: 7,721 statute miles.

This bayou country state sports excellent fishing, both fresh and salt water. The most popular freshwater species is the largemouth bass, with catfish and crappie ranking close behind. The state has an abundance of fresh water that harbors many sunfish species. The coastline, tidewaters, and offshore islands are noted for very good saltwater

One of the finest largemouth bass fishing lakes in the United States is Toledo Bond Reservoir on the Texas-Louisiana border. The reservoir is a manmade "drowned forest" lake. *Courtesy Evinrude Motors.*

fishing for channel bass, spotted weakfish, black drum, Spanish mackerel, king mackerel, cobia, and tarpon. The great number of offshore oil rigs and platforms have become important sports fish havens, and as a result Louisiana is growing in importance as an offshore sports-fishing state. Big strides are being made in bill-fishing in Louisiana offshore waters. Such areas as the Mississippi River delta, Toledo Bend Reservoir, Lake Ponchatrain, and Black Lake are synonymous with good fishing. The Louisiana bayou country is the birthplace of some excellent seafood recipes.

MAINE

Land area: 62,992 square miles; inland water area: 3,616 square miles; coastline: 228 statute miles; tidal coastline: 3,478 statute miles.

Excellent inland and coastal fishing is found in our northeasternmost state. Lakes and rivers have handlocked salmon, brook trout, lake trout, and smallmouth bass. Excellent fishing is found in the Kennebec and Penobscot Rivers. Many of the state's coastal streams offer good sea-run brown trout and striped bass fishing. Off-coast fishing includes striped bass, pollock, mackerel, and big bluefin tuna, with most of the fishing being out of Boothbay Harbor.

MARYLAND

Land area: 9,891 square miles; inland water area: 686 square miles; coastline: 31 statute miles; tidal coastline: 3,190 statute miles.

Maryland is noted for its fine bass fishing in famed Chesapeake Bay. Good runs of white and yellow perch in the tidal streams provide a bonus to striper fishing. Other important saltwater species are channel bass, black drum, blackfish, sea trout, flounders, and kingfish. School tuna, white marlin, and dolphin are found in Maryland's offshore waters. Streams in the interior of the state feature some good trout fishing.

MASSACHUSETTS

Land area: 7,833 square miles; inland water area: 424 square miles; coastline: 192 statute miles; tidal coastline: 1,519 statute miles.

Massachusetts is noted for its fine saltwater fishing for striped bass, bluefish, pollock, haddock, flounders, cod, and mackerel. Some of the East Coast's finest flounder fishing can be enjoyed in Quincy, which is just outside of Boston. The Connecticut River, Quabbin Reservoir, streams, and ponds offer excellent freshwater fishing for trout, yellow perch, bluegills, and crappie. Overall Massachusetts is right in the ranks of the top sports-fishing states.

MICHIGAN

Land area: 56,818 square miles; inland water area: 1,398 square miles.

With over three thousand miles of Great Lakes shoreline plus eleven thousand lakes and thirty-six thousand statute miles of rivers and streams, Michigan is right up there near the top of the sports-fishing ladder. In recent years coho fishing has boomed Michigan's fishing on a hemispheric plane. Trout used to be the state's best offering in fishing. Now cohos have taken over. The lower portions of the state feature good largemouth bass and panfish action. The famed Au Sable River is one that no trout fisherman should never pass unchallenged. Michigan is a great fishing state that the traveling angler should make a point of visiting.

MINNESOTA

Land area: 79,289 square miles; inland water area: 4,779 square miles.

Minnesota is another of our great sport-fishing states. It has some twelve thousand lakes and probably the largest walleye population of any state. Northern pike, muskellunge, bass, and panfish attract great numbers of sports fishermen to Minnesota. Trout fishing ranks high in the state, since Minnesota has over two thousand miles of streams plus several lakes holding trout. In addition to fishable waters within the state, Minnesota also has a long shoreline on Lake Superior. Lake Pepin is the Minnesota lake where water skiing was invented in 1922 by Ralph Samuelson.

MISSISSIPPI

Land area: 47,358 square miles; inland water area: 358 square miles; coastline: 44 statute miles; tidal coastline: 359 statute miles.

Mississippi is noted for its fine catfish fishing. In addition, four major flood—control reservoirs with Ross Barnett the best known provide excellent bass, crappie, and bream fishing. The state has a number of small, manmade lakes alive with bass and bluegills. The state also has some beautiful streams that offer fine float fishing. Coastal saltwater fishing fills the bill of those who like to angle the brackish waters of tidal rivers. The Mississippi gulf coast is growing in stature for the offshore fisherman seeking billfish, king mackerel, cobia, and bonita. Enid, Sardis, Grenada, and Arkabutla Lakes form Mississippi's "Great Lakes."

MISSOURI

Land area: 69,046 square miles; inland water area: 640 square miles.

Bull Shoals Lake and the Ozarks spell fine fishing for Missouri. Bull Shoals is a huge impoundment that offers excellent largemouth bass, crappie, white bass, catfish, walleye, and sunfish action. In addition to Bull Shoals, there are many small lakes, Ozark streams, and farm ponds. The Ozark streams boast some very good trout fishing. The Lake of Ozarks has 1,375 miles of fine shoreline fishing.

MONTANA

Land area: 145,603 square miles; inland water area: 1,535 square miles.

Montana is called the Big Sky Country because of

its rich mountain beauty. Montana is also the trout fisherman's dreamland. The Missouri, Madison, Big Hole, and Yellowstone Rivers are all noted for excellent trout fishing. Flathead Lake, thirty-eight miles long with 120,000 surface acres and at an elevation of three thousand feet, offers excellent fishing for Mackinaw, rainbow, and Dolly Varden trout, salmon, whitefish, bass, and perch. There are hundreds of glacier-fed lakes and small mountain streams that will delight the trout fisherman. Eight- and ten-pound trout are not uncommon, and five-pounders can be found in almost every daily catch. Montana's fishing is seasonal because of the weather.

NEBRASKA

Land area: 76,522 square miles; inland water area: 705 square miles.

The most productive body of water in this state is twenty-five-mile-long Lewis and Clark Reservoir. The state has many streams and small lakes that hold largemouth bass, pike, white bass, walleye, sauger, paddlefish, crappie, and bluegill. Many of the state's streams provide good trout fishing.

Country mill ponds have been favorite fishing holes for years. They yield bass, bream, crappie, and catfish. *Courtesy Mercury Motors.*

NEVADA

Land area: 109,880 square miles; inland water area: 651 square miles.

The big water in this state is Lake Mead, which covers 229 square miles, and is renowned for its fine bass fishing. In an otherwise desert state, Nevada has brown, rainbow, and cutthroat trout in some of its larger lakes and streams. One may not go to Nevada specifically to fish, but one going into the state should never go without fishing tackle.

NEW HAMPSHIRE

Land area: 9,033 square miles; inland water area: 271 square miles; coastline: 13 statute miles; tidal coastline: 131 statute miles.

New Hampshire's great south bay area provides fine fishing for smelt, flounders, striped bass, and mackerel. The numerous lakes in the southern portion of the state have good smallmouth bass fishing, while brown, brook, and rainbow trout dominate streams in the northern part of the state. Lake Winnepesaukee is one of the state's best fishing areas.

NEW JERSEY

Land area: 7,532 square miles; inland water area: 304 square miles; coastline: 130 statute miles; tidal coastline: 1,792 statute miles.

New Jersey offers both fresh- and saltwater fishing. The main saltwater fish include striped bass, bluefish, white marlin, and bluefin tuna. The state's seaports have an abundance of party and charter sports-fishing boats. The Delaware River offers good smallmouth bass fishing, and there is considerable trout fishing in the state's streams and lakes, thanks to good annual stocking programs.

NEW MEXICO

Land area: 121,445 square miles; inland water area: 221 square miles.

New Mexico may be something of a desert state but it has some fine fishing waters. Anglers seeking largemouth bass, white bass, walleye, sunfish, and catfish can find them in the warm waters in the low-lying portions of the state. The highland parts with their vast mountain ranges have fine trout fishing in Elephant Butte Lake and the tumbling rivers like the Red and Rio Grande. The trout are big and varied and include rainbows and browns. Navajo Lake has both cold- and warm-water fish, with trout, and salmon in the cold parts and bass and sunfish in the warm waters. The San Juan River is good for brown, cutthroat, and rainbow trout.

NEW YORK

Land area: 47,869 square miles; inland water area: 1,707 square miles; coastline: 127 statute miles; tidal coastline: 1,850 statute miles.

Long Island is the gateway to the Atlantic Ocean with Long Island Sound offering good saltwater fishing. Coastal waters have striped bass, bluefish, tautog, weakfish, and flounders. Waters out of Montauk boast cod, striped bass, bluefish, and sharks. The state's inland waters yield good trout fishing, especially in Westchester County, the Beaverkill River, and the Ten-Mile River. Just about every outlying county in the state has some good trout waters.

NORTH CAROLINA

Land area: 48,880 square miles; inland water area: 3,706 square miles; coastline: 301 statute miles; tidal coastline: 3,375 statute miles.

Because of the state's nearness to the Gulf Stream, North Carolina's coastal and offshore waters excel in fishing for marlin, tuna, mackerel, bonito, dolphin, channel bass, striped bass, and bluefish. The state's freshwater fishing is equally famed with lakes, streams, and farm ponds offering largemouth bass, smallmouth bass, catfish, sunfish, and a variety of trout. Any fisherman visiting North Carolina should make a point of sampling its fishing.

Placidity is the word for Merchants Mill Pond, a quiet corner of Gates County, North Carolina. This is typical of waters found in the Southern and Gulf Coast states. All offer excellent bass fishing. *Courtesy Georgia Pacific.*

NORTH DAKOTA

Land area: 69,280 square miles; inland water area: 1,385 square miles.

North Dakota's main gamefish is the northern pike. Other species in good supply include walleye, sauger, white bass, largemouth bass, and various trout species. Reservoirs and lakes make up the fishing waters since there are virtually no streams of note. The biggest single fishing area is Garrison Reservoir with its three hundred thousand surface acres. Other notable fishing spots include Butte Reservoir and Lake Darling. North Dakota's winters can be very severe, and as a result the state's fishing is highly seasonal.

OHIO

Land area: 41,018 square miles; inland water area: 204 square miles.

The bulk of Ohio's fishing is in the state's numerous lakes. Fish species in good supply include muskellunge, walleye, northern pike, largemouth bass, smallmouth bass, white bass, crappie, sunfish, and bullheads. Much of northern Ohio is bordered by Lake Erie. In addition to this and the inland lakes, there are thousands of farm ponds. Rivers like the Muskingum and Huron support smallmouth bass, but in general much of Ohio's stream fishing has suffered from pollution. Wolf Run, Piedmont, Indian Lake, Seneca, and Salt Fork are good fishing lakes.

OKLAHOMA

Land area: 68,984 square miles; inland water area: 935 square miles.

Oklahoma's fishing is good the year around. Its many reservoirs, lakes, and ponds support largemouth bass, white bass, and sunfish. The Illinois River starts in the Ozarks and meanders hundreds of miles in eastern Oklahoma and offers some fine smallmouth bass fishing. Some of Oklahoma's reservoirs are being stocked with striped bass. There has been introduction of trout in some of the streams in the eastern portion of the state. Tenkiller Reservoir, which stills the Tahlequah River, has one of the largest flathead catfish populations in the state. Oklahoma's flathead catfish grow to enormous size and are found in many of the state's lakes. Lake Texoma on the Oklahoma-Texas border is noted for its largemouth bass and white bass fishing.

OREGON

Land area: 96,209 square miles; inland water area: 772 square miles; coastline: 296 statute miles; tidal coastline: 1,410 statute miles.

Oregon sports very good fresh- and saltwater fishing. The state has fine striped bass, trout, salmon, and steelhead fishing, and its many inland streams feature some truly great trout fishing. Rivers well known to trout and salmon fishermen include the Rouge, Klamath, and Crescent. Striped bass are found in the lower section of the Coos River, and some of the state's reservoirs include warm water species such as largemouth bass and sunfish. Klamath Lake's western shoreline has many coves fringed with heavy woods, offering beautiful scenery to backdrop its fine fishing.

PENNSYLVANIA

Land area: 45,025 square miles; inland water area: 308 square miles; coastline: none; tidal coastline: 89 statute miles.

Pennyslvania's headliners are trout and smallmouth bass. The Pocono region with its many lakes supports trout, walleye, bass, and assorted sunfish. Harvey's Lake and Cystal Lake are among the state's largest and most popular. Waters like the Allegheny River and Big Pine Creek in the north central part of the state are fine for trout fishing. The best smallmouth bass water in the state is the Delaware River.

RHODE ISLAND

Land area: 1,049 square miles; inland water area: 165 square miles; coastline: 40 statute miles; tidal coastline: 384 statute miles.

Rhode Island may be our smallest state but its 384 statute miles of tidal coastline offer some of the finest saltwater fishing, especially surf fishing, to be found in the United States. Great numbers of surf fishermen migrate to the coast in May when big schools of striped bass move into coastal waters. These fish range from schoolies of four and five pounds to tackle busters scaling fifty and sixty pounds. Fine bluefish runs follow later in the summer. A lot of partyboats operate out of the state's ports to carry fishermen out for cod and bottom fish species. Many boats operate out of Port Judith for the big bluefin tuna that invade offshore waters. Narrangansett Bay is one of the most complete fishing and boating areas on the northeast U.S. coast. There is trout fishing in the state's streams and ponds, but with such good saltwater fishing, and trout fishing is rather neglected.

SOUTH CAROLINA

Land area: 30,280 square miles; inland water area: 775 square miles; coastline: 187 statute miles; tidal coastline: 2,876 statute miles.

The state boasts good saltwater fishing for channel bass, black drum, flounders, sea trout, and whiting close to shore and bluefish, mackerel, cogia, barracuda, and bonito offshore. Lake Hartwell is one of the state's top lakes, and the Santee-Cooper Reservoir ranks high for freshwater fishing, and already stripers up to fifty pounds have been taken from this impoundment. The state has a lot of water supporting good largemouth bass, crappie, and sunfish fishing. Overall South Carolina is an important sports-fishing state.

SOUTH DAKOTA

Land area: 75,956 square miles; inland water area: 1,091 square miles.

Rivers, streams, impoundments, and farm ponds offer a wide variety of fishing. There is excellent trout fishing in waters in the Black Hills region. Trout fishing is very good in such impoundments as Pactala Reservoir, Center Lake, and streams like Rapid Creek. Some of the lakes have walleye, northern pike, and perch. Most of the farm ponds have some largemouth bass and sunfish. Sharpe, Francis Case, and Lewis and Clark Lakes total 583,000 surface acres and range from 37 to 110 miles in length. Lake Oahe is 210 feet deep.

TENNESSEE

Land area: 41,367 square miles; inland water area: 877 square miles.

Tennessee ranks as one of the top fishing states in the southern United States. The state's generally mild temperatures and many lakes and streams provide a variety of fish and fishing. Largemouth and smallmouth bass are the main species, with Dale Hollow Reservoir offering unusually good bass action. An earthquake in 1811 created Reelfoot Lake in the northwest corner of the state. Waters from the Mississippi River crept into the depression to fill this 14,500-acre lake. The rainbow is the most common of the trout found in the state's many streams. Fishing is generally good on a year-round basis in this mountainous Southern state.

TEXAS

Land area: 262,970 square miles; inland water area: 4,369 square miles; coastline: 367 statute miles; tidal coastline: 3,359 statute miles.

Texas ranks as one of the best fishing states in the nation. Its many and huge lakes—Armistad, Texoma, San Rayburn, Buchana, Travis, and Caddo to mention a few—offer excellent bass and crappie fishing. Rivers, streams, and farm ponds in the heavily timbered eastern portion of the state are noted for excellent fishing for catfish. Texas is equally noted for fine saltwater fishing for channel bass, spotted sea trout (speckled trout to Texans), flounders, croakers, pompano, jackfish, Spanish mackerel, and cobia. Offshore waters off the upper Texas coast provide good fishing for red snapper, amberjacks, king mackerel, dolphin, and grouper. The lower coast's offshore waters are good for king mackerel, dolphin, billfish, and occasionally tuna.

UTAH

Land area: 82,381 miles; inland water area: 2,535 square miles.

Utah's main fish is the trout with specimens in excess of five pounds regularly taken from Tish Lake and the Unita Mountain lakes. Bear Lake, a notably clean lake, offers very good fishing.

VERMONT

Land area: 9,274 square miles; inland water area: 335 square miles.

Vermont boasts good trout fishing with its lakes and streams supporting rainbow, brown, and brook trout. The Willoughby River is famous for its spring rainbow trout run with fish to ten pounds taken regularly. Streams like Otter Creek and Battenkoll offer excellent trout fishing because of little fishing pressure. The upper Conn River has warm-water fishing for bass and sunfish. Lake Champlain, which forms the western border of much of Vermont, is the largest body of fresh water east of the Great Lakes.

VIRGINIA

Land area: 38,841 square miles; inland water area: 976 square miles; coastline: 112 statute miles; tidal coastline: 3,315 statute miles.

Virginia's inland waters in the Piedmont and Blue Ridge regions support brook, rainbow, and brown trout plus largemouth, smallmouth, and spotted bass and sunfish. Tidal salt waters afford excellent channel bass, striped bass, croaker, flounder, sea trout, shad, and white perch fishing. Surf fishing is a way of life on the Virginia beaches. The state's offshore waters are very good for marlin, bonito, and mackerel. Virginia's eastern shore is separated from

the mainland by Chesapeake Bay and is a peninsula ringed by bays and inlets that provide unusually good saltwater fishing.

WASHINGTON

Land area: 61,663 square miles; inland water area: 1,529 square miles; coastline: 157 statute miles; tidal coastline: 3,026 statute miles.

Saltwater salmon fishing is great at Westport, Neah Bay, and inside of Puget Sound. Other saltwater species in abundance include flounders, lingcod, and rockfish. The state's inland lakes and streams have fine fishing for rainbow, steelhead, Kokanee, Dolly Varden, cutthroat, brown, and brook trout. There are also local trout species such as Montana and Yellowstone. Washington has good fishing for chinook and coho salmon. The eastern part of the state is dotted with rivers and small lakes, many with splendid scenic backdrops.

WEST VIRGINIA

Land area: 24,084 square miles; inland water area: 97 square miles.

This state has good trout waters in the Appalachian Highlands with the Cranberry River and Shavers Fork River ranking as standouts. The trout include rainbow, brook, and brown. The state's streams also support good smallmouth bass fishing. Muskellunge, walleye, largemouth bass, catfish, and sunfish are also found in the state. The Greenbrier and Elk Rivers and impoundments like Sutton and Bluestone Reservoirs offer good fishing for warm-water species.

WISCONSIN

Land area: 54,464 square miles; inland water area: 1,690 square miles.

It is quite difficult to drive more than a dozen or so miles in rural Wisconsin without running into a picturesque lake or stream, all of which offer good fishing. The most sought-after fish in Wisconsin is the muskellunge, which is generally found in the northern lake districts. Other species in lakes and rivers are northern pike, rainbow, brook and brown trout, plus warm-water species including rock bass, smallmouth bass, crappie, bullheads, and sunfish. In addition to its inland waters the state has vast shorelines on Lake Michigan and Lake Superior.

Wisconsin's waters have always been noted for excellent fishing. The state has thousands of fishing lakes. *Courtesy Mercury Motors photo.*

This fisherman is hooked fast to a northern pike in a Canadian lake. The Canadian wilderness offers superb fishing. *Courtesy Canadian Government Office of Tourism.*

WYOMING

Land area: 97,281 square miles; inland water area: 633 square miles.

Wyoming has some twenty thousand statute miles in fishing streams, and the state ranks as one of the top fishing areas in the United States for natural trout fishing. The trout species include rainbow, brook, brown, cutthroat, and Mackinaw. The state's waters also hold grayling, Rocky Mountain whitefish, largemouth bass, black crappie, and sunfish. Many of the areas can be reached only by hike-in or horseback and offer splendid fishing. The state's fishing is augumented with some wonderful scenery. Outstanding fishing areas include the Snake River, Jackson Lake (glacier-made lake four hundred feet deep with 25,730 surface acres), and Jenny Lake.

CANADA

Land area: 3,851,908 square miles; inland water area: 291,571 square miles; Atlantic coastline: 14,790 statute miles; Arctic coastline: 32,555 statute miles; Hudson Bay and Straits coastline: 6,765 statute miles; Pacific coastline: 5,560 statute miles; Great Lakes coastline: 4,726 statute miles.

Canada's coastline is one of the largest in the world and is comprised of 17,860 statute miles mainland and 41,810 statute miles of islands. Inland lakes make up 7.6 percent of Canada's total area.

The nation's fishing is governed by the weather and ranges from ice-out to ice-in, meaning from thaw to freeze. This period can range from about four months in the nation's northern reaches to eight to nine months in the southern regions. Canada offers fishing in virgin lakes and with many million lakes of twenty acres or more—the boast is no idle one. Canada is renowned more for its freshwater fishing than the saltwater counterpart. Smallmouth bass, northern pike, walleyes, yellow perch, and muskellunge are found in the southern lakes. Pike, walleyes, Arctic grayling, lake trout, and char are found in the lakes that extend to Canada's northern regions. The main streams and mountain lakes in the Canadian Rockies are famed for excellent trout fishing. Salmon are found in the nation's east and west coastal rivers. Canadian fishing is indeed memorable because of the splendid to breathtaking scenery that backgrounds so many of its lakes and streams.

Canada's Northwest Territory offers excellent lake and river fishing. These anglers are working the Talson River for lake trout.

The author with a string of lake trout caught on a fly-in trip to a wilderness lake in Canada's Northwest Territory.

Fish grew big in Canadian waters. Texas angler Harv Boughton with a thirty-seven-pound lake trout caught from Black Lake in Saskatchewan Province.

MEXICO

Land area: 761,662 square miles; eastern coastline: 1,774 statute miles; western coastline: 4,438 statute miles.

With its long coastline, especially on the Pacific side, Mexico boasts having the finest blue-water fishing to be found in North America. Excellent sailfish, marlin, dolphin, bonito, and roosterfish action is to be found out of just about every port on the Pacific Coast. Mexico's east coast on the Gulf of Mexico is noted for billfish, tarpon, dolphin, roosterfish, channel bass, spotted weakfish, and snook. Mexico's northern interior from the eastern slopes of its mountainous spine to the east coast has numerous lakes that offer excellent largemouth bass fishing. Some of the better-known waters include Don Martin Lake, Lake Guerrero, and Sugar Lake.

PART III
How To Cook Seafood

Some Useful American, English and Metric Equivalent Measures

U. S. Liquid Measures	*Metric*
1 gallon	3.785 liters
1 quart	.946 liters
1 fluid ounce	29.573 mililiters

U. S. Dry Measures	*Metric*
1 quart	1.101 liters
1 pint	.550 liters
1 teaspoon	4.9 cubic centimeters
1 tablespoon	14.8 cubic centimeters
1 cup	236.6 cubic centimeters

U. S.	*English*
1.032 dry quarts	1 quart
1.201 liquid quarts	1 quart
1.201 gallons	1 gallon
1 English pint	20 fluid ounces
1 American pint	16 fluid ounces
1 American cup	8 fluid ounces
8 American tablespoons	4 fluid ounces
1 American tablespoon	½ fluid ounce
3 American teaspoons	½ fluid ounce
1 English tablespoon	⅔ to 1 fluid ounce (approx.)
1 English tablespoon	4 teaspoons

The American measuring tablespoon holds ¼ oz. flour

30

How To Cook Fish

The taste and table quality of fish meat will be no better than the care you give the fish between the time you catch it and the time it goes over the cooking fires. Fish flesh, like that of animals and fowl, begins to deteriorate as soon as the creature dies. The difference lies in the fact that fish meat deteriorates so very much more rapidly.

There are two ways of taking care of your catch until it is taken home. One is to keep it alive on a stringer or in a live box. There is no major problem here if the fish is properly strung and if there is sufficient circulation of water in the live box. Correct stringing calls for running the stringer through both lips. This permits the fish to open and close its mouth to maintain a flow of water through and over the gills. Never run the stringer through the mouth and out the gills or visa verca and expect the creature to survive for any reasonable length of time. Stringing in this manner seriously restricts the fish's breathing apparatus. Yes, fish breathe. Oxygen is absorbed from the water as it passes through and over the gills. Improper stringing simply results in suffocation of the fish. Whether the fish is put on a string or in a live box, it is easier to keep alive in cool weather and water than it is in warm weather and water.

The second way to care for your catch is to field dress it as soon as it is caught. In the case of some fish species, this is an absolute must if you want untainted meat. Some species, especially those heavy in fat and rich in oil, must be processed early, otherwise you may end up with meat that has a bit of a "bite" in the taste.

Fish should be cleaned as soon as possible. Thoroughly wash the fish before storing in a cooler.

The secret in proper field dressing is to keep the fish clean, dry, and cool. The meat that is kept moist and warm will spoil because bacteria thrive under these conditions. Proper field dressing calls for removing entrails, the gills, and all kidney tissue along the backbone. Flush out the body cavity and wipe it dry. Carefully wrap the meat in foil or waxed paper and store with ice in a cooler until the fish can be brought home and finally prepared either for cooking or freezer storage. Be careful not to store fish for lengthy periods with the flesh in direct contact with the ice. A couple of hours won't hurt,

167

A good cooler is an excellent way to store your fish until you have the chance to clean them. Place the fish atop the ice in the chest and do not allow the fish to soak in just cold water.

but fish flesh kept for a day or so in direct contact with ice will lose flavor.

Personally I prefer field dressing to taking the catch home whole. The parts discarded can be returned to the water as food for scavangers. That beats having the stuff raise a stink in the garbage can at home.

If the fish is to go into the freezer, wrap securely in freezer paper, using care to squeeze all the air out of the package. Label the package as to the kind of fish contained and the date of putting it in the freezer. Some frozen fish store well for months; the freezer storage life of other species may be just a few weeks. This does not mean that the meat goes bad while it is frozen. Instead it tends to "dry out," and a fish with a month freeze life but stored for six months is certain to have the taste, flavor, and consistency of dry cotton.

Frozen fish should be thawed in the refrigerator (place it there the night before you plan to use it) or under cold running water. Never thaw fish at room temperature or with warm water. After the fish has thawed out, it will generally keep up to twenty-four hours in a cold refrigerator. Under no circumstances refreeze fish, or for that matter any marine products. What can't be consumed should be discarded.

Any fish to be consumed within a day or two can be stored in the coldest place in your refrigerator. When the time comes for preparing it for the pan or oven, give it a thorough cleaning and then dry the meat again.

There are several methods of preparing fish, with pan-frying being the most common. Generally

speaking the fish should be salted, rolled in corn meal or an egg-cornmeal-flour batter, and cooked over a medium flame. Use butter or good cooking oil and brown each side. Fry until the skin is crisp, but do not cover the pan for it will create steam and destroy crispness. A second frying method is that of deep-fry. The secret here is to bring the cooking oil to the proper temperature (a range of 350 to 380 degrees). In deep-frying the fish is cut into pieces that are dipped in a batter of flour and bread crumbs in a flour-egg-bread crumb mix. Completely submerge the fish in the hot cooking oil. When done the pieces will rise to the top. Remove and drain off excess oil.

The secret of good-tasting fried fish is to use fresh, good quality cooking oil. With some fried foods the cooking oil can be strained and used again. You can do this with potatoes. But never do it with fish. Fish have a distinct flavor and taste, and in frying, the cooking oil will pick up this flavor. If the oil is used over and over for fish, it will result in strong-tasting fish.

This fifteen-pound cobia makes choice eating, but the fish will spoil quickly if left untended on the floor of the boat.

A second method of cooking fish is baking. This is usually done with whole fish or portions of a large fish. There are three ways to bake: (1) a very hot oven for a short period, (2) a medium oven for a longer time, or (3) simmering for a considerable time in milk, bullion, or other flavored stock that does not cover the fish.

A third method is to broil, which is an excellent way to prepare fatty fish or fish with high oil content. It is important to heat the oven and the broiling pan in order to ensure even cooking. The meat must be frequently basted with butter. A substitute for basting can be a strip of bacon or each fish or fillet.

The important thing in cooking fish, whether it is pan-frying, deep-frying, baking, or broiling, is not to overdo it. Cooking breaks down tissue, making it easier to chew and digest. Fish meat is quite tender to begin with and overcooking will cause the meat to become hard, tough, and lose flavor. The naturally tender meat of fish cooks quickly and easily. Side dishes to go with the main fish dinner should be prepared prior to cooking the fish itself. With red meats and fowl the opposite is more generally the case. When the meat of fish is sufficiently cooked, it should be firm but should flake easily. You should be able to separate the meat from the bones easily with a fork. If the meat is mushy, it is undercooked; if it crumbles very easily into hard bits and is tasteless, it is overcooked.

There are some distinct advantages in eating fish. Most fish meats contain food elements that our bodies need but can't manufacture; fish are high in minerals that are an aid in bone and tooth building; fish are high in food value and proteins but low in fats and calories; and finally as stated earlier in this chapter, fish can be a time-saver in that it can be cooked in a short time. The only time fish are cooked for long periods is in the making of chowders.

Frying, baking, and broiling are what can be described as "plain vanilla" ways of preparing fish for the table. Frying, pan or deep, is the practical way to cook fish out on the trail or for the shore lunch or supper. The modern camper, truck, or van, and the modern cruiser have adequate space and equipment to permit baking and broiling in addition to frying.

There is nothing wrong with this "plain vanilla" cooking, and a lot of people go through life having never eaten fish prepared in any other ways. Man's taste buds are the spawners of recipes that truly activate the savory glands.

Fish recipes as well as those for other viands vary from one section of the country to another, and in a way they reflect the nature and culture of the people of a particular region. A few examples will suffice to drive the point home. Consider the states along the

Texas fisherman Mike Aleman has a string of fine-eating spotted weakfish. Fish this size may not break tackle but they make the choicest eating.

Gulf of Mexico and in particular Texas and Louisiana. Note how often the side dish to a fish dinner is rice. Note also how many Texas fish recipes are heavy with seasoning; Louisiana recipes just as heavy in seasoning but with the addition of many spices. Gulf Coasters lean heavy to seafood gumbos; New Englanders go equally strong for fish chowders. The European taste is reflected in those recipes calling for cooking fish in wines, ales, and beers.

Although many of the recipes in this book list specific fish, substitutes can be readily made if one stays within the general family of the fish listed. As an example, a recipe stipulating channel bass can also be used with striped bass, black drum, or covina substituted; a recipe for Spanish mackerel will serve equally well for other members of the mackerel family.

SMOKED FISH LOG

2 cups flaked fish or 1 pound smoked fish fillets
1 8-ounce package cream cheese, softened
1 tablespoon lemon juice
2 teaspoons grated onion
1 teaspoon horse radish
1 teaspoon liquid smoke (if not smoked fish)
¼ teaspoon salt
½ cup chopped pecans
2 tablespoons chopped parsley

Poach, drain, and flake fish. Combine cheese, lemon juice, onion horse radish, liquid smoke, salt, and fish; mix thoroughly. Chill for several hours. Combine pecans and parsley. Shape mixture into a log, and roll in nut mixture. Makes 2 cups spread. Serve with crackers. Serves 4.

BAKED FISH EN PAPILLOTE

2 pounds fish fillets
1 green pepper, sliced
1 onion, sliced
¼ cup melted butter or margarine
2 tablespoons lemon juice
2 teaspoons salt
1 teaspoon paprika
dash of pepper

Rinse fish and pat dry. Brush with half the butter and sprinkle with the seasonings. Place plastic-type cooking bag in a baking dish. Add remaining butter, lemon juice, green pepper, and onion to the bag. Use a broad spatula and slip fish into bag on vegetables. Close bag and puncture a few holes according to instructions with the bag. Bake in preheated oven, 375 degrees F., for 20 to 25 minutes, or until fish flakes easily when tested with a fork. Slit bag and serve directly to plates or arrange dish and garnish with cooked green pepper, onion, and fresh lemon wedges. Spoon juices in bag over each serving. Serves 6.

REDFISH MEXICALI

This recipe originated on the southern portion of the Texas coast. The chili powder and liquid hot pepper sauce reflect the influence of Mexican cooking that is so prevalent in south Texas and along the border with Mexico.

2 pounds redfish fillets (other fresh fish fillets can be
    substituted)
2 tablespoons salad oil
2 tablespoons soy sauce

2 tablespoons Worcestershire sauce
1 teaspoon paprika
½ teaspoon chili powder
½ teaspoon garlic powder
dash of liquid hot pepper sauce

Place fillets in a single layer, skin side down, on a well-greased broil-and-serve platter, 16 x 10 inches. Combine remaining ingredients. Pour sauce over fillets. Broil about 4 inches from source of heat for 10 to 15 minutes, or until fish flakes easily when tested with a fork. Baste once during broiling with sauce in pan. Garnish with lemon wedges. Serves 6.

TEXAS FRIED GAFFTOPS

Elsewhere in this book is a special chapter on recipes for catfish. All of the recipes listed therein are for freshwater catfish species. The following recipe is a Texas favorite for the gafftopsail catfish, a saltwater catfish that enjoys the nickname of "tourist trout" because it lures so many inlanders to the Texas coast each spring when gafftopsail catfish runs of great proportions occur.

6 skinned, pan-dressed gafftopsail catfish (one pound
    each)
2 teaspoons salt
¼ teaspoon pepper
2 eggs
2 tablespoons milk
2 cups cornmeal

Wash and dry fish. Sprinkle both sides with salt and pepper. Beat eggs slightly and blend in the milk. Dip fish in eggs and roll in cornmeal. Place fish in a heavy frying pan with about ⅛ inch melted fat, hot but not smoking. Fry at a moderate heat. When fish is brown on one side, turn carefully and brown the other side. Cooking time is about 10 minutes, depending upon the thickness of the fish. Drain on absorbent paper. Serve immediately on a hot platter, plain or with a sauce. Serves 6.

SCHOONER STEAKS FLAMINGO

The red snapper is one of the most popular of all food fish in the states bordering the Gulf of Mexico. Either baked or broiled, the red snapper is a feature seafood attraction in quality restaurants in the many resort cities on the Gulf Coast.

2 pounds of red snapper steaks
1 teaspoon salt
dash of pepper
1 cup grated cheese

1 tablespoon prepared mustard
2 teaspoons horse radish
2 tablespoons chili sauce
¼ cup melted butter or margarine

Wash and dry the fish and cut steaks into serving-size portions. Sprinkle both sides with salt and pepper. Combine cheese, mustard, horse radish, and chili sauce. Place fish on a greased broiler pan about 2 inches from source of heat. Brush with butter and broil 5 to 8 minutes or until lightly browned. Turn carefully and brush other side with butter and broil 5 to 8 minutes longer or until fish flakes easily when tested with a fork. Place cheese mixture on top of fish. Return to broiler for 1 to 2 minutes, or until cheese melts and browns. Serves 6.

BAKED RED SNAPPER WITH SOUR CREAM STUFFING

1 dressed red snapper (three or four pounds)
1½ teaspoons salt
Sour Cream Stuffing
2 tablespoons melted fat or oil
        Sour Cream Stuffing:
¾ cup chopped celery
½ cup chopped onion
¼ cup melted fat or oil
1 quart dry bread crumbs
½ cup sour cream
¼ cup diced peeled lemon
2 tablespoons grated lemon rind
1 teaspoon paprika
1 teaspoon salt

Clean, wash, and dry fish. Sprinkle inside and out with salt. Cook celery and onion in fat until tender. Combine all stuffing ingredients and mix thoroughly. Stuff fish loosely and close opening with skewers or toothpicks. Place fish in a well-greased baking pan and brush with fat. Bake in a moderate oven, 350 degrees F., for 40 to 60 minutes, or until fish flakes easily when tested with a fork. Baste occasionally with fat. Remove skewers or toothpicks before serving. Serves 6.

RED SNAPPER PAYSANNE

2 pounds red snapper steaks
½ teaspoon salt
¼ teaspoon white pepper
1 4-ounce can sliced mushrooms, drained
¼ cup catsup
2 tablespoons melted butter or margarine
½ teaspoon liquid smoke

Wash and dry fish. Cut steaks into serving-size

portions. Place in a greased baking dish, and sprinkle with salt and pepper. Combine remaining ingredients and spread over top of the fish. Bake in a moderate oven, 350 degrees F., for 25 to 30 minutes, or until fish flakes easily when tested with a fork. Makes 6 servings.

BROILED RED SNAPPER LAFITTE

2 pounds red snapper fillets
2 tablespoons melted fat or oil
2 tablespoons lemon juice
1 teaspoon salt
½ teaspoon paprika
dash of pepper

Cut fillets into 6 portions. Place skin side down on well-greased baking pan. Combine remaining ingredients and pour over fish. Broil about 4 inches from source of heat for 10 to 15 minutes, or until fish flakes easily when tested with a fork. Baste once during broiling with sauce in pan. Garnish with toasted almonds if desired. Serves 6.

SNAPPY SNAPPER

2 pounds red snapper fillets
½ cup frozen orange juice concentrate, thawed
¼ cup salad oil
¼ cup soy sauce
¼ cup cider vinegar
½ teaspoon salt
chopped parsley

Wash and dry fillets. Cut fillets into 6 portions. Place fish in a single layer, skin side up, on a well-greased baking pan. Combine remaining ingredients except parsley. Brush fish with sauce. Broil about 4 inches from source of heat for 5 minutes. Turn fish carefully and brush with sauce. Broil 5 to 7 minutes longer, or until lightly browned and fish flakes easily when tested with a fork. Sprinkle with parsley. Serves 6.

SPICY SNAPPER

2 pounds red snapper fillets
⅔ cup tomato juice
3 tablespoons vinegar
2 tablespoons salad oil
1 envelope (⅝ ounce) old-fashioned French dressing mix

Wash and dry fish. Skin fillets and cut into serving-size portions. Place fish in a single layer in a shallow baking dish. Combine remaining ingredients and mix thoroughly. Pour sauce over fish and let stand for 30 minutes, turning once. Remove fish, reserving sauce for basting. Place fish on a well-greased broiler pan. Broil about 4 inches from source of heat for 4 to 5 minutes. Turn carefully and brush with sauce. Broil 4 to 5 minutes longer, or until fish flakes easily when tested with a fork. Serves 6.

BAKED FLOUNDER WITH SHRIMP SAUCE

The flounder is an excellent fish to use in gourmet recipes because of its mild flavor, firm and very white meat. It is a fish that can be baked or broiled whole, or filleted and prepared in a wide variety of ways. It is also a species in which there is relatively little waste. When a fish is gutted and headed the weight loss can be as much as fifty percent. In the case of the flounder this same processing results in a loss of as little as fifteen percent of the fish's total weight.

2 pound flounder, pan dressed
¼ cup margarine or cooking oil
1 teaspoon salt
1 cup sliced fresh mushrooms (2 4-ounce cans sliced mushrooms, drained, can be substituted)
1 10½-ounce can condensed cream of shrimp soup
¼ cup half-and-half or milk
2 tablespoons dry sherry
¼ teaspoon rosemary
¼ teaspoon paprika
chopped parsley

Place fish in shallow 2-quart baking dish. Drizzle 2 tablespoons melted margarine or cooking oil over fish and sprinkle with salt. Bake in moderate oven, 350 degrees F., for 25 to 30 minutes, or until fish flakes easily when tested with a fork. Baste with pan juices several times during baking. While fish is baking, cook mushrooms until tender in remaining 2 tablespoons melted margarine or cooking oil. Add soup, half-and-half or milk, sherry, rosemary, and paprika; stir and heat thoroughly. Spoon sauce over fish and sprinkle with parsley. Makes 6 servings.

BAKED FLOUNDER IN WINE SAUCE

2-pound flounder, pan dressed
½ teaspoon salt
dash of pepper
3 tomatoes, sliced
2 tablespoons flour
2 tablespoons melted butter or margarine
½ cup skim milk
⅓ cup dry white wine
½ teaspoon crushed basil
chopped parsley

Sprinkle flounder on both sides with salt and pepper. Place fish in a greased baking dish, and arrange tomatoes over top. Sprinkle with salt and pepper. Blend flour into butter. Add milk gradually and cook until thick and smooth, stirring constantly. Remove from heat and stir in wine and basil. Pour sauce over top of tomatoes. Bake in a moderate oven, 350 degrees F., for 25 to 30 minutes or until fish flakes easily when tested with a fork. Sprinkle with parsley. Serves 6.

SOUTHERN BROILED FLOUNDER

2 pounds flounder fillets
¼ cup melted fat or oil
1 teaspoon salt
dash of pepper
2 4-ounce cans mushroom stems and pieces, drained
1 cup grated cheese
1 tablespoons chopped parsley

Cut fillets into serving-size pieces. Combine fat, salt, and pepper; mix thoroughly. Chop mushrooms. Combine mushrooms, cheese, and parsley. Place fish in a well-greased broiler pan and brush with fat. Broil about 3 inches from source of heat for 3 to 4 minutes. Turn carefully and brush with fat. Broil 3 to 4 minutes longer, or until fish flakes easily when tested with a fork. Spread mushroom mixture on fish and broil 2 to 3 minutes longer, or until lightly browned. Serves 6.

FLOUNDER CURRY

2 pounds flounder fillets
1 cup thinly sliced celery
1 cup thinly sliced onion
1 tablespoon melted fat or oil
1 teaspoon curry powder
1 teaspoon salt
dash of pepper
¾ cup skim milk
paprika

Skin fillets and place in a single layer in a greased baking dish. Cook the celery and onion in fat for 5 minutes. Stir in seasonings and milk. Spread over fish. Bake in a moderate oven, 350 degrees F., for 25 to 30 minutes or until fish flakes easily when tested with a fork. Sprinkle with paprika. Serves 6.

FLOUNDER STUFFED WITH CRAB

2 pan-dress flounders (¾ pounds each)
crab stuffing
⅓ cup lemon juice
2 teaspoons salt
¾ cup melted butter or margarine
paprika

Crab Stuffing:

1 pound blue crab meat
½ cup chopped onion
⅓ cup chopped celery
⅓ cup chopped green pepper
⅓ cup melted fat or oil
2 cloves garlic, finely chopped
2 cups soft bread cubes
3 eggs beaten
1 tablespoon chopped parsley
2 teaspoons salt
½ teaspoon pepper

Clean, wash, and dry fish. To make a pocket for the stuffing, lay the fish flat on a cutting board, light side down. Use sharp knife to cut down the center of the fish along the backbone from the tail to about 1 inch from the head. Turn the knife flat and cut the flesh along both sides of the backbone to the tail allowing the knife to run over the rib bones. Place fish in a single layer on a well-greased baking pan. To make stuffing, drain crab meat and remove any remaining shell or cartilage. Cook onion, celery, green pepper, and garlic in fat until tender. Combine bread cubes, eggs, parsley, salt, pepper, cooked vegetables, and crab meat; mix thoroughly. Stuff fish loosely. Combine remaining ingredients and mix well. Brush fish with sauce. Bake in a moderate oven, 350 degrees F., or until fish flakes easily when tested with a fork. Serves 6.

BROILED PACIFIC COD WITH TOMATO AND CHEESE

2 pounds Pacific cod fillets
2 tablespoons melted butter or margarine
2 teaspoons salt
1 8-ounce can tomato sauce
2 small onion, chopped
½ cup grated American or cheddar cheese

Wash and dry fish fillets, and cut into 6 portions. Arrange fish in well-greased baking pan; brush with melted fat, and sprinkle with salt. Broil about 3 inches from source of heat for about 8 minutes. Pour tomato sauce over fish and sprinkle with onion and cheese. Broil until cheese melts and fish flakes easily when tested with a fork; cooking time about 4 minutes. Serves 6.

OVEN-BARBECUED LINGCOD

2 pounds lingcod (Pacific ocean perch can be
    substituted)
½ cup cooking oil
1 teaspoon salt
dash of pepper
1 clove garlic, minced
1 cup shredded American or cheddar cheese
1 cup fine bread, cracker, or cereal crumbs
1 cup commercial barbecue sauce

Clean, wash, and dry fish. Cut into 6 serving portions. Combine oil, salt, pepper, and garlic. Mix cheese and crumbs. Dip each piece into oil; drain; roll in cheese-crumb mixture. Arrange the fish in well-greased baking pan. Bake in hot oven, 450 degrees F., for 10 minutes. Heat barbecue sauce and spoon half of the sauce over the fish. Keep remaining sauce hot. Cook fish an additional 5 minutes or until fish flakes easily when tested with a fork. Serve with the remaining barbecue sauce. Makes 6 servings.

HALIBUT IN ORANGE-GRAPE SAUCE

2 pounds halibut steaks
2 cups boiling water
2 tablespoons lemon juice
1 teaspoon salt
1 tablespoon cornstarch
1 tablespoon sugar
½ cup orange juice
½ cup cold water
2 teaspoons grated orange rind
1 teaspoon lemon juice
1 11-ounce can mandarin orange segments, drained
a cup seeded green grape halves

Wash and dry fish and cut into 6 serving portions. Place fish in a well-greased, large frying pan. Add boiling water, lemon juice, and salt. Cover, simmer for 8 to 10 minutes, or until fish flakes easily when tested with a fork. While fish is cooking, prepare sauce. Combine cornstarch and sugar in small saucepan. Stir in orange juice and cold water. Cook slowly, stirring constantly, until thickened. Stir in orange rind, lemon juice, and fruits; heat. Transfer cooked, drained fish carefully to hot serving platter. Spoon sauce over fish. Makes 6 servings.

BROILED SALMON WITH HERB SAUCE

2 salmon steaks
¼ cup butter or margarine

¼ cup dry white wine
1 tablespoon chopped parsley
¼ teaspoon finely herbs blend
1 clove garlic, sliced
1 teaspoon salt

Combine butter or margarine, wine, parsley, herbs, and garlic; heat slowly until fat is melted. Let stand 15 minutes. Sprinkle salmon steaks with salt. Place fish on a well-greased broiler pan and brush with sauce. Broil about 3 inches from heat source, 4 to 6 minutes. Turn carefully; brush with sauce. Broil 4 to 6 minutes longer, or until fish flakes easily when tested with a fork. Baste steaks with sauce several times while broiling. Serves 6.

RAINBOW TROUT WITH MUSHROOM-HERB STUFFING

6 pan-dressed rainbow trout (brown, brook, or other
    species of freshwater trout can be substituted)
2 teaspoons salt
4 cups soft bread cubes (½ inch)
⅔ cup butter or margarine
1 cup sliced fresh mushrooms
⅔ cup sliced green onions
¼ cup chopped parsley
2 tablespoons chopped pimiento
4 teaspoons lemon juice
½ teaspoon marjoram

Clean, wash, and dry fish. Sprinkle 1½ teaspoons salt evenly over inside and outside of fish. Sauté bread cubes in ½ cup butter or margarine until lightly browned, stirring frequently. Add mushrooms and onion, cook until mushrooms are tender. Stir in remaining salt, parsley, pimiento, lemon juice, and marjoram; toss lightly. Stuff fish, and arrange in single layer in a well-greased baking pan. Brush with remaining melted butter or margarine. Bake in a moderate oven, 350 degrees F., 25 to 30 minutes, or until fish flakes easily when tested with a fork. Can be served plain or with a sauce. Makes 6 servings.

BAKED STRIPER FILLETS

2 pounds striped bass fillets (channel bass or black
    drum can be substituted)
2 teaspoons lemon juice
dash of pepper
6 slices bacon, chopped
½ cup soft bread crumbs
2 tablespoons chopped parsley
¾ cup thinly sliced onion
2 tablespoons bacon fat

Skin fillets; wash and dry. Place fillets in a single layer in a greased baking fish. Sprinkle with lemon juice and pepper. Fry bacon until crisp. Remove bacon from fat. Add to bread crumbs and parsley. Cook onion in bacon fat until tender. Spread onion over fish. Sprinkle crumb mixture over top of onion. Bake in a moderate oven, 350 degrees F., for 25 to 30 minutes, or until fish flakes easily when tested with a fork. Serves 6.

CAPE COD FISH BALLS

Cape Cod fish balls is one of New England's most famous seafood dishes. There are a number of versions of this dish, with the versions differing according to various spices added.

1 pound salt codfish
instant mashed potatoes
water
salt
1 egg
2 egg yolks
shortening or vegetable oil for frying

Place codfish in large frying pan; cover with cold water. Heat to boiling; cover. Simmer 10 minutes, or until fish flakes easily when tested with a fork. Drain, Flake fish with fork. Prepare four cups instant mashed potatoes with water, salt, and butter or margarine, following directions on label, but omit milk called for. Beat in egg and egg yolks; fold in codfish. Melt sufficient shortening or vegetable oil in deep-fat fryer or large saucepan to fill two-thirds full. Head to 375 degrees F. Drop cod mixture by tablespoonfuls into fat; fry, turning once, for 1 minute or until crispy-golden. Lift out with slotted spoon. Drain, and serve hot. Makes about 2 dozen balls for 6 servings.

CIOPPINO

This is a seafood dish that includes what can be called a duke's mixture of fish, clams, and shrimp. It is a specialty of the Pacific Northwest and a favorite in San Francisco. With minor variations in spices and seasonings, the dish is also called Pacific cioppino, Northwest cioppino, and San Francisco or Frisco cioppino.

1½ pounds halibut, lingcod, rockfish, or sea bass,
    pan-dressed
2 cups sliced onion
2 cloves garlic, finely chopped
¼ cup cooking or olive oil
1 12-ounce can Italian tomatoes, undrained

1 8-ounce can tomato sauce
1 cup water
¼ cup chopped parsley
2 teaspoons salt
1 teaspoon basil
½ teaspoon oregano
¼ teaspoon pepper
1 dozen clams in shell, washed
1 cup cooked, peeled, Pacific pink shrimp

Wash and dry fish, and cut into 1½-inch chunks. Cook onion and garlic in oil until onion is tender but not brown. Add tomatoes, tomato sauce, water, parsley, basil, oregano, and pepper. Cover and simmer gently for about 30 minutes. Add fish chunks; cover and simmer 10 to 20 minutes. Add clams in shells and shrimp; cover. Cook 10 minutes longer, or until fish flakes easily when tested with a fork. Serves 6 to 8.

STUFFED SALMON WITH EGG SAUCE

1 dressed salmon, about four pounds (rockfish can be substituted)
1½ teaspoons salt
1½ cups diced celery
1½ cups chopped onion
1 clove garlic, finely minced
1 small bay leaf, crumbled
½ cup butter or margarine
4 cups soft bread crumbs
2 tablespoons chopped parsley
½ teaspoon rosemary
dash of pepper
    Egg Sauce:
2 tablespoons butter or margarine
2 tablespoons flour
½ teaspoon salt
dash white pepper
1 cup milk
¼ cup half-and-half (milk-cream)
1 tablespoon lemon juice
2 hard-boiled eggs, coarsely chopped
2 tablespoons diced pimiento

Clean, wash, and dry fish. Sprinkle one teaspoon salt over inside cavity of fish, and place in a well-greased baking pan. Cook celery, onion, garlic, and bay leaf in ⅓ cup butter or margarine until vegetables are tender. All remaining salt, bread crumbs, parsley, rosemary, and pepper; toss lightly. Stuff fish loosely; brush with remaining butter or margarine. Cover fins and tail of fish loosely with foil. Bake in moderate oven, 350 degrees F., for 45 to 60 minutes, or until fish flakes easily when tested with a fork. Serve with egg sauce. Serves 6.

PACIFIC SEA BASS FILLETS

1½ pounds sea bass fillets
½ cup lemon or lime juice
¾ cup flour
1½ teaspoons salt
½ cup sesame seeds
olive oil

Wash and dry fillets and cut into 6 portions. Place fish in shallow baking pan. Pour lemon or lime juice over fillets and let stand for 1 hour. Turn once. Combine flour and salt. Roll fillets in flour mixture; dip in lemon or lime juice again and roll in sesame seeds. Fry fillets in olive oil until nicely browned on one side; turn carefully and brown the other side. Fish is done when it flakes easily when tested with a fork. Cooking time is 8 to 10 minutes, depending upon thickness of fillets. Serve with lemon butter. Serves 6.

STEAMED FISH

1 sea bass (1½ to 2 pounds)
1 tablespoon chopped leek
1 teaspoon shredded ginger or powdered ginger
½ teaspoon salt
dill weed
soy sauce
1 garlic clove
1 tablespoon peanut oil or vegetable oil
2 teaspoons sesame oil

Clean, wash, and dry fish. Combine leek, ginger, and salt; rub into fish. Sprinkle lightly with dill; add a few drops of soy sauce. Steam in a pot or steamer for about 15 minutes. Turn over and steam for another 5 minutes. Crush garlic clove into peanut oil and sesame oil, cook over high heat until garlic is slightly browned. Strain oils to remove garlic. Brush oils over fish, just prior to removing from heat. Serves 4.

HALIBUT WITH RICE

2 pounds halibut (lingcod, sea bass, rockfish, or salmon can be substituted)
4 slices bacon, diced
2 tablespoons butter or margarine
1 cup chopped onion
1 clove garlic, finely minced
1½ cups uncooked rice (not instant)
3 cups boiling water
⅓ cup chili sauce
2 chicken bouillon cubes
2 teaspoons salt
pinch of saffron
1 10-ounce package frozen peas

Clean, wash, and dry fish; cut into 1-inch chunks. Fry bacon until crisp. Remove pieces from pan; drain on absorbent paper. Add butter or margarine to bacon drippings, and cook onion and garlic in drippings until tender. Add rice, boiling water, chili sauce, bouillon cubes, salt, and saffron; mix well. Return to a boil; cover and cook slowly for 10 minutes. Add fish, bacon, and peas; cover and cook 10 minutes longer, or until rice and peas are tender and fish flakes easily when tested with a fork. Makes 6 servings.

ALASKAN FISHERMAN'S STEW

2 pounds salmon (rockfish, lingcod, Pacific ocean
     perch, or halibut can be substituted)
1½ cups sliced celery
½ cup chopped onion
1 clove garlic, minced
¼ cup butter or margarine
2 16-ounce cans tomatoes, undrained
1 8-ounce can tomato sauce
2 teaspoons salt
½ teaspoon paprika
½ teaspoon chili powder
¼ teaspoon pepper
1 7-ounce package spaghetti, uncooked
2 cups boiling water
¼ cup grated Parmesan cheese

Clean, wash, and dry fish, and cut into one-inch chunks. Cook celery, onion, and garlic in butter or margarine in large, heavy pan until tender. Add tomatoes, tomato sauce, and seasonings. Bring to a simmer; cover; cook slowly 15 to 20 minutes. Add uncooked spaghetti and boiling water; mix; cover pan. Cook slowly about 10 minutes, or until spaghetti is almost tender. Add fish; cover; cook slowly about 10 minutes, or until fish flakes easily when tested with a fork. Serve hot with cheese sprinkled on top. Makes 6 servings.

FISH POT PIE

1½ pounds fish fillets (meat from any firm fish)
1 cup cooked diced carrots
1 cup cooked peas
1 10½-ounce can condensed chicken soup
½ cup water
1 cup biscuit mix

Skin fillets and cut into ½-inch pieces (1 cans of tuna fish may be substituted). Combine carrots, peas, and fish cubes, and place in well-greased 1½-quart casserole. Combine soup and water, and stir over low heat until smooth. Pour over fish.

Prepare biscuit mix as directed on package and cover casserole mixture. Bake at 450 degrees F., for 30 minutes or until crust is light brown. Makes 6 servings.

BACK BAY CHOWDER

1 pound fish fillets (meat from any firm fish)
½ cup chopped onion
2 tablespoons melted fat
2 cups potatoes cut into small pieces
1 cup boiling water
¾ teaspoon salt
pepper to season
2 cups milk
1 8-ounce can cream-style yellow corn

Skin fillets and cut into ½-inch pieces (2 cans of square. Cook chopped onion in fat until soft. Add potatoes, water, salt, pepper, and fish cubes. Cover and simmer for 15 minutes or until potatoes are cooked. Add milk and corn, and continue heating until piping hot. Serves 6.

CHANNEL BASS AU GRATIN

2 pounds channel bass steaks or fillets (striped bass,
     black drum, flounder, or halibut can be
     substituted)
1½ teaspoons salt
dash of pepper
¼ cup flour
2 tablespoons grated onion
1 10½-ounce can condensed cream of celery soup
1 cup grated cheese
2 tablespoons chopped parsley
paprika

Wash and dry fish and cut into serving-size portions. Add seasonings to flour. Roll fish in flour and place in a well-greased, shallow 1½-quart casserole. Add onion soup and spread over fish. Top with cheese and parsley. Sprinkle with paprika. Bake in moderate oven at 350 degrees F., for 25 to 30 minutes, or until fish flakes easily when tested with a fork. Serves 6.

CHANNEL BASS IN WINE SAUCE

2 pounds channel bass fillets (striped bass, black
     drum, or flounder can be substituted)
1½ teaspoons salt
dash of pepper
3 tomatoes, sliced
½ teaspoon salt
dash of pepper
2 tablespoons flour

2 tablespoons melted margarine
½ cup skim milk
⅓ cup dry white wine
½ teaspoon crushed basil
chopped parsley

Wash and skin fillets. Sprinkle fillets on both sides with salt and pepper. Place fillets in a single layer in greased baking dish, approximately 12 x 8 x 2. Arrange tomatoes over top of fillets. Sprinkle with salt and pepper. Blend flour into butter. Add milk gradually and cool until thick and smooth, stirring constantly. Remove from heat and stir in wine and basil. Pour sauce over top of tomatoes. Bake in moderate oven 350 degrees F., for 25 to 30 minutes or until fish flakes easily when tested with a fork. Sprinkle with parsley. Serves 6.

SWEET AND SOUR REDFISH

2 pounds channel bass, a species known as redfish
    on Gulf Coast (striped bass, black drum
    flounder, or halibut can be substituted)
1 20-ounce can pineapple chunks
1¼ cups liquid (pineapple syrup and water)
¼ cup cider vinegar
¼ cup brown sugar, packed
3 tablespoons cornstarch
1 tablespoon soy sauce
1½ teaspoons salt
½ teaspoon garlic salt
3 tablespoons cooking oil
1 6-ounce can water chestnuts, drained and sliced
1 medium green pepper, cut in 1-inch squares
1 medium tomato, cut in thin wedges
6 servings hot, fluffy rice

Cut fish into 1-inch pieces. Drain pineapple chunks, reserve syrup. Add water to syrup to measure 1½ cups liquid. Combine liquid, vinegar, brown sugar, cornstarch, soy sauce, and salts; blend well. Cook fish in oil in 12-inch frying pan or Chinese wok over moderate heat, turning pieces carefully until fish is firm. Add liquid mixture and cook, stirring carefully, until sauce is thick and clear. Add remaining ingredients, mix carefully. Cook just until vegetables are heated and fish flakes easily when tested with a fork. Serve with rice. Serves 6.

FESTIVE DRUM

2 pounds black drum fillets (channel bass or striped
    bass can be substituted)
½ cup French dressing
1½ cups crushed cheese crackers
2 tablespoons melted fat or oil
paprika

Large black drum have course meat and are often riddled with worms along their backbones. Small ones like the one held by Texas angler Vince Stiglich Jr. make very good table fare.

Skin fillets and cut into serving-size portions. Dip fish in dressing and roll in cracker crumbs. Place on a well-greased cookie sheet. Drizzle fat over fish. Sprinkle with paprika. Bake in very hot oven 500 degrees F., for 10 to 12 minutes, or until fish flakes easily when tested with a fork. Serves 6.

SMOKED FISH WITH WILD RICE-MUSHROOM STUFFING

1 dressed red snapper, 3 to 4 pounds (striped bass,
    channel bass, or black drum can be
    substituted)
2 teaspoons salt
¼ teaspoon pepper
4 slices precooked bacon
¼ cup thinly sliced green onion and tops
wild rice-mushroom stuffing
        Wild Rice-Mushroom Stuffing:
1 4-ounce package wild rice
4 tablespoons margarine or cooking oil
½ cup chopped onion
½ cup chopped celery
1 2½-ounce jar sliced mushrooms

¼ cup chopped parsley
¼ teaspoon pepper

Clean, wash, and dry fish. Sprinkle inside and out with salt and pepper. Make stuffing next. Cook wild rice according to directions on package. Sauté vegetables in margarine or cooking oil until vegetables are tender. Combine all ingredients and mix thoroughly. Makes approximately 2½ cups stuffing. Stuff fish loosely. Close opening with small skewers or toothpicks. Place precooked bacon on top of fish and sprinkle with sliced onions. Place fish on well-greased grill inside smoke cover. Close hood. Smoke over low coals for approximately 90 minutes, or until fish flakes easily when tested with a fork. Remove skewers. Serves 6.

BAKED HADDOCK

2 pounds haddock fillets
2 teaspoons lemon juice
dash of pepper
6 slices bacon, chopped
½ cup soft bread crumbs
2 tablespoons chopped parsley
¾ cup thinly sliced onion
2 tablespoons bacon fat

Wash and skin fillets and place in a single layer in a greased baking dish. Sprinkle with lemon juice and pepper. Fry bacon until crisp. Remove bacon from fat. Add to bread crumbs and parsley. Cook onion in bacon fat until tender. Spread onion over fish. Sprinkle crumb mixture over top of onion. Bake in a moderate oven 350 degrees F., for 25 to 30 minutes, or until fish flakes easily when tested with a fork. Serves 6.

SMOKED FISH ORIENTAL

1 pound smoked whitefish
1 16-ounce can bean sprouts, drained
6 eggs, beaten
½ cup finely chopped green onion
dash of pepper
Foo Yung sauce
1 tablespoon toasted sesame seeds

Wash fish and remove skin and bones. Flake fish. Combine all ingredients except sauce and sesame seeds. Pour ⅓ cup fish mixture onto a hot greased griddle or frying pan. Fry at a moderate heat for 2 to 3 minutes or until brown. Turn carefully and fry 2 to 3 minutes longer or until brown. Drain on absorbent paper. Pour Foo Yung sauce over patties and sprinkle with sesame seeds. Serves 6.

BROILED SEA BASS

2 pounds sea bass fillets
½ cup pineapple juice
¼ cup steak sauce
1 teaspoon salt
dash of pepper

Wash and skin fillets and cut into serving-size portions. Place fish in a single layer in a shallow baking pan. Combine remaining ingredients and pour over fish. Let stand for 30 minutes, turning once. Remove fish, reserving sauce for basting. Place fish on a well-greased broiler pan. Broil about 4 inches from source of heat for 4 to 6 minutes. Turn carefully and brush with sauce. Broil 4 to 6 minutes longer or until fish flakes easily when tested with a fork. Serves 6.

COD CURRY

2 pounds cod fillets
1 cup thinly sliced celery
1 cup thinly sliced onion
1 tablespoon melted fat or oil
1 teaspoon curry powder
1 teaspoon salt
¾ cup skim milk
paprika

Wash and skin fillets and place in a single layer in a greased baking dish. Cook the celery and onion in fat for five minutes. Stir in seasonings and milk. Spread over fish. Bake in a moderate oven 350 degrees F., for 25 minutes, or until fish flakes easily when tested with a fork. Sprinkle with paprika. Makes 6 servings.

SESAME RAINBOW TROUT

6 pan-dressed rainbow trout
¼ cup melted fat or oil
¼ cup sesame seeds
2 tablespoons lemon juice
½ teaspoon salt
dash of pepper

Clean, wash, and dry fish. Combine remaining ingredients. Place fish in a well-greased, hinged wire grill. Baste fish with sauce. Cook about 4 inches from moderately hot coals for 5 to 7 minutes. Baste with sauce. Turn and cook for 5 to 7 minutes more, or until fish flakes easily when tested with a fork. Serves 6.

HALIBUT ITALIAN STYLE

2 pounds halibut steaks (flounder can be substituted)
2 cups Italian dressing
2 tablespoons lemon juice
2 teaspoons salt
¼ teaspoon pepper
paprika

Wash and cut steaks into serving-size portions and place in a single layer in a shallow baking dish. Combine remaining ingredients except paprika. Pour sauce over fish and let stand for 30 minutes, turning once. Remove fish, reserving sauce for basting. Place fish in well-greased, hinged wire grills. Sprinkle with paprika. Cook about 4 inches from moderately hot coals for 8 minutes. Baste with sauce and sprinkle with paprika. Turn and cook for 7 to 10 minutes longer, or until fish flakes easily when tested with a fork. Serves 6.

GRILLED SWORDFISH

2 pounds swordfish steaks
½ cup melted fat or oil
⅓ cup lemon juice
½ cup chopped onion
2 tablespoons capers and juice
2 tablespoons catsup
1 tablespoon salt
2 teaspoons Worcestershire sauce
2 teaspoons sugar
4 bay leaves, crushed
2 cloves garlic, finely chopped
¼ teaspoon pepper
paprika

Wash steaks and cut into serving-size portions and place in a single layer in a shallow baking pan. Combine remaining ingredients, except paprika. Pour sauce over fish and let stand for 30 minutes, turning once. Remove fish, reserving sauce for basting. Place fish in well-greased, hinged wire grill. Sprinkle with paprika. Cook about 4 inches from moderately hot coals for 8 minutes. Baste with sauce and sprinkle with paprika. Turn and cook for 7 to 8 minutes longer, or until fish flakes easily when tested with a fork. Serves 6.

SEA BASS WESTERN STYLE

2 pounds sea bass steaks
¼ cup orange juice
¼ cup soy sauce
2 tablespoons catsup
2 tablespoons melted fat or oil
2 tablespoons chopped parsley
1 tablespoon lemon juice
1 clove garlic, finely chopped
½ teaspoon oregano
½ teaspoon pepper

Wash fish and cut into serving-size portions and place in single layer in shallow baking dish. Combine remaining ingredients. Pour sauce over fish and let stand for 30 minutes, turning once. Remove fish, reserving sauce for basting. Place fish in well-greased, hinged wire grills. Cook about 4 inches from moderately hot coals for 8 minutes. Baste with sauce. Turn and cook for 7 minutes more, or until fish flakes easily when tested with a fork. Makes 6 servings.

SMOKY BARBECUED MACKEREL

2 pounds mackerel fillets (any of the many mackerel species can be used)
½ cup vinegar
½ cup salad oil
2 tablespoons grated lemon rind
1 tablespoon hickory liquid smoke
1 tablespoon brown sugar
2 teaspoons salt
½ teaspoon Worcestershire sauce
2 bay leaves
dash white pepper
dash liquid hot pepper sauce
paprika

Combine all ingredients except paprika and bring to the boiling point. Cool. Cut fillets into serving-size portions, and place in a single layer in a shallow baking pan. Pour sauce over fish and let stand for 30 minutes, turning once. Place fish in well-greased, hinged wire grills. Cook on a barbecue grill about 4 inches from moderately hot coals for 8 minutes. Baste with remaining sauce. Turn and cook 7 to 9 minutes longer or until fish flakes easily when tested with a fork. Sprinkle with paprika. Serves 6.

HADDOCK IN CREAM SAUCE

1 pound haddock fillets
¼ cup beer
1 pint heavy whipping cream
7 scallions, cut up (including greens)
1 teaspoon butter
salt and pepper to taste

Marinate fish fillets in beer for half hour before cooking. Remove fish from marinade and place in baking pan. Pour heavy cream over fish and then

179

cover with scallions, adding one teaspoon butter, salt, and pepper. Cook in 350 degree F., oven for 18 to 20 minutes or until fish flakes easily when tested with a fork. Serves 4.

PLANKED RED SNAPPER

2 pounds red snapper fillets (channel bass, striped
    bass, etc., can be substituted)
2 tablespoons cooking oil
2 tablespoons lemon juice
1 teaspoon salt
½ teaspoon paprika
dash of pepper
seasoned hot mashed potatoes
seasoned hot cooked vegetables (peas, carrots,
    broccoli, asparagus, etc.)

Place fillets in a single layer, skin side down, on a preheated, oiled plank or well-greased bake-and-serve platter, 18 x 13 inches. Combine remaining ingredients, except vegetables, and mix well. Pour sauce over fish. Bake in a moderate oven, 350 degrees F., for 20 to 25 minutes or until fish flakes easily when tested with a fork. Remove from oven and arrange the hot mashed potatoes and other vegetables around the fish. Drizzle with melted butter and return to oven briefly until brown. Serves 6.

OVEN-FRIED FILLETS

2 pounds fresh fillets
½ cup milk
1 teaspoon salt
1½ cups cereal crumbs or toasted dry bread crumbs.
¼ cup melted fat or oil

Combine milk and salt. Dip fillets in milk and roll in crumbs. Place fish in a single layer, skin side down, on a well-greased baking pan, 15 x 10 inches. Pour fat over fish. Bake in hot oven, 500 degrees F., for 10 to 15 minutes or until fish are brown and flake easily when tested with a fork. Serves 6.

FILLETS IN TOMATO-CHEESE SAUCE

2 pounds fresh fish fillets
1 can cream of tomato soup
2 tablespoons chopped onion

¾ teaspoon salt
pepper to season
1 cup grated cheese

Place fillets in a well-greased baking dish, 12 x 8. Combine soup, onion, salt, and pepper and pour over fish. Sprinkle with grated cheese and bake at 350 degrees F., for 25 to 30 minutes, or until fish flakes easily when tested with a fork. Serves 6.

FISH IN CHIPS

2 pounds fresh fish fillets
¼ cup lemon juice
2 tablespoons Italian salad dressing
2 cups (4 to 5 ounces) crushed potato chips
½ cup grated Parmesan cheese
¼ cup chopped parsley
1½ teaspoons paprika
½ teaspoon thyme
2 tablespoons salad oil

Cut fillets into serving-size pieces. Combine lemon juice and dressing. Combine potato chips, cheese, parsley, and seasonings. Dip fish in juice mixture and roll in chip mixture. Place fish, skin side down, on a well-greased baking sheet, 15 x 12 inches. Drizzle fat over fish. Bake in very hot oven 500 degrees F., for 10 to 15 minutes or until fish flakes easily when tested with a fork. Serves 6.

TEXAS TATER SALAD

1½ pounds fresh fish fillets
2 cups cooked potatoes, cut into small pieces
3 eggs, hard boiled and chopped
½ cup grated carrot
⅔ cup salad dressing
2 tablespoons chopped onion
1 teaspoon salt
pepper to season

Place fillets in boiling, salted water. Cover and simmer 10 minutes or until fish flakes easily when tested with a fork. Drain. Remove skin and bones; flake. Mix all ingredients together and place in refrigerator until cold. Serve on lettuce. Serves 6.

31

Catfish Favorites

Catfish recipes deserve a chapter alone. The catfish, like the Fourth of July and baseball, is about as American as you can get. Streams, parks, streets, and even some hamlets have been named in honor of the fish. "Catfish" is a popular nickname and there are some sports celebrities who answer to it. This delicately flavored, firm-fleshed fish stands tall in America's food heritage.

There are in excess of twenty species of catfish and close relatives found in North American waters. But for flavor the one that stands above all others is the channel catfish, a species valued highly as a sports fish and a commercial fish. The channel catfish has been studied intensely and today they are raised in artificially formed lakes throughout the South and south-central states. These catfish farms make up a multimillion-dollar-a-year industry. Today Mississippi River drainage areas of Arkansas, Missouri, Mississippi, and Louisiana are rich with catfish farms. Catfish farming reached significant commercial importance in the late 1940s with the production of bait minnows. Then in the 1950s land made idle by rice-crop rotation on Arkansas farms was flooded to form lakes for the raising of commercial catfish species.

There was nothing haphazard about the ventures. Fish culturists followed scientific propagation and rearing techniques. Proper environment called for specially designed spawning and rearing ponds. Brood stock was carefully selected and feed rations scientifically balanced. Scientific management techniques were followed throughout. The resulting product that we enjoy today is better flavored and more succulent than those catfish of the same species found in the wild. But whether your catfish

comes from the wild or from a fish farm you can rest assured it will provide supreme dining pleasure.

Since the commercial catfish industry grew up in the South and in the Mississippi River system, it should come as no surprise that many of the recipes bear Southland names.

The channel catfish is king of the clan as far as eating is concerned. However, if channel catfish meat is not available, meat from blue catfish, white catfish, or flathead catfish can be substituted in the following recipes.

BAYOU CATFISH

6 skinned, pan-dressed catfish
1 cup dry white wine
½ cup melted fat or oil
1 4-ounce can mushroom stems and pieces, drained
¼ cup chopped green onions
2 tablespoons lemon juice
2 tablespoons chopped parsley
2 teaspoons salt
¼ teaspoon crushed bay leaves
¼ teaspoon pepper
¼ teaspoon thyme

Clean, wash, and dry fish. Cut 6 squares of heavy-duty aluminum foil, 18 inches wide. Grease lightly. Place each fish on one half of each square of foil. Combine remaining ingredients. Pour sauce over fish, using approximately ⅓ cup of sauce for each fish. Fold other half of foil over fish and seal edges by making double folds in the foil. Place packages of fish on barbecue grill about 6 inches from moderately hot coals. Cook for 20 to 25 minutes, or until fish flakes easily when tested with a fork. To serve, cut a big crisscross in the top of each package and fold the foil back. Makes 6 servings.

NEW ORLEANS CATFISH

2 pounds of catfish steaks
½ teaspoon salt
dash of pepper
2 cups cooked rice
2 tablespoons grated onion
½ teaspoon curry powder
6 thin lemon slices
¼ cup butter or margarine
chopped parsley

Cut fish into 6 portions and place in a well-greased baking dish, 13 x 9 x 2. Sprinkle fish with salt and pepper. Combine rice, onion, and curry powder, and spread over fish. Top with lemon slices and dot with butter. Cover and bake in moderate oven 350 degrees F., for 25 to 30 minutes or until fish flakes easily when tested with a fork. Remove cover the last few minutes of cooking to allow for slight browning. Sprinkle with parsley. Serves 6.

CAJUN COUNTRY CATFISH

6 skinned, pan-dressed catfish
½ cup tomato sauce
2 packages (¾ ounce each) cheese-garlic salad
    dressing mix
2 tablespoons melted fat or oil
2 tablespoons chopped parsley
2 tablespoons grated Parmesan cheese

Clean, wash and dry fish. Combine remaining ingredients except cheese. Brush fish inside and out with the sauce. Place in well-greased baking dish and brush with remaining sauce and sprinkle with cheese. Let stand for 30 minutes. Bake in a moderate oven 350 degrees F., for 25 to 30 minutes or until fish flakes easily when tested with a fork. Turn oven control to broil. Place fish about 3 inches from source of heat and broil for 1 to 2 minutes or until crisp and lightly brown. Service for 6.

DIXIELAND CATFISH

6 skinned, pan-dressed catfish
½ cup French dressing
12 thin lemon slices
paprika

Clean, wash, and dry fish. Brush inside and out with dressing. Cut 6 lemon slices in half, and place 2 halves in each body cavity. Place fish in a well-

greased baking dish. Place a lemon slice on each fish, and brush top of fish with remaining dressing. Sprinkle with paprika. Bake in moderate oven 350 degrees F., for 30 to 35 minutes of until fish flakes easily when tested with a fork. Serves 6.

SOUTHERN PLANTATION
CATFISH

6 unskinned, pan-dressed catfish
2 teaspoons salt
orange-rice stuffing
2 tablespoons melted fat or oil
2 tablespoons orange juice
        Orange-Rice Stuffing:
1 cup chopped celery with leaves
¼ cup chopped onion
¼ cup melted fat or oil
¼ cup water
¼ cup orange juice
2 tablespoons lemon juice
1 tablespoon grated orange rind
¾ teaspoon salt
1 cup precooked rice
½ cup toasted, blanched, slivered almonds

Prepare orange-rice stuffing first. Cook celery and onion in fat until tender. Add water, juices, orange rind, and salt, and bring to a boil. Add rice and stir to moisten. Cover and remove from heat. Let stand 5 minutes. Add almonds and mix thoroughly. Clean, wash, and dry fish. Sprinkle inside and out with salt. Fill fish with orange-rice stuffing and close openings will small skewers or toothpicks. Place fish in a well-greased baking pan. Combine fat and orange juice, and brush fish with the mixture. Bake in moderate oven 350 degrees F., for 25 to 30 minutes or until fish flakes easily when tested with a fork. Baste occasionally with fat mixture. Remove skewers before serving. Serves 6.

SMOKY BROILED CATFISH

6 skinned, pan-dressed catfish
⅓ cup soy sauce
3 tablespoons melted fat or oil
1 tablespoon liquid smoke
1 clove garlic, finely chopped
½ teaspoon ginger
½ teaspoon salt
lemon wedges

Clean, wash, and dry fish. Combine remaining ingredients except lemon wedges and mix thoroughly. Brush inside of fish with sauce. Place fish on a well-greased broiler pan and brush with sauce. Broil about 3 inches from source of heat for 4 to 6 minutes. Turn carefully and brush other side with sauce. Broil 4 to 6 minutes longer, basting occasionally, until fish flakes easily when tested with a fork. Serve with lemon wedges. Makes 6 servings.

COUNTRY FRIED CATFISH

10 unskinned, pan-dressed catfish (six ounces each)
2 large eggs, beaten
¼ cup milk
1½ teaspoons salt
¼ teaspoon pepper
2 cups all-purpose flour
2 cups dry bread crumbs

Wash fish thoroughly. Combine eggs, milk, salt, and pepper. Combine flour and crumbs. Dip fish in egg mixture and roll in flour mixture. Fry in deep fat 350 degrees F., for 3 to 5 minutes, or until fish flakes easily when tested with a fork. Drain on absorbent paper. Serve with tartar or seafood sauce. Serves 6.

SAUCY BROILED CATFISH

6 skinned, pan-dressed catfish
1 cup melted fat or oil
¼ cup chopped parsley
2 tablespoons catsup
2 tablespoons wine vinegar
2 cloves garlic, finely chopped
2 teaspoons basil
1 teaspoon salt
¼ teaspoon pepper

Clean, wash, and dry fish. Place in a single layer in a shallow baking dish. Combine remaining ingredients. Pour sauce over fish and let stand for 30 minutes, turning once. Remove fish, reserving sauce for basting. Place fish on a well-greased broiler pan, and brush with sauce. Broil about 3 inches from source of heat for 5 to 7 minutes, or until lightly browned, basting twice. Turn carefully and brush other side with sauce. Broil 5 to 7 minutes longer, basting occasionally, or until fish is brown and flakes easily when tested with a fork. Serves 6.

TENNESSEE FRIED CATFISH

6 skinned, pan-dressed catfish
2 tablespoons salt
¼ teaspoon pepper
2 eggs
2 tablespoons milk
2 cups cornmeal

Clean, wash, and dry fish. Sprinkle both sides with salt and pepper. Beat eggs slightly and blend in the milk. Dip fish in the eggs and roll in cornmeal. Place fish in heavy frying pan with ⅛ inch melted fat, hot but not smoking. Fry at a moderate heat. When fish is brown on one side, turn carefully and brown the other side. Depending upon thickness of the fish, cooking time is about 10 minutes. Drain on absorbent paper. Serve immediately on a hot platter, plain or with a sauce. Service for 6.

SESAME CATFISH

6 skinned, pan-dressed catfish
½ cup melted fat or oil
½ cup sesame seeds
4 tablespoons lemon juice
1 teaspoon salt
dash pepper

Clean, wash, and dry fish. Place fish in a well-greased hinged, wire grill. Combine remaining ingredients. Baste fish with sauce. Cook about 4 inches from moderately hot coals for 8 minutes. Baste with sauce. Turn and cook for 7 to 9 minutes longer, or until fish flakes easily when tested with a fork. Serves 6.

CATFISH GUMBO

1 pound skinned catfish fillets
½ cup chopped celery
½ cup chopped green pepper
½ cup chopped onion
1 clove garlic, finely chopped
¼ cup melted fat or oil
2 beef bouillon cubes
2 cups boiling water
1 16-ounce can of tomatoes
1 10-ounce package frozen okra, sliced
2 teaspoons salt
¼ teaspoon pepper
¼ teaspoon thyme
1 whole bay leaf
dash Tabasco
1½ cups hot cooked rice

Cut fillets into 1-inch pieces. Cook celery, green pepper, onion, and garlic in fat until tender. Dissolve bouillon cubes in water. Add bouillon, tomatoes, okra, and seasonings. Cover and simmer for 30 minutes. Add fish. Cover and simmer for 15 minutes longer, or until the fish flakes easily when tested with a fork. Remove bay leaf. Place ¼ cup of rice in each of 6 soup bowls and fill with gumbo. Serves 6.

CONTINENTAL CATFISH

6 skinned, pan-dressed catfish
1 teaspoon salt
dash pepper
1 cup chopped parsley
¼ cup butter or margarine, softened
1 egg, beaten
¼ cup milk
1 teaspoon salt
¾ cup dry bread crumbs
½ cup grated Swiss cheese
3 tablespoons melted fat or oil

Clean, wash, and dry fish. Sprinkle inside and out with salt and pepper. Add parsley to butter and mix thoroughly. Spread inside of each fish with approximately 1 tablespoon of parsley butter. Combine egg, milk, and salt. Combine crumbs and cheese. Dip fish in egg mixture and roll in crumb mixture. Place on a well-greased cooky sheet, 15½ x 12 inches. Sprinkle remaining crumb mixture over top of fish. Drizzle with fat. Bake in extremely hot oven, 500 degrees F., for 15 to 20 minutes or until fish flakes easily when tested with a fork. Serves 6.

CATFISH CAPER

2 pounds skinned catfish fillets
½ cup melted fat or oil
⅓ cup lemon juice
¼ cup chopped onion
2 tablespoons capers and juice
2 tablespoons catsup
1 tablespoon salt
2 teaspoons Worcestershire sauce
2 teaspoons sugar
4 bay leaves, crushed
2 cloves garlic, finely chopped
¼ teaspoon pepper
paprika

Place fillets in a single layer in a shallow baking pan. Combine remaining ingredients except paprika. Pour sauce over fillets and let stand for 30 minutes, turning once. Remove fillets, reserving sauce for basting. Place fillets in well-greased hinged wire grills. Sprinkle with paprika. Cook about 4 inches from moderately hot coals for 7 to 10 minutes. Baste with sauce and sprinkle with paprika. Turn and cook for 7 to 10 minutes longer, or until fish flakes easily when tested with a fork. Makes 6 servings.

CRISPY CATFISH

6 skinned, pan-dressed catfish
½ cup evaporated milk

1 tablespoon salt
dash pepper
1 cup flour
½ cup yellow cornmeal
2 teaspoons paprika
12 slices bacon

Clean, wash, and dry fish. Combine milk, salt, and pepper. Combine flour, cornmeal, and paprika. Dip fish in milk mixture and roll in flour mixture. Fry bacon in heavy pan until crisp. Remove bacon, reserving fat for frying. Drain bacon on absorbent paper. Fry fish in hot fat for 4 minutes. Turn carefully and fry for 4 to 6 minutes longer, or until fish is brown and flakes easily when tested with a fork. Drain on absorbent paper. Serve with bacon. Serves 6.

PATIO CATFISH

6 skinned, pan-dressed catfish
¾ cup melted butter or margarine
⅓ cup lemon juice
2 teaspoons salt
paprika

Clean, wash, and dry fish. Combine butter, lemon juice, and salt. Cut 6 pieces of heavy-duty aluminum foil, 18 x 18 inches each. Grease lightly. Place 2 tablespoons of sauce on foil. Place fish in sauce. Top each fish with 2 tablespoons sauce and sprinkle with paprika. Bring the foil up over the fish and close all edges with tight double folds. Make 6 packages. Place packages on a grill about 6 inches from moderately hot coals. Cook for 25 to 30 minutes, or until fish flakes easily when tested with a fork. Serves 6.

ZIPPY BROILED CATFISH

6 skinned, pan-dressed catfish
4 tablespoons lemon juice
2 teaspoons salt
dash pepper
1 cup flour
1⅓ cups Italian salad dressing
Lemon wedges
parsley

Clean, wash, and dry fish. Brush inside of fish with lemon juice; sprinkle with salt and pepper. Roll fish in flour. Shake off excess flour. Place fish on a well-greased broiler pan. Brush with salad dressing. Broil about 4 inches from source of heat for 4 to 6 minutes, basting occasionally. Turn carefully and brush with salad dressing. Broil 4 to 6 minutes longer, or until fish flakes easily when tested with a fork. Garnish with lemon wedges and parsley. Serves 6.

Our neighbors across the border in Canada have some delightful recipes for fish found in the provinces. Most Americans, however, are not familiar with fine Canadian piscatorial treats because they frequently associate northland fishing with the rustic hunting and fishing lodge and the so common shore lunch. The reason is simple. On almost all fishing trips to the Canadian out-of-the-way lakes and rivers, the midday meal is a shore lunch left to the hands of the guides, who frequently are Indians. They do an admirable job shore-lunch style, which means pan-frying or deep-frying. Don't fret for a second that I might be selling the shore lunches short. It is indeed a treat to take a flopping fish off the stringer, slice off slabs of meat and immediately cook it. The meat off such a fish has a far firmer texture and delightful flavor than the same meat that has been frozen or been kept on ice for several days.

By all means try the shore-lunch style of cooking fish. It is indeed a treat. For added zest to your eating pleasure here are a few mouth-watering Canadian favorites.

BAKED MUSKELLUNGE WITH FRUIT STUFFING

1 5-pound muskellunge (pike or walleye make good
    substitutes) with head and tail cut off
1 cup chopped, dried apricots
1 cup chopped apple
4 cups bread crumbs
½ cup melted butter or cooking oil
½ cup diced celery
¼ cup water and lemon juice
½ teaspoon mint
salt and pepper to taste

The ingredients of this recipe will fill a 5-pound fish that has been headed, tailed, and boned. Ingredients can be increased proportionately for larger fish. Thoroughly mix the stuffing and put in cavity of fish. Tie the fish in several places to hold the stuffing in place and then place in oiled roasting pan with ¼ cup of water and lemon juice. Bake in moderate oven, 10 minutes per inch stuffed thickness. Baste frequently with the liquid. Serves 6 to 8.

SALMON, TROUT BRAISED IN FOIL

Slice salmon or trout and place in cups made of aluminum foil. Add salt, pepper, a few onion rings, thyme, one teaspoon mustard to one can of cream of mushroom soup (cream of celery can be substituted). Close cups and cook atop coals for approximately 20 minutes. Use fish 1½ to 2 pounds in size.

SALMON, TROUT BISQUE

1 pound salmon or trout
¼ cup chopped onion
¼ cup diced celery
¼ cup butter or cooking oil
3 tablespoons flour
1½ teaspoons salt
3 cups milk and fish liquid
1 cup tomato juice
2 tablespoons chopped parsley

Boil the salmon or trout, saving the liquid. Add milk to this liquid to make three cups. Cook onion and celery in butter or cooking oil in a deep, heavy pan until tender and then blend in the flour and salt. Add liquid slowly, stir constantly, and cook until mixture thickens. Stir in tomato juice and parsley and bring to a slow simmer. This dish is best when served quite hot. Serves 4.

FISH FILLETS WITH ORANGE BUTTER SAUCE

2 pounds of fillets from trout, walleye, pike, bass, or muskellunge
grated rind of one orange
¼ cup orange juice
¼ cup melted butter
pepper and salt

Sprinkle fillets with salt and pepper and place in a greased baking dish. Grate orange rind and squeeze juice from orange. Mix juice with melted butter and pour over the fillets. Sprinkle with orange rind and bake in hot oven for 10 minutes per inch thickness. Serves 6.

WHITEFISH FILLETS IN MARGUERY SAUCE

2 pounds whitefish fillets
½ cup white wine
3 tablespoons melted butter
½ sliced lemon
1 tablespoon lemon juice
½ teaspoon salt
1 tablespoon flour
1 tablespoon butter or fat hot wine liquid
1 egg yolk
3 tablespoons cream
1 teaspoon sugar
chopped parsley
pepper

Salt and pepper fillets and place in greased baking dish. Mix wine, fat, and lemon juice and pour over the fillets. Place lemon slices on top and bake in hot oven for 10 minutes per inch thickness. At the same time blend fat and flour in top of a double boiler. When the fillets are cooked, pour off the hot wine liquid and add slowly to flour mixture, stirring constantly until mixture thickens. Add the egg yolk beaten with cream and sugar and cook 1 minute

longer. Pour over the fillets and serve garnished with the chopped parsley. Serves 6.

POACHED FILLETS WITH BEER SAUCE

2 walleye, pike, or muskellunge fillets cut into service size
1 pint ale or lager beer
2 ounces of butter
1 tablespoon cooking oil
1 minced onion
1 chopped tomato
1 tablespoon flour
1 teaspoon vinegar
pepper, salt, and tarragon

This is a recipe derived from northern Germany and Scandanavian tastes. Mix the ale or lager beer, oil, onion, seasonings, and tomato in cooking pot and marinate the fillets for an hour. Bring to a light boil for 15 to 20 minutes, testing the fillets with fork. Remove the fillets. Melt butter in a saucepan and stir in the flour to make a smooth paste. Pour a little of the hot mixture into this paste, and then stir both into the hot beer mixture and cook until it thickens. Serve with the fish fillets. Use the sauce immediately, since it is one that does not keep as a left over. Serves 6.

CANADIAN FISH CHOWDER

2 pounds of pike, walleye, or muskellunge fillets
3 cups water
3 tablespoons of butter or cooking oil
1 cup of chopped celery
2 medium onions, chopped
3 cups of diced potatoes
1 cup of diced carrots
2 cups of milk
salt, pepper, pinch of thyme, sage, and tarragon

Cook fillets in salted water for 10 minutes. Cook onions and celery in butter or cooking oil until tender. Add milk, potatoes and carrots, seasonings, along with water from the fish fillets. Cook for an additional 15 to 20 minutes, or until the potatoes and carrots are very tender. Flake the fish fillets and add to the mixture. Serves 6 to 8.

33

Rough Fish Recipes

Many people, fishermen included, tend to look down their noses in regards to some species of fish. With them it has to be a choice fish or else. During the lean years of World War II a lot of people ate shark meat and liked it, only very few knew they were eating shark. The meat was marketed as "gray fish." The prejudice against eating shark meat probably stems from two facts: (1) sharks are scavangers, and (2) sharks have been known to eat people. There are other fish species that are not eaten because they are viewed as baitfish with which to catch gamefish. The mullet is a prime example of this. Another of the rough fish is the carp. The rough fish recipes that follow are representative of sections of the country or nations. The several mullet recipes recorded were born in Florida, mainly in the Keys and Key West. Most of the carp recipes stem from Central Europe and the Slavic nations.

ZESTY MULLET FILLETS

2 pounds of mullet fillets
¼ cup French dressing
1 tablespoon lemon juice
1 tablespoon grated onion
2 teaspoons salt
dash of pepper

Wash and cut fillets into serving-size portions. Combine remaining ingredients. Baste fish with sauce. Place in a well-greased, hinged wire grill. Cook about 4 inches from moderately hot coals for 8 minutes. Baste with sauce. Turn and cook for 7 to 10 minutes longer, or until fish flakes easily when tested with a fork. Serves 6.

KEY LIME MULLET

2 pounds mullet fillets
1 teaspoon salt
dash of pepper
¼ cup lime juice
3 tablespoons butter or margarine, melted
paprika
lime wedges

Wash and skin fillets and cut into serving-size portions. Place in a single layer in a shallow baking dish. Sprinkle with salt and pepper. Pour lime juice over fish and let stand for 30 minutes, turning once. Remove fish, reserving sauce for basting. Place fish in a well-greased broiler pan. Combine butter and juice. Brush fish with butter mixture and sprinkle with paprika. Broil about 4 inches from source of heat for 8 to 10 minutes, or until fish flakes easily when tested with a fork. Serve with lime wedges. Makes 6 servings.

SERBIAN CARP

Although most of the carp recipes reflect an European taste, the fish is actually a native of Asia. It made its way into Europe and later into the United States via transplant. The carp has met little acceptance as a food fish in the United States because it has so many bones and because few people know how to properly dress the fish. After catching and before cleaning, hang the carp by its head and cut off the tail to freely bleed the fish. Skin and fillet the fish and discard all of the dark meat on each side. This dark meat is quite strong-tasting.

2 pounds carp fillets
¼ pound butter
2 finely chopped onions
3 tablespoons tomato paste
¼ pound chopped mushrooms
salt and red pepper
flour and water

Roll fillets in flour seasoned with salt and red pepper. Sear in butter. After removing carp, sauté onions and mushrooms. Add tomato paste and a little water. Put carp in and stew until well done, or until fish flakes when tested with a fork. Serves 6.

CARP IN BEER

Here's a carp recipe that reflects the German, Austrian, and Bohemian influence. The dark beer and gingerbread make this dish a real delight.

2 pounds carp fillets
2 12-ounce cans of dark beer
1 medium onion
1 stalk celery, chopped
1 bay leaf
½ teaspoon thyme
1 teaspoon salt
1 sprig parsley
¼ pound butter or margarine
½ cup gingerbread crumbs

Mince onion and add celery, bay leaf, thyme, parsley, beer, and salt. Bring to a boil. Cut carp into serving-size portions and place in sauce. Cook for 10 to 15 minutes on low fire. Remove carp from sauce and thicken sauce with gingerbread crumbs. Strain sauce and stir in butter. The sauce must be creamy and hot. Pour over carp. Serves 6.

CARP CHOWDER

2 pounds carp fillets
2 stalks chopped celery
¼ cup butter or margarine
1 chopped onion
¼ cup flour
dash of thyme
salt and pepper
water

Simmer carp, onions, celery, thyme, salt, and pepper slowly in water for 30 minutes. Thicken with a mixture of butter and flour. Serves 6.

CARP CAKES

1 cup flaked, cooked carp
3 cups mashed potatoes

1 egg beaten
2 tablespoons bacon grease
½ tablespoon butter or margarine
½ teaspoon pepper
½ teaspoon salt
⅛ teaspoon paprika

Mix carp, potatoes, bacon grease, butter, salt, pepper, and paprika; then add beaten egg. Shape into cakes and fry in hot grease until golden brown. Serves 6.

SHARK STEAKS

Unless you happen to be visiting some of the South Pacific islands, you will not run into any fish markets selling shark meat. Consequently if you want to try this recipe, go out and catch your own shark. Bleed the fish immediately after it is caught. Select the whitest meat you can find on the fish and cut out steaks. The meat can be improved by soaking for several hours in vinegar.

4 shark steaks, 1-inch thick
⅛ pound butter
¼ teaspoon salt
⅛ teaspoon pepper
1 8-ounce can of pineapple rings, save juice
1½ teaspoon powdered ginger

Wash and dry the fish, and brown steaks on each side in butter in frying pan. Pour in juice from can of pineapple, cover tightly, and steam for 5 minutes. Place a pineapple ring on each steak and steam for 5 minutes more, or until meat flakes easily when tested with a fork. Sprinkle with ginger and serve. Makes 4 servings.

NORTH SEA EEL

Most eel caught on hook and line are caught by accident, and then if the angler is not up on his marine life, he visions his catch as something of a sea serpent. He cuts off his line, glad to get rid of the creature. Those folks familiar with eels handle them gingerly because they are slimy, slippery creatures armed with a mouthful of teeth that can inflict a nasty bite. Cleaning the creature is no easy job. Slit the neck of the eel, tie a string around it, and tie the other end to something solid. Then with the aid of pliers, pull off the skin. Slit the stomach, remove the entrails, and wash thoroughly. When you cook eel it is a lot like frog legs in that the meat jumps and twitches. Here's how to avoid that. Cut the eel into 2-inch pieces and slit along the backbone of each piece. This cuts the muscle so the meat will not jump while cooking. Eel meat should be parboiled for several minutes before cooking.

1 dressed eel, cut in 2-inch pieces
½ cup olive oil
2 cloves garlic, crushed
1 tablespoon chopped parsley
1 tablespoon lemon juice
pinch of red pepper
¼ teaspoon salt
⅛ teaspoon pepper

Combine oil, parsley, garlic, lemon juice, and seasonings. Marinate the eel in mixture for at least 15 minutes, the longer, the better. Place in a broiler pan and broil for 5 minutes on each side. Serves 6.

PECONIC BAY BLOWFISH

Tickle the fish on the belly and it puffs itself up into a round ball. It is a ridiculous-looking fish, and it is one that most fishermen throw away. In the eyes of a lot of fishermen the blowfish is nothing but a bait-stealer best described with colorful oaths. The fish when cleaned properly is a solid chunk of white meat that is quite delicious. The blowfish is a bear to clean. Its skin is tough and prickly, and one must wear gloves to clean the fish. Cut through the fish directly behind the head. Grab the skin and peel it off the way one takes off a glove. The innards will fall out and you will have solid white meat that faintly resembles a frog's leg.

8 to 10 blowfish, cleaned and dressed
¼ cup olive oil
½ cup Chablis or other white wine
1 teaspoon rosemary
¼ teaspoon salt
⅛ teaspoon black pepper

Place fish in baking dish, pour on oil and wine, and sprinkle with seasonings. Bake in hot oven 425 degrees F., for 25 minutes. Serves 4 to 6 depending upon size of fish.

34

How To Cook Shrimp

Shrimp can be prepared boiled, fried, baked, and in gumbo. The quickest and simplest way to prepare shrimp is to boil the crustaceans. It is easiest to head the shrimp first; the remaining portion, which is called a tail, can be boiled in tap water with a touch of salt added or with commercially prepared shrimp or crab boils. The boil mixtures are sold by the package and are simply mixtures of a number of spices. A good reason for cooking the tails still in the shells is that cooking makes them easiest to clean. With a shrimp deveiner one can remove the vein (also called dirt track) from the groove on the crustacean's back and the remaining shell all in one motion. The meat then can be served either hot or chilled with various dips and hot sauces. The shrimp can also be used in cocktails and salads either whole or cut into pieces, depending upon the size of the shrimp available.

When shrimp are to be fried, they should be cleaned raw and then dipped in a batter—cornmeal, cornmeal and egg, or milk, flour, and egg. Dip and roll the shrimp in the batter and fry in hot cooking oil. Make sure the oil is deep enough to completely cover the shrimp. Fry until golden brown, but exercise care not to overfry, since this can make your shrimp quite tough.

You can live a full life on "plain Jane" cooking. If you want to add a new dimension to your shrimp-eating enjoyment, try the following recipes.

SMOKED SHRIMP

2 pounds raw jumbo shrimp, peeled and cleaned
½ cup buttery-flavored vegetable oil
seasoned salt

Use large shrimp if jumbos are not available, but do not go smaller than large shrimp because of shrinkage in cooking. Place the shrimp on a well-greased outdoor grill over low coals. Brush the shrimp generously with the buttery-flavored oil and sprinkle with seasoned salt. Close the hook and smoke for 15 minutes. Turn turn the shrimp over and baste and smoke for another 4 or 5 minutes. Serve the shrimp with remoulade, tartar, or cocktail sauce. This recipe will serve 6 adults.

PEPPERED SHRIMP AND EGG

Bored with starting the day off with the usual bacon and egg breakfast? Yes, the great American breakfast day after day can become a bore. Here's a recipe that will start your day with a new flavor. It is called peppered shrimp and egg.

½ pound cooked, peeled and deveined shrimp
3 slices bacon
½ cup chopped onion
¾ cup chopped green pepper
½ teaspoon salt
¼ teaspoon cayenne pepper
6 eggs, beaten
¼ cup coffee cream
½ teaspoon Worchestershire sauce

Fry bacon until it is crisp and then drain on absorbent paper. Crumble the bacon. Cook onion and green pepper in the bacon fat until tender. Add seasonings and shrimp and heat. Combine the eggs, cream, Worchestershire sauce, and bacon. Add to shrimp mixture and cook until the eggs are firm, stirring occasionally. The preparation will serve 6 adults.

SHRIMP HURRY CURRY

Shrimp Hurry Curry, a recipe concocted by the Texas Parks and Wildlife Department, has a bit of the Oriental and exotic about it. Curry is a traditional spice used in India and China. It is a spice, however, that is to be taken lightly. Always use a light hand and preferably follow a kitchen-tested recipe where curry powder is concerned. A little of it goes a long way, and too much will only mask other flavors.

1½ pounds raw, peeled and cleaned shrimp (frozen
    shrimp can be substituted for fresh)
1 10-ounce can frozen cream of shrimp soup
1 10-ounce can condensed cream of mushroom soup
2 tablespoons butter or margarine
¾ cup sour cream
1½ curry powder
2 tablespoons chopped parsley
rice, toast points, or patty shells for 6 portions

Thaw the frozen ingredients. Melt butter in a 10-inch frying pan. Add shrimp and cook over a low heat for not more than 5 minutes, stirring frequently. Add the soups and stir until thoroughly blended. Stir in the cream, curry powder, and parsley. Heat and serve over hot, fluffy rice, toast points, or in patty shells. Serves 6.

SHRIMP-CHEESE DREAMS

½ pound cooked, peeled, and cleaned shrimp
6 ounces cream cheese, softened
½ cup chopped pecans
½ cup crushed pineapple, drained
¼ cup chopped rice olives
1 tablespoon lemon juice
6 slices each, white and wholewheat bread, buttered

Chop the shrimp and combine all the ingredients except the bread. Spread 6 slices of white bread with approximately ½ cup of the shrimp mixture. Cover with 6 slices of whole wheat bread. Cut each sandwich diagonally into 4 triangles.

SHRIMP MIAMI

Frequently a recipe is named after the area, state, or city in which it was first popularized. Shrimp Miami is such a dish. It is one that can be served hot or cold, either as an appetizer or entree. It makes an excellent party dish in that it can be cooked ahead of time and served well chilled, or if you prefer it can be prepared at the last minute and served hot from a chafing dish. This is one of those recipes in which the main ingredient must be exactly so. This recipe calls for fresh, raw shrimp. Don't use cooked shrimp because they will become tough and flavorless. Since the vermouth in the recipe adds only flavor, it is all right to serve this dish to children and teetotalers.

2 pounds shrimp, fresh and in shell
¼ cup olive or salad oil
½ teaspoon white pepper
¼ cup extra dry vermouth
2 tablespoons lemon juice
2 teaspoons salt

Peel the shrimp, leaving the last section of the shell on. Remove sand veins and wash. Preheat electric frying pan to 320 degrees F. Add oil, salt, pepper, and shrimp. Cook for 8 to 10 minutes or until the shrimp are tender and pink, stirring frequently. Increase the temperature to 420 degrees F. Add the vermouth and lemon juice, and cook 1 minute longer, stirring constantly. Drain, and serve hot or cold as an appetizer or entree. The recipe will serve 6 adults.

SHRIMP JAMBALAYA

For really fine shrimp jambalaya turn to the bayou country of Louisiana. This shrimp jambalaya is a culinary delight with the tantalizing seafood aroma that smells of old New Orleans during Mardi Gras time. This recipe features shrimp simmered in a base of tomatoes and rice and seasoned with bay leaves, cloves, and a touch of thyme.

1 pound peeled and deveined shrimp, fresh or
    frozen
1 cup chopped green pepper
½ cup chopped onion
2 cloves garlic, finely chopped
¼ cup melted fat or cooking oil
1 16-ounce can of tomatoes
1½ cups water
1 cup uncooked rice
½ teaspoon crushed whole thyme
3 clove buds
¼ teaspoon salt
1 bay leaf
¼ cup chopped parsley
dash of pepper

Cook green pepper, onion, and garlic in fat until tender. Add all the remaining ingredients except the parsley and shrimp. Cover and cook for 20 minutes. Add the shrimp and cook for an additional 5 to 10 minutes, or until shrimp are done and rice is tender. Stir occasionally. Add the parsley at the end of the cooking period. Remove bay leaf and clove buds just before serving. Recipe makes servings for 6 adults.

SHRIMP CREOLE

A whole new era of dining dawned when the French invented cuisine à las Creole. Shrimp Creole is an old-time favorite that will please the young as well as the old. It is one of those recipes that has stood the test of time and is as popular today as when it was first introduced.

1 pound raw, cleaned shrimp
1 large onion, chopped
2 cloves garlic, chopped
1 green bell pepper, chopped
½ cup chopped celery
¼ cup chopped parsley
1 six-ounce can tomato paste
1 one-pound can tomatoes
1 cup water
1 teaspoon chili powder
1 teaspoon sugar
1 tablespoon Worcestershire sauce
1 bay leaf
1 teaspoon gumbo filé
1 tablespoon salt
¼ teaspoon pepper
dash cayenne pepper

Sauté the onion, garlic, celery, green pepper, and parsley in fat. Add the tomatoes, tomato paste, water, chili powder, sugar, Worcestershire sauce, bay leaf, salt, pepper, and cayenne. Simmer slowly for 1 hour. Add raw shrimp and gumbo filé, and cook 3 to 5 minutes more. Serve over fluffy white rice. Serving is for 6.

PICKLED SHRIMP

2 pounds shrimp, fresh or frozen
2 medium onions
1½ cups vegetable oil
1½ cups white vinegar
½ cup sugar
1½ teaspoons salt
1½ teaspoons celery seed
4 tablespoons capers with juice

Place peeled and deveined shrimp in boiling salted water for 3 to 5 minutes, or until pink and tender. Drain and rinse with cold water, then chill. Make alternate layers of shrimp and onion rings in a

sealable container. Mix remaining ingredients and pour over shrimp and onions. Seal and place in refrigerator for 6 hours or more, shaking or inverting occasionally. Remove shrimp from marinade and serve. Serves 6.

SHRIMP CARMEL

3 pound shrimp, shelled and deveined
2 4-ounce cans water chestnuts, drained and sliced
½ cup butter
2 teaspoons garlic salt
⅛ teaspoon Tabasco
1 large green pepper, cut in rings
1 tablespoons minced onion
½ teaspoon salt
½ teaspoon dried tarragon

Prepare in a foil pan made from several large pieces of heavy-duty aluminum foil, at least one-half-inch deep. Place butter, garlic salt, and Tabasco in foil pan and set on grill. Add shrimp and remaining ingredients. Cook 20 to 30 minutes. Grill 6 to 8 inches from heat. Serve immediately. About 6 servings.

SOY BARBECUED SHRIMP

2 pounds fresh shrimp, shelled and deveined
2 cloves garlic
½ teaspoon salt
½ cup soy sauce
½ cup lemon juice
½ teaspoon pepper
3 tablespoons finely chopped parsley
2 teaspoons dehydrated onion flakes

Arrange shrimp in a shallow dish. Mash garlic with salt in small bowl. Stir in remaining ingredients. Pour marinade over shrimp and thread shrimp on skewers. Grill 3 minutes, basting with marinade. Turn and grill 5 minutes more, basting several times. Use any remaining marinade as dip. Serves 4 adults.

SHRIMP MINI-PIES

½ pound shrimp, peeled and deveined
3 tablespoons mayonnaise or salad dressing
2 tablespoons lemon juice
1 tablespoon chopped sweet pickle
1 teaspoon horseradish
1 teaspoon prepared mustard
1 teaspoon salt
pastry for 1 pie crust (9 inch)

Cook shrimp 3 minutes in boiling water. Drain,

cool, and grind or finely chop shrimp. Combine all ingredients except pastry. Mix thoroughly. Roll pastry very thin, about ⅛ inch, and cut into 2½-inch circles. Place a teaspoonful of shrimp mixture in center of each circle. Moisten edges with cold water, fold over, and press edges together with a fork. Place on a tray and keep chilled until ready to fry. Cook in hot oil for 2 to 3 minutes, or until golden brown. Makes approximately 40 hors d'oeuvres.

SHRIMP SUPREME

3 pounds shrimp, peeled and deveined
2 4-ounce cans slick mushrooms, drained
⅔ cup melted butter or margarine
½ cup chopped parsley
¼ cup chopped onion
2 tablespoons lemon juice
2 tablespoons chili sauce
1 teaspoon garlic salt
½ teaspoon teaspoon garlic salt
dash Worcestershire sauce
dash liquid hot pepper sauce

Cut 6 squares of heavy-duty aluminum foil, 12 inches each. Divide shrimp into 6 portions. Place each portion of shrimp on one half of each square of foil. Place mushrooms on top of shrimp. Combine remaining ingredients. Fold other half of foil over shrimp and seal edges by making double folds in the foil. Place packages about 4 inches from moderately hot coals. Cook about 20 minutes. To serve, cut around the edges and fold the foil back. Serves 6.

CANTONESE SHRIMP AND BEANS

1½ pounds shrimp, peeled and deveined
1½ teaspoons chicken stock base
1 cup boiling water
¼ cup thinly sliced green onion
1 clove garlic, crushed
1 tablespoon salad oil
1 teaspoon salt
½ teaspoon ginger
1 9-ounce package frozen cut green beans
1 tablespoon cornstarch
1 tablespoon cold water
dash of pepper

Dissolve chick stock base in boiling water. Cook onion, garlic, and shrimp in oil for 3 minutes, stirring frequently. If necessary add a little of the chicken broth to prevent sticking. Stir in salt, ginger, pepper, green beans, and chicken broth. Cover and simmer 5 to 7 minutes longer, or until beans are cooked but still slightly crisp. Combine cornstarch and water. Add cornstarch mixture to shrimp and cook until thick and clear, stirring constantly. Dish will serve 6.

SHRIMP ALMANDINE

1 pound shrimp, peeled and deveined
1 cup blanced, slivered almonds
½ cup melted butter or margarine
½ teaspoon salt
2 tablespoons chopped parsley
dash of pepper
toast points

Cook shrimp 3 minutes in boiling water and then cool. Sauté almonds in butter until lightly brown. Remove almonds. Add shrimp and sauté until lightly brown. Add seasonings, parsley, and almonds. Serve on toast points. Serves 6.

SHRIMP REMOULADE

1 pound shrimp, peeled and deveined
2 cloves garlic, finely chopped
⅓ cup horseradish mustard
2 tablespoons catsup
2½ teaspoons paprika
¾ teaspoon cayenne pepper
1 teaspoon salt
⅓ cup tarragon vinegar
½ cup olive or salad oil
½ cup chopped green onions and lettuce tops

Cook shrimp 3 minutes in boiling water and then cool. Combine all ingredients except shrimp and lettuce; shake well. Marinate shrimp in the sauce for several hours in refrigerator. Serve on lettuce. Serves 6.

SHRIMP ORIENTAL

1 pound shrimp, peeled and deveined
¼ cup lemon juice
1 cup flour
3 eggs, beaten
1½ teaspoons salt

Pour lemon juice over shrimp and let stand 10 minutes. Cut shrimp almost through lengthwise and spread open. Place flour in paper bag. Add shrimp and shake well. Combine egg and salt. Dip each shrimp in egg. Place shrimp in a heavy frying pan that conatins about ⅛ inch fat, hot but not smoking. Fry at moderate heat. When shrimp are brown on one side, turn carefully and brown on the other side. Total cooking time approximately 4 minutes. Drain on absorbent paper before serving. Serves 6.

SHRIMP PIZZA

¾ pound small shrimp, peeled and deveined
⅓ cup chopped onion
9 cloves garlic, finely chopped
½ cup olive or salad oil
3 6-ounce cans Italian-style tomato paste
1½ teaspoons oregano
⅓ cup chopped parsley
¾ pound Mozzarella cheese, sliced thin
3 unbaked pizza crusts (9 inches each)

Cook onion and garlic in olive oil until tender. Add tomato paste and simmer for 5 minutes. Remove from heat; add oregano and parsley. Place pizza crusts on greased baking sheets. Cover each crust with ⅓ of the sauce, arrange ⅓ of the shrimp over the sauce, and cover with ⅓ of the cheese. Bake in a hot oven for 20 minutes or until crust is brown and cheese melts. Makes three pies; serves 6.

SHRIMP NEWBURG

1 pound shrimp, peeled and deveined
¼ cup butter or margarine
2½ tablespoons flour
¾ teaspoon salt
1 pint coffee cream
2 egg yolks, beaten
2 tablespoons sherry
dash cayenne pepper
dash nutmeg
toast points

Cook shrimp 3 minutes in boiling water and then cool. Melt butter or margarine and blend in flour and seasonings. Add cream gradually and cook until thick and smooth, stirring constantly. Stir a little of the hot sauce into egg yolks; add to remaining sauce, stirring constantly. Add shrimp and heat. Remove from heat and slowly stir in sherry. Serve immediately on toast points. Serves 6.

SHRIMP DEJOUGHE

¾ pound shrimp, peeled and deveined
1 cup dry bread crumbs
½ cup melted butter or margarine
¼ cup chopped green onions and tops
2 cloves garlic, finely chopped
2 teaspoons chopped parsley
1 teaspoon chervil
1 teaspoon tarragon vinegar
1 teaspoon crushed whole thyme
¼ teaspoon nutmeg
dash of mace
½ cup sherry

Chill shrimp with ice water for 5 minutes. Drain. Combine crumbs, butter, onion, garlic, parsley, chervil, vinegar, thyme, nutmeg, mace, and sherry. Place alternate layers of shrimp and crumb mixture in a well-greased 1-quart casserole. Combine 2 tablespoons of melted butter or margarine with ½ cup of dry bread crumbs, and sprinkle over top of casserole. Bake in a moderate oven or until brown. Serves 6.

SHRIMP ROCKEFELLER

1 pound shrimp, peeled and deveined
2 12-ounce packages frozen, chopped spinach
½ cup butter or margarine
1½ teaspoons Worcestershire sauce
2 teaspoons anchovy paste
½ teaspoon salt
¼ teaspoon Tabasco
1 teaspoon celery salt
½ cup chopped green onions and tops
2 cloves garlic, finely chopped
½ cup chopped parsley
1 cup chopped lettuce
3 slices white bread, crusts removed
¾ cup water
2 tablespoons melted butter or margarine
½ cup dry bread crumbs
¼ cup grated Parmesan cheese

Thaw spinach and drain. Melt butter and blend in seasonings. Add vegetables and simmer 10 minutes, or until tender. Moisten bread with water, add vegetables, and mix well. Place shrimp in 6 well-greased individual shells or 10-ounce casseroles, reserving 6 shrimp for top. Cover with vegetable mixture. Combine butter and crumbs. Sprinkle buttered crumbs and cheese over top of each shell. Place a shrimp on top, and bake in hot oven for 15 minutes or until brown. Serves 6.

SHRIMP GUMBO

1 pound shrimp, peeled and deveined
2 cups sliced fresh okra or 1 10-ounce package
    frozen okra, sliced
⅓ cup shortening, melted
⅔ cup chopped green onions and tops
3 cloves garlic, finely chopped
1½ teaspoons salt
½ teaspoon pepper
2 cups hot water
1 cup canned tomatoes
2 whole bay leaves
6 drops Tabasco
1½ cups cooked rice

Sauté okra in shortening about 10 minutes, or until okra appears dry, stirring constantly. Add onion, garlic, salt, pepper, and shrimp. Cook about 5 minutes. Add water, tomatoes, and bay leaves. Cover and simmer 20 minutes. Remove bay leaves. Add Tabasco. Place ¼ cup of rice in bottom of 6 soup bowls, fill with gumbo.

GULF COAST SHRIMP BOIL

2 pounds shrimp, peeled and deveined
3 bay leaves
1 tablespoon whole allspice
1½ teaspoons crushed red peppers
2 teaspoons whole black peppers
2 teaspoons whole cloves
2 quarts water
2 medium onions, sliced
6 cloves garlic
2 lemons, sliced
¼ cup salt

Tie spices in a piece of cheesecloth. To the water add onion, garlic, lemon, salt, and bag of seasonings; bring to a boil. Add shrimp; cover and return to the boiling point. Simmer 3 to 5 minutes, depending upon size of shrimp. Remove from heat and let stand in spiced water for 3 minutes. Drain and chill. Serve garnished with whole spices and lemon slices. Serves 6.

SHRIMP VICTORIA

1 pound medium shrimp, peeled and deveined
¼ cup butter or margarine

1 small onion, finely chopped
1 6-ounce can mushroom buttons, drained
1 tablespoon flour
¼ teaspoon salt
dash cayenne pepper
1 cup sour cream
3 cups cooked rice

Melt butter or margarine in blazer pan of chafing dish over direct moderate heat. Add shrimp and onion, and sauté for 10 to 15 minutes, or until shrimp are tender. Add mushrooms and cook 5 more minutes. Sprinkle in flour, salt, and pepper; mix well. Stir in sour cream and cook gently for 10 minutes, but do not allow mixture to boil. Serve over rice. Serves 6.

BATTER FRIED SHRIMP

1 pound medium shrimp, peeled and deveined
1 cup sifted flour
1 tablespoon sugar
1½ teaspoons baking powder
½ teaspoon seasoned salt
½ teaspoon chili powder
2 beaten eggs
⅓ cup milk
1 tablespoon oil

Sift dry ingredients into a bowl. Add remaining ingredients and stir until smooth. Dip shrimp in batter and drain well. Cook in hot oil 350 degrees F., 3 to 4 minutes or until golden brown. Drain on absorbent paper and allow to cool slightly. Serve plain or with seafood or tartar sauce. Serves 4.

35

Clam, Oyster, Scallop Recipes

Mollusks—clams, oysters, and scallops—are true seafood delicacies and are among the few seafoods that are often eaten raw. Fish can be eaten raw but are consumed rarely thus by the civilized world. This same civilized world readily accepts eating clams, oysters, and scallops raw and in good taste. It may take a bit of doing getting the first raw one down, but once one gets the hang of it, it is quite difficult limiting one's intake. And when these tasty meats are dipped in sauces, it is all the more easy to consume large numbers of mollusk meats.

OYSTERS ON THE HALF SHELL

36 fresh oysters in shells
crushed ice
cocktail sauce
lemon wedges
parsley

Wash off shells and open oysters. Arrange crushed ice in six shallow bowls or soup plates. Place six half-shell oysters on the ice with a small container of cocktail sauce in the center for each plate. Garnish with lemon wedges and parsley. Makes 6 servings.

OYSTER ROAST

36 oysters in the shell
melted butter or margarine

Wash oyster shells thoroughly. Place oysters on a grill about 4 inches from hot coals. Roast for 10 to 15 minutes, or until shells begin to open. Serve in shells with melted butter or margarine. Serves 6.

OYSTER KABOBS

2 12-ounce jars of oysters
⅓ cup French dressing
20 cocktail tomatoes or tomato wedges
10 slices of bacon, cut in half
¼ cup melted fat or cooking oil
1½ teaspoons salt
⅛ teaspoon pepper

Drain oysters and place in a shallow baking dish. Pour dressing over oysters and let stand 30 minutes. Wash tomatoes and remove stems. Remove oysters, reserving dressing for basting. Roll each piece of bacon around two or three oysters, depending on size of oysters. Place oysters and tomatoes on short skewers, and place the kabobs on a well-greased broiler pan. Combine fat, salt, pepper, and reserved dressing, mixing thoroughly. Brush kabobs with the seasoned fat. Broil for 4 to 5 minutes about 3 inches from source of heat. Turn kabobs carefully and brush with fat. Broil 4 to 5 minutes longer, or until the bacon is crisp. Serves 6.

ANGELS ON HORSEBACK

1 12-ounce jar of oysters
2 tablespoons chopped parsley
½ teaspoon salt
paprika
pepper
10 slices of bacon, cut in thirds

Drain oysters and sprinkle with parsley and seasonings. Place an oyster on each piece of bacon. Wrap bacon around oyster and secure with a toothpick. Place oysters on a broiler pan. Broil about

4 inches from source of heat for 8 to 10 minutes, or until the bacon is crisp. Turn carefully. Broil 4 to 5 minutes, or until bacon is crisp. Makes approximately 30 hors d'oeuvres.

SCALLOPED OYSTERS

1 pint oysters
2 cups cracker crumbs
½ teaspoon salt
⅛ teaspoon pepper
½ cup melted butter or margarine
¼ teaspoon Worcestershire sauce
1 cup milk

Drain oysters. Combine cracker crumbs, salt, pepper, and butter or margarine. Sprinkle one-third in a greased casserole, and cover with a layer of oysters. Repeat layer. Add Worcestershire sauce to milk and pour over contents of dish. Sprinkle remaining crumbs over top. Bake in moderate oven at 350 degrees F., 30 minutes or until brown. Makes 6 servings.

OYSTER PICKUP

1 12-ounce jar oysters
2 cups oyster liquor and water
1 package (1¾ ounces) cream of leek soup mix
1 cup milk
1 tablespoon chopped parsley

Drain oysters, reserving liquor. Add oyster liquor and water to soup mix and bring to a boil, stirring constantly. Reduce heat and simmer for 10 minutes. Add milk and heat, sirring occasionally. Add oysters and heat 3 to 5 minutes longer, or until edges of oysters begin to curl. Sprinkle with parsley. Makes 6 servings.

OYSTER-MUSHROOM STEW

24 fresh oysters
1 10½-ounce can of cream of mushroom soup
2 cups oyster liquor and milk
¼ cup butter or margarine
½ teaspoon sherry
½ teaspoon salt
paprika

Drain oysters and reserve liquor. Combine all ingredients except oysters and sherry in a 3-quart saucepan. Heat, stirring occasionally. Add oysters. Heat 3 to 5 minutes longer or until edges of oysters begin to curl. Add sherry. Sprinkle with paprika. Makes 6 servings.

SOUTHERN FRIED OYSTER

24 oysters
2 eggs, beaten
1 cup cracker crumbs
⅓ cup flour

Drain oysters. Mix eggs, cracker crumbs and flour with sufficient milk to make a soupy paste. Roll each oyster thoroughly in the paste. Fry oysters in hot deep fry for 2 to 3 minutes, or until golden brown. Serves 6.

CHESAPEAKE BAY CLAM BAKE

6 dozen soft-shell clams
12 small onions
6 medium baking potatoes
6 ears of corn, in husks
12 live blue crabs
lemon wedges
melted butter or margarine

Wash clam shells thoroughly. Peel onions and wash potatoes. Par-boil onions and potatoes for 15 minutes; drain. Remove cornsilk from corn and replace husks. Cut 12 pieces of cheesecloth and 12 pieces of heavy-duty aluminum, 18 x 36 inches each. Place 2 pieces of cheesecloth on top of 2 pieces of foil. Place 2 onions, a potato, ear of corn, 12 clams, and 2 crabs on cheesecloth. Tie the cheesecloth up over the food. Pour 1 cup of water over the package. Bring edges of foil together and seal tightly. Make 6 packages. Place packages about 4 inches from hot coals. Cover with hood or aluminum foil. Cook for 45 to 60 minutes, or until onions and potatoes are cooked. Serve with lemon wedges and butter. Serves 6.

PACIFIC CLAM CHOWDER

2 cups clam juice (nectar from steamed clams)
1 bouillon cube
½ cup chopped onion
½ clove garlic, minced
3 tablespoons butter or margarine
¼ cup flour
½ bay leaf
1 cup milk
1 cup drained, minced, cooked clams
1 cup drained, cooked noodles
paprika

Combine clam juice and bouillon cube. Bring to a boil and stir until dissolved. Sauté onion and garlic in butter or margarine until tender; stir in flour.

Add clam juice and cook, stirring constantly until thick. Add bay leaf. Stir in milk, clams, and noodles; heat thoroughly. Serve in bowls; sprinkle with paprika. Serves 6.

PACIFIC CLAM AND CORN CHOWDER

8 ounces minced clams
1 cup clam liquid and water
3 slices bacon, chopped
1 cup chopped onion
2 cups diced raw potatoes
1½ cups drained whole-kernel corn
3 cups milk
2 tablespoons flour
1 tablespoon butter or margarine
1 teaspoon celery salt
1 teaspoon salt
dash white pepper
½ cup coarse cracker crumbs

Drain clams; reserve liquid. Add water to clam liquid to make 1 cup. Fry bacon until crisp; add onion and cook until tender. Add potatoes and clam liquid and water. Cover. Simmer gently until the potatoes are tender, then add corn and milk. Blend flour and butter or margarine and stir into chowder. Cook slowly until mixture thickens slightly, stirring constantly. Add seasonings and clams and simmer for 5 minutes. Top with cracker crumbs and serve hot. Serves 6.

DEVILED CLAMS

1 pint clams
1 clove garlic, minced
2 tablespoons chopped onion
½ cup chopped celery
¼ cup melted butter or margarine
1 tablespoon flour
¾ teaspoon salt
¼ teaspoon pepper
¼ teaspoon thyme
3 drops Tabasco
1 tablespoon chili sauce
1 egg, beaten
½ cup cracker meal
2 tablespoons chopped parsley
2 tablespoons butter or margarine, melted
½ cup dry bread crumbs

Drain and chop clams. Cook garlic, onion, and celery in butter or margarine until tender. Blend in flour and seasonings. Add clams and cook until thick, stirring constantly. Stir a little of the hot sauce into egg; add egg mixture to remaining sauce,

stirring constantly. Add cracker meal and parsley. Fill 6 well-greased individual shells or casseroles. Combine butter or margarine and crumbs and sprinkle over top of each shell. Bake in hot oven of 400 degrees F., for 10 minutes or until brown. Serves 6.

SCALLOP KABOBS

1 pound scallops
1 13½-ounce can pineapple chunks, drained
1 4-ounce can button mushrooms, drained 1 green
   pepper, diced into 1-inch squares
¼ cup salad oil
¼ cup lemon juice
¼ cup chopped parsley
¼ cup soy sauce
½ teaspoon salt
12 slices bacon
dash pepper

Rinse scallops in cold water to remove any shell particles. Place scallops, pineapple, mushrooms, and green pepper in a bowl. Combine oil, lemon juice, parsley, soy sauce, salt, and pepper. Pour sauce over scallop mixture and let stand for 30 minutes, stirring occasionally. Fry bacon until cooked but not crisp. Cut each slice in half. Using long skewers, alternate scallops, pineapple, mushrooms, green pepper, and bacon until skewers are filled. Cook about 4 inches from moderately hot coals for 6 minutes. Turn and cook for 5 to 6 minutes longer. Serves 6.

CHARCOAL BROILED SCALLOPS

2 pounds scallops
½ cup melted fat or oil
¼ cup lemon juice
2 teaspoons salt
¼ teaspoon white pepper
½ pound sliced bacon
paprika

Rinse scallops in cold water to remove shell particles. Place scallops in bowl. Combine fat, lemon juice, salt, and pepper. Pour sauce over scallops and let stand for 30 minutes, stirring constantly. Cut each slice of bacon in half lengthwise and then crosswise. Remove scallops, reserving sauce for basting. Wrap each scallop with a piece of bacon and fasten with a toothpick. Place scallops in well-greased, hinged wire grills. Sprinkle with paprika. Cook about four inches from moderately hot coals for five minutes. Baste with sauce and sprinkle with paprika. Turn and cook for five to six minutes longer or until bacon is crisp. Makes 6 servings.

SCALLOP SALAD BOWL

1½ pounds scallops
1½ cups water
3 tablespoons lemon juice
1½ teaspoons salt
3 peppercorns
3 slices onion
½ cup tarragon vinegar
⅓ cup salad oil
⅓ cup sugar
1 clove garlic, sliced
1½ cups diagonally sliced celery
6 servings crips salad greens
¾ cup sliced radishes
3 hard-cooked eggs, sliced
1 pint cherry tomatoes, cut in half, or two tomatoes, cut in wedges
¼ pound cheddar cheese, cut in thin strips

Rinse scallops with cold water and drain well. Combine water, lemon juice, ½ teaspoon salt, peppercorns, and onion in saucepan; bring to a boil. Simmer 5 minutes. Add scallops; cover and simmer gently 5 to 10 minutes, or until scallops are tender. Drain scallops. Combine vinegar, oil, sugar, remaining 1 teaspoon salt, and garlic; stir until sugar is dissolved. Pour over scallops. Cover and chill several hours. Add celery; mix and drain; save marinade. Arrange greens in large salad bowl. Pile scallops and celery in center of bowl, and arrange remaining foods in groups around scallops in crisp salad greens. Serve with reserved marinade or, if preferred, favorite French or oil-and-vinegar dressing. Serves 6.

OYSTERS ROCKEFELLER

Oysters Rockefeller is not a main dish but an appetizer, and it is probably one of the most famous oyster recipes in America. The story of how the recipe got its name is interesting. The recipe was concocted by Jules Alciatore at Antoine's in New Orleans. It was a recipe so rich that it was named after the then wealthiest man in the country.

18 large oysters on the half shell
6 tablespoons butter or margarine
½ cup fine dry bread crumbs
2 cups fresh spinach leaves, washed and stemmed
½ cup parsley sprigs
½ cup diced celery
2 tablespoons diced onion
1 tablespoon Pernod liqueur

¼ teaspoon salt
3 drops liquid red pepper seasoning

Melt butter or margarine in saucepan, add bread crumbs and sauté for one minute, stirring constantly. Combine butter mixture, spinach, parsley, celery, onion, Pernod, salt, and pepper seasoning. Blend and stir mixture until smooth. Pour into small bowl and place in refrigerator until ready to use. Arrange oysters on a bed of rock salt in six individual headproof dishes, placing three in each dish. The rock salt steadies oyster shells and retains heat. Top each oyster with a tablespoonful of the spinach mixture. Broil 3 minutes, or just until the topping is lightly browned and heated through. Serve immediately. Serves 6.

NEW ENGLAND CLAM CHOWDER

2 10½-ounce cans minced clams
1 8-ounce bottle clam juice
3 slices bacon, chopped
1 large onion, chopped
4 medium potatoes, pared and diced
3 cups water
1 teaspoon salt
¼ teaspoon pepper
1 envelope nonfat dry milk
3 tablespoons flour
2 tablespoons minced parsley

Cook bacon until crisp. Drain on absorbent paper and reserve. Add onion to bacon drippings in saucepan and sauté until soft. Add potatoes, 2 cups of water, salt, and pepper; cover. Simmer for 15 minutes or until potatoes are tender. Remove from heat. Drain liquid from clams into a 4-cup measure; reserve clams. Add bottled clam juice and remaining cup of water. Combine dry milk with flour in small bowl; stir briskly into clam liquids in cup. Add to potato mixture in saucepan. Cook, stirring constantly, over medium heat, until chowder thickens and bubbles for 1 minute. Add clams; heat until piping-hot. Ladle into soup bowls; sprinkle with parsley and reserved bacon. Service for 6.

HERB-BAKED SCALLOPS

2 pounds sea scallops
½ cup butter or margarine
3 tablespoons chopped parsley
1½ teaspoons leaf basil, crumbled
1 teaspoon salt
¼ teaspoon pepper

Wash clams in cold water and drain thoroughly

with absorbent paper. Place in a single layer in a large shallow baking dish, dot with butter or margarine, and sprinkle with parsley, basil, salt, and pepper. Bake in moderate oven 350 degrees F., 5 minutes. Stir scallops to coat well with butter mixture. Bake 20 minutes longer or until tender. Buttery sauce from dish can be used over baked or mashed potatotes. Serves 6.

OYSTER FRITTERS

3 dozen fresh shucked oysters
1 cup flour
1 teaspoon salt
dash cayenne pepper
⅔ cup water
2 tablespoons cooking oil
1 egg yolk, beaten
1 egg white, stiffly beaten

Drain oysters and spread out on paper towels to remove excess moisture. Sift dry ingredients together. Combine water, fat, and egg yolks. Add gradually to dry ingredients, stirring only until batter is blended. Let stand for 1 hour. Fold in egg white. Dip oysters in batter. Fry immediately in deep fat 375 degrees F., for 3 or 4 minutes until golden brown. Drain on absorbent paper. Serve with cocktail or tartar sauce. Serves 6.

OYSTER STEW

3 dozen fresh shucked oysters
2 slices bacon, chopped
⅓ cup chopped onion
1 10-ounce can frozen condensed cream of potato
    soup
4 cups oyster liquid and half-and-half cream
1¼ teaspoons salt
dash white pepper
chopped parsley

Drain oysters, reserving liquid. Fry bacon until crisp. Remove bacon from fat. Cook onion in bacon fat until tender. Add soup, oyster liquid, cream and seasonings; heat, stirring occasionally. Add bacon and oysters. Heat for 3 to 5 minutes longer or until edges of oysters begin to curl. Sprinkle with parsley. Serves 6.

OYSTER-CORNBREAD STUFFING

The traditional Thanksgiving Day meal calls for a plump turkey with rich dressing. For an added delight go beyond the usual cornbread stuffing and add an unusual ingredient—oysters.

12 ounces fresh oysters
1 cup chopped celery
1 cup chopped onion
¼ cup butter or margarine
3½ cups toasted cornbread
½ cup chicken broth
1 teaspoon poultry seasoning
1 teaspoon sage

Drain oysters. Cook celery and onion in butter or margarine until tender. Add oysters and cook 3 to 5 minutes or until edges begin to curl. Combine all ingredients and mix thoroughly. Makes approximately 4 cups stuffing, enough for a 4-pound ready-to-cook bird. For 5-9-pound bird, 2 times stuffing recipe; for 10-15-pound bird; 3 times stuffing recipe; for 16-20-pound bird, 4 times stuffing recipe; for 21-25-pound bird, 5 times stuffing recipe. If stuffing is baked separately, it should be placed in a well-greased shallow bake-and-serve dish and baked at 350 degrees F. for 25 to 30 minutes.

36

Crab and Lobster Goodies

Crab and lobster meat can be served in many ways and to fit many occasions. These meats make excellent main dishes and some supreme cocktails and salads.

EASY CRAB CASSEROLE

  1 pound blue crab meat
  1 10½-ounce can condensed cream of mushroom
      soup
  ½ cup cooked peas
  dash of pepper
  ½ cup grated cheese
  paprika

Remove any shell or cartilage from crab meat. Combine soup, peas, pepper, and crab meat. Place in 6 well-greased individual shells or 5-ounce custard cups. Sprinkle cheese and paprika over top of crab mixture. Bake in a moderate oven, 350 degrees F., for 20 to 25 minutes or until brown. Serves 6.

CRAB CANAPES

  1 pound blue crab meat
  3 tablespoons mayonnaise or salad dressing
  1 tablespoon prepared mustard
  12 slices white bread
  ¼ teaspoon salt
  dash pepper
  1 tablespoon lemon juice
  ¼ cup grated Parmesan cheese
  2 tablespoons dry bread crumbs

Remove any shell or cartilage from crab meat. Combine mayonnaise, seasonings, lemon juice, and

This is a female blue crab in "sponge." Female blue crabs in this stage should be returned to the water unharmed. In some coastal states they are illegal to keep when in "sponge."

crab meat. Remove crusts and toast bread. Spread crab mixture on each slice of toast. Combine cheese and crumbs; sprinkle over top of each slice of toast. Cut each slice into 6 pieces. Place on a broiler pan about 3 inches from source of heat. Broil for 2 to 3 minutes, or until brown. Makes approximately 72 canapes.

SOUTHWEST CRAB SALAD BOWL

  1 pound blue crab meat
  1 quart mixed salad greens
  2 tomatoes, cut into wedges
  ½ cup pitted ripe olives, sliced
  ¼ cup chopped green onion

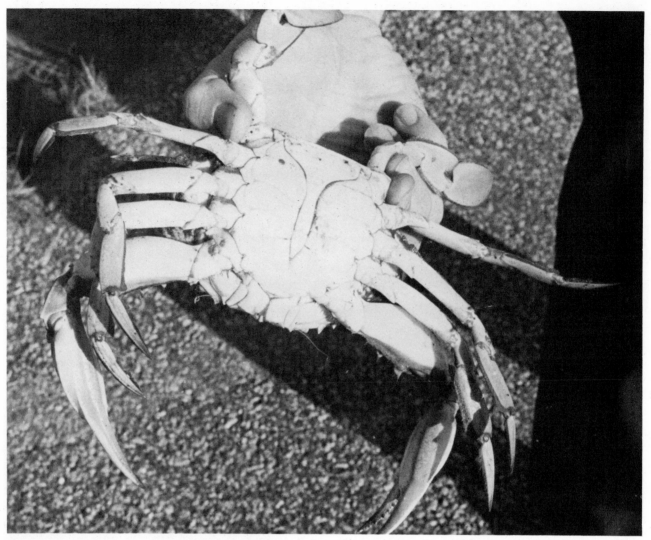

This is the male blue crab. Meat from the male blue is far superior to that from the female blue crab.

½ cut shredded natural Cheddar cheese
corn chips or tortilla chips
              Southwest Dressing:
½ cup mashed avocado
⅓ cup sour cream
2 tablespoons lemon juice
½ teaspoon sugar
¼ teaspoon chile powder
½ teaspoon salt
¼ teaspoon Tabasco sauce
1 clove garlic, crushed.

Remove any remaining shell or cartilage from crab meat. Combine crab, salad greens, tomatoes, olives, and onion. Combine all ingredients for Southwest Dressing and mix until smooth. Chill. Add dressing to the salad and toss lightly. Sprinkle with cheese, and garnish with whole ripe olives.

Serve immediately with corn or tortilla chips. Serves 8.

CHEESE-CRAB FONDUE

8 ounces blue crab meat (lumpted lobster meat can be substituted)
1 10-ounce can frozen condensed cream of shrimp soup
¼ cup milk or half-and-half cream
½ cup shredded American or Cheddar cheese
2 teaspoons lemon juice
dash paprika
dash white pepper
2 tablespoons sherry

Remove remaining shell or cartilage from crab meat. If lobster meat is substituted, break into lumps. Thaw shrimp soup and combine with milk in fondue pot. Cover, heat over direct moderate flame, stirring often. Fold in remaining ingredients except for sherry. Adjust heat to low flame. Stir in sherry just before serving. Serve with Melba toast, toast points, or in patty shells. If mixture needs thinning, use milk. Makes approximately 2¾ cups. Serves 6.

CRAB LOUIS

1 cup crab meat
1 cup mayonnaise
¼ cup heavy cream, whipped
¼ cup chili sauce
¼ cup chopped green onion
2 medium heads iceberg lettuce or romaine, shredded
4 medium tomatoes, cut in wedges
4 hard-boiled eggs, sliced

Blend mayonnaise with cream, chili sauce, onion, and pepper. Arrange lettuce on large platter, and top lettuce with remaining ingredients. Serve with dressing. Serves 6.

GRILLED LOBSTER TAILS

6 lobster tails (eight ounces each)
¼ cup melted butter or margarine
2 tablespoons lemon juice
½ teaspoon salt
melted butter or margarine

Cut lobster tails in half lengthwise. Remove swimmerettes and sharp edges. Cut 6 squares of heavy-duty aluminum foil, 12 inches each. Place each lobster tail on one half of each square of foil. Combine butter, lemon juice, and salt. Baste lobster meat with sauce. Fold other half of foil over lobster tail and seal edges by making double folds in the foil. Place packages, shell side down, about 5 inches from coals. Cook for 20 minutes. Remove lobster tails from foil. Place lobster tails on grill, flesh side down, and cook for 2 to 3 minutes longer, or until lightly browned. Serve with melted butter or margarine. Serves 6.

KING CRAB-CELERY VICTOR

1½ pounds king crab meat (blue crab can be substituted)
2 celery hearts
2 chicken bouillon cubes
3 cups boiling water
1 cup French dressing
6 large lettuce cups
pepper

Remove any remaining shell or cartilage from crab meat. Trim celery hearts so they are about 5 inches long. Cut each heart into thirds lengthwise. Place celery in 10-inch frying pan. Dissolve bouillon cubes in boiling water and pour over celery. Cover pan and simmer for 10 to 15 minutes, or until celery is tender. Let celery cool in bouillon. Drain. Place celery in a shallow baking dish. Pour French dressing over celery and chill for at least 2 hours. Remove celery from dressing. Drain. Place in lettuce cups. Sprinkle with pepper. Place approximately ¼ cup of crab meat on celery. Serves 6.

CRAB DIVAN

2¼ pounds crab meat (king, dungeness, or blue crab)
2 20-ounce packages frozen broccoli spears
2 tablespoons flour
1 teaspoon salt
¼ teaspoon pepper
1 tablespoon melted butter or margarine
½ cup skim milk
¼ cup grated American cheese
1 1-pound can tomatoes, drained
2 tablespoons crushed cornflakes

Remove any remaining shell or cartilage from crab meat. If crab meat is in large pieces, cut into 1-inch pieces. Cook broccoli half as long as directed on package. Drain thoroughly and place in a greased baking dish, 8 x 8 x 2. Spread crab meat over top of broccoli. Blend flour and seasonings into butter or margarine. Add milk gradually and cook until thick and smooth, stirring constantly. Add cheese and stir until melted. Stir in tomatoes. Pour sauce over crab meat. Sprinkle with crushed cornflakes. Bake in hot oven, 400 degrees F., for 20 to 25 minutes or until lightly browned. Serves 6.

CHEF'S SALAD CHESAPEAKE

1½ pounds blue crab meat
1 10-ounce package frozen asparagus spears
6 lettuce cups
lemon-caper dressing
3 hardboiled eggs, sliced
paprika

Remove any shell or cartilage from crab meat. Flake crab meat. Cook asparagus spears to package directions. Drain and chill. Place three asparagus spears in each lettuce cup. Place about ⅓ cup crab meat on asparagus. Cover with approximately two tablespoons of lemon-caper dressing. Top with three slices of hardboiled egg. Sprinkle with paprika. Serves 6.

SWEET AND SOUR KING CRAB

¾ pound king crab meat
1 cup sliced onion
1 small green pepper, cut in 1-inch squares
¼ cup butter or margarine
1 20-ounce can pineapple chunks in heavy syrup
½ cup sugar
2 tablespoons cornstarch
½ teaspoon dry mustard
¼ teaspoon salt
½ cup white vinegar
1 tablespoon soy sauce
⅔ cup cherry tomato halves or thin tomato wedges
6 servings hot, cooked seasoned, plain, or almond
    rice or chow-mein noodles

Sauté onion and green pepper in butter or margarine until onion is tender but not browned. Drain pineapple; reserve syrup. Combine sugar, cornstarch, mustard, and salt. Stir in pineapple syrup, vinegar, and soy sauce; mix well; add to onion-green pepper mixture. Cook, stirring constantly, until thick and clear. Fold in pineapple chunks, crab meat, and tomatoes. Heat; serve over rice or noodles. 6 servings.

CRAB ELEGANT

¾ pound dungeness crab meat (blue crab or king
    crab, flaked, can be substituted)
1 cup celery, sliced
1 cup fresh mushrooms, sliced
1 4-ounce can sliced mushrooms, drained
¼ cup sliced green onions
3 tablespoons flour
¾ teaspoon salt
dash white pepper
1 cup milk
½ cup half-and-half milk and cream
¼ cup sherry
½ teaspoon Worcestershire sauce
2 tablespoons diced pimiento
1 ripe avocado, peeled and sliced
6 servings hot, fluffy rice

Cook celery in butter or margarine until tender. Add mushrooms and onion, and cook until onion is tender. Blend in flour, salt, and pepper. Stir in milk and half-and-half milk-cream; cook until thickened, stirring constantly. Add sherry, Worcestershire sauce, crab meat, and pimiento; mix carefully. Place over low heat and bring to serving temperature, stirring often. Serve on rice; garnish with avocado slices. Serves 6.

BAKED STUFFED LOBSTER

4 small live lobsters (1¼ pounds each)
1 cup melted butter or margarine
2¾ cups unsalted soda cracker crumbs
1 cup chopped parsley
2 teaspoons paprika
1 teaspoon salt

Drop live lobsters into large kettle of rapidly boiling salted water; cover. Cook over high heat for 8 to 10 minutes, or until lobsters turn bright red. Remove with tongs at once, drain, and let cool enough to handle. Place each lobster on its back and cut down middle from head to tail with scissors, being careful not to cut through hard shell of back. Place lobster open so it will be flat (if necessary, crack back shell in several places). Remove pick coral (roe), green tomalley (liver), stomach sac from back of head, black vein running from head to tail, and spongy gray tissue. Brush meat with some of the melted butter or margarine. Place lobsters on cooky sheet. Mix cracker crumbs, parsley, paprika, and salt in bowl; drizzle with remaining melted butter or margarine. Toss lightly to mix, divide evenly and pack into opened lobsters. Bake in hot oven, 425 degrees F., 15 minutes, or until meat is hot and crumb topping is golden. Place on individual large serving platters; garnish with water cress or lemon wedges. Serves 4 to 6.

BAKED CRAB MEAT REMICK

1 pound crab meat
6 slices bacon, cooked and crumbled
1½ cups mayonnaise or salad dressing
½ cup chili sauce
1 teaspoon tarragon vinegar
1 teaspoon dry mustard
½ teaspoon paprika
¼ teaspoon celery salt
few drops of Tabasco

Remove any shell or cartilage from crab meat. Flake meat and place in 6 scallop shells or individual baking dishes; sprinkle with bacon. Place shells in large pan for easy handling. Heat in moderate oven, 350 degrees F., 5 minutes while fixing topping. Blend mayonnaise or salad dressing, chili sauce, vinegar, mustard, paprika, celery salt, and Tabasco seasoning in small bowl. Spoon over hot crab mixture. Broil, 4 to 5 inches from heat, for 1 minute, or just until hot. Makes 6 servings.

Boiled blue crab claws and bodies. Pick the meat out of the shells and use it in cocktails, baked casseroles, or gumbo for gourmet seafood eating.

CHESAPEAKE CRAB IMPERIAL

2 pounds blue crab meat
1 egg
⅔ cup finely diced green pepper
¼ cup finely diced pimiento
2 teaspoons dry mustard
2 teaspoons salt
¼ teaspoon white pepper
¾ cup mayonnaise or salad dressing
paprika

Remove any shell or cartilage from crab meat. Flake meat. Beat egg in medium size bowl. Stir in green pepper, pimiento, mustard, salt, pepper, and all but two tablespoons of the mayonnaise or salad dressing until well blended. Fold in crab meat. Spoon into 6 10-ounce custard cups. Sprinkle each with 1 teaspoon remaining mayonnaise or salad dressing; sprinkle with paprika. Bake in moderate oven, 350 degrees F., 15 minutes or just until hot. Makes 6 servings.

37

How To Buy Seafood

One of the truisms of sports fishing is that ten percent of the fishermen catch ninety percent of the fish. Where eating fish is concerned, there is a parallel—only it runs 180 degrees in the opposite direction. Namely it is that ninety percent of the fish eaten are purchased in the fish market, while only ten percent are caught by sports fishermen. Obviously, then, unless you happen to be in the ten percent of the sports fishermen who catch all those fish, the marine life that wends its way to your dinner table will come out of a fish market.

It requires skill and know-how to catch fish. There is no skill involved when it comes to exchanging money across the counter for fish. Know-how, however, is extremely important if one is to purchase prime fish, and obviously if the product is going to decorate your dinner table, you want fresh fish.

HOW TO KNOW GOOD FISH

The ability to recognize fresh fish is necessary when whole fish are purchased. One who trades at the same fish market all the time and one who gets to know the operator can place his faith in the dealer's hands. If one has to select on his own, then here are the things to look for in fresh fish: bright, clear, bulging eyes; reddish pink gills; elastic flesh; fins that spring back when pressed, and no objectionable odors. When the fish is purchased dressed, in steaks or fillets, it should have a moist look and be almost odorless. If the meat appears dry and curled at the edges, you can be sure it isn't fresh.

HOW MUCH TO BUY

A serving of fish is usually one-third to one-half pound of edible meat. Where steaks, fillets, or sticks are involved, allow one-third pound per person; hence a family of six would require two pounds of fish. For dressed fish allow one-half pound per person, or three pounds for the same family of six. Remember in dressed fish there is some waste in bones and skin. Where whole fish are concerned, allow one pound per person. There is considerable weight loss in waste, since the whole fish is as it comes out of the water. It still must be eviscerated, scaled or skinned, and have head, fins, and tail removed.

HOW FISH ARE MARKETED

Fish are marketed in various forms for different uses. If one is to buy intelligently, one must know these forms or cuts. They are as follows:

Whole—The fish as it comes out of the water. Before cooking, it must be scaled or skinned and eviscerated. It may or may not have head, tail, and fins removed prior to cooking. This depends upon how the fish is to be cooked.

Drawn—This is a whole, eviscerated fish, usually with head, fins, and tail not removed.

Dressed—This is a whole fish eviscerated and scaled or skinned with head, tail, and fins removed.

Steaks—Cross section slices from large dressed fish. These are ready for use.

Fillets—Side of the fish, cut lengthwise away from the backbone. These are ready for use.

Sticks and portions—These are pieces of fish cut from large fish or blocks of frozen fillets. They are uniform in size ranging from one to several ounces. These are ready to use.

STORING FISH

Fish are highly perishable and must be handled with care. Fresh fish should be carefully wrapped in waxed paper, plastic, or aluminum foil, packed in ice or kept in the coldest part of the refrigerator. It should be used within twenty to thirty-six hours of purchase. If it is to be kept for a longer period, then it should be carefully wrapped in plastic or aluminum foil and frozen. Carefully squeeze all air out of the package to prevent "freezer burn." The frozen fish can then be stored at minus ten degrees Fahrenheit or lower until ready for use. Dressed frozen fish, steaks, and fillets may be cooked in frozen form but extra cooking time is required. Thawing is necessary for cleaning and dressing whole and drawn fish. The accepted practice is to thaw at refrigerator temperature (forty to forty-five degrees) or in cold running water. Fish that have been thawed should be held at refrigerator temperature only long enough to permit ease of preparation. Never refreeze partially thawed or thawed fish.

CRUSTACEANS AND MOLLUSKS

Almost all shellfish consumed are purchased at the seafood market. There are people who harvest their own, but in the overall picture they represent a decimal fraction of a percentage point. Shellfish are divided into two general classifications: crustaceans (crabs, shrimp, lobsters, and crayfish) mollusks (oysters, clams, and scallops). All shellfish, whether mollusks or crustaceans, are among the most delicate and perishable of foods. All shellfish must be kept well refrigerated until preparation time.

SHRIMP

Depending upon the species and from what waters they are taken, raw shrimp range in color from reddish brown to greenish-gray. The common varieties of shrimp include: white, brown or grooved, pink, and red or royal. When cooked all are similar in appearance, flavor, yield, and texture.

Shrimp are marketed in the following forms: whole, headed, peeled, and deveined; cooked in shell; cooked, peeled, and deveined; fresh frozen and breaded frozen. Shrimp are commonly sold by the pound. Shrimp sizes are designated by the count or tails per pound and nonpeeled they are divided into the following categories: fifteen and under, sixteen to twenty, twenty-one to twenty-five, twenty-six to thirty, thirty-one to forty-two, forty-three and over. Terms to describe shrimp corresponding to the number per pound are jumbo, large, medium, medium-small, small, and cocktail.

How much shrimp to buy depends upon the manner in which they are to be served. When stuffed, jumbo and large shrimp with fifteen tails and under or sixteen to twenty tails per pound should be used. Figure on servings of a half dozen stuffed shrimp per person and buy accordingly. When shrimp are desired for simple batter-dip and deep-frying, buy shrimp in the twenty-one to twenty-five to twenty-six to thirty counts and allow for a dozen per adult. Smaller shrimp, thirty-one to forty-three or forty-three and over count, are best for cocktails and salads. For cocktails figure nine to a dozen per adult, depending upon the size of the shrimp. If shrimp are to be used in a salad, allow for one-third pound per adult.

Shrimp are also sold as broken pieces for use in salads and mixed dishes when shape is unimportant. Shrimp—headed, peeled, and deveined—are also sold frozen in five-pound boxes. Breaded uncooked shrimp ready for deep-frying, and precooked breaded shrimp ready for heat-and-serve are sold by the package in eight-, ten-, twelve-, fourteen-, and sixteen-ounce sizes.

CRABS

The varieties of edible crabs available in North America include: hard-shell or blue crab from the Atlantic Oceans and Gulf of Mexico waters, dungeness crab from Pacific waters, and king and tanner or queen crabs from Pacific waters off Alaska. Soft-shell crabs are molted blue crabs that have shed their hard shells.

Crabs are marketed as follows: live; cooked in the shell; fresh rough dressed; pasteurized or frozen meat; and canned. Crabs are almost always sold alive or freshly cooked in the shells in areas near the fishing grounds. Hard-shell crabs are frequently cooked alive by steaming or boiling almost as soon as they are brought to market places. In the case of the blue crabs, the hard back shells are broken off before boiling or steaming to save space in the cooking pots. Crab meat is extremely perishable and must be refrigerated or packed in ice until used. The meat is often picked from the cooked crabs and shipped in iced containers.

Cooked blue crab meat is sold in the following

forms: lump; flake and lump, and claw. A description of these forms follows:

Lump meat—This meat is white and comes from the larger body muscles. It is often called "special" or back-fin.

Flake meat—This meat is white, smaller bits than lump, and comes from the body part of the crab.

Flake and lump meat—It is what the term implies, a mixture of both white meats.

Claw meat—This meat comes from the crab claws. The outer surface of the mat is brownish, while the inner portion is white. This meat is jucier than body white meat.

Soft-shell crabs are sold both fresh and frozen. They are marketed by size or number to the pounds. They are cleaned prior to freezing, and when cooked may be eaten shell and all. Soft-shell crabs are usually served deep-fried or sautéed.

The king crab is the largest found in waters bordering North America. These huge crabs range from five to twenty pounds. The leg meat is available cooked or frozen in five-pound blocks; cooked and frozen leg sections in shells are available whole or split. The whole legs can be broiled, baked in the shell, or served cold with a sauce.

When blue crabs are sold alive or whole, figure on a dozen to serve three adults. With blue crab meat already picked from the shell figure on a pound to serve three adults if the meat is baked or stuffed in aluminum shells. A pound of picked crab meat will serve eight adults if used for cocktails. A pound will serve six adults when the meat is used to make gumbo.

LOBSTERS

Live Maine or northern lobsters can be purchased for shipment throughout the country, and through the use of holding tanks they can be kept alive for days. This lobster is not to be confused with crayfish or rock lobsters. The northern or Maine lobster runs from three-fourths of a pound to three pounds, sometimes over. Edible meat comes from both the tail and claws, whereas with crayfish and rock lobsters, only the tails are marketable. Rock lobster tails scale from one-quarter of a pound to a pound in size and are imported frozen in this country mainly from Australia, New Zealand, and South Africa.

Lobsters are sold in four forms: live; cooked in the shell; fresh or frozen meat; and canned meat. Only in producing areas will one find fresh lobsters cooked in the shell and lobster meat in large quantities.

Whole lobsters can be steamed, boiled, broiled, or baked stuffed and served in the shell. The meat is also used in salads, cocktails, sandwiches, chowders, bisques, and in Newburg. Lobster tails are usually broiled, baked, boiled, and baked stuffed.

OYSTERS

Oysters are found in the tidal waters of the Atlantic and Pacific coasts and the Gulf of Mexico. They vary in flavor, size, and texture as a result of the waters from which they are harvested. Those dredged from the Atlantic and Gulf coasts are known as eastern oysters. Usually, however, they are marketed under the name of the state or specific waters from which they are taken—Chesapeake Bay oysters, Maryland Oysters, Galveston Bay oysters, Louisiana oysters, etc. The giant Japanese oyster is taken from the Pacific, while Puget Sound yields the small, delicately flavored Olympic oyster.

Oysters are sold live, fresh or frozen shucked, and canned. Oysters in the shell are sold by the bushel, sack, and barrel and should be alive when purchased. When an oyster is alive, its shell is closed tightly. Oysters with shells that do not close when handled are dead and are unfit to eat. Oysters in the shell can be kept alive and fresh if refrigerated at forty degrees or lower (but not below freezing).

Fresh shucked oysters should be plump with a natural cream color and have a clear liquid free from shell particles. They should be packed in metal containers or waxed cartons, and when properly refrigerated will keep for a week to ten days. Shucked oysters are sold by the pint, quart, and gallon.

Eastern oysters are designated by terms that indicate the number of meats (individual oysters) to a gallon. Small oysters run 301 to 500 per gallon. Selects run 211 to 300, and this is the size generally preferred for frying. Extra selects run 160 to 210.

Oysters may be served raw on the shell or baked on the half shell with various toppings or sauces. Shucked oysters can be batter-dipped and fried, escalloped, or used in stews, bisques, chowders, or for making stuffing mixtures.

CLAMS

Clams in shells should be alive when purchased. Hard-shell clams that have gaping shells that will not close when handled are dead and should be discarded. With other varieties of clams, the siphon or neck of a live clam will twitch when touched. Clams in the shells are marketed by the peck, bushel, and barrel, and will remain fresh and alive for several days if refrigerated at about forty degrees.

Fresh shucked clams should be plump with free liquid and free from bits of shell. When refrigerated or packed in ice, they will remain fresh for a week to ten days. They are usually marketed by the gallon, sometimes quart, for chowder, frying, or sauced entrees. Frozen shucked clams should not be thawed until ready for use, and once thawed, they should never be refrozen.

Soft-shelled clams can be steamed and served with the sauce in which they were cooked and with drawn butter. Cherrystone and little neck clams can be served raw on the halfshell.

SCALLOPS

Large sea scallops, inhabitants of offshore banks and deep water, are used extensively in quality food operations. Bay scallops come from inshore waters. They are small and considered a delicacy. They are expensive since they are found in limited supply. Both the sea and bay scallops have white, sweet, firm meat. Scallops can be broiled; breaded, and deep-fried; sautéed; en brochette; au gratin; in Newburg; and in soups and chowders.

Glossary
of Fishing Terms

ALGAE: Simple plants, most of which live under water.

ANADROMOUS: Fish that spend part of their lives in salt water and part in fresh water.

ANCHOVY: A major food source of Pacific fish; the most popular of Pacific Coast baitfish.

ANTI-REVERSE: A device that permits line to be pulled from a reel on which the handle remains stationary.

AUTOMATIC REEL: A reel that has a wind-up spring, which when released takes up line.

BACKLASH: Line tangle caused by overrunning of the reel spool.

BAIL Line pickup device on a spinning reel.

BAIT-CASTING: Casting of lures or plugs that imitate baitfish.

BAIT-CASTING REEL: Conventional spool or revolving spool reel used for bait-casting fishing.

BAIT-FISHING: Fishing with natural baits such as shrimp, minnows, worms, etc.

BAITFISH: Any kind of small fish used for bait.

BALANCED TACKLE: Tackle selected so that rod, reel, and line are correctly balanced for efficient fishing.

BALL-BEARING SWIVEL: Swivel with ball bearings and used to join leader and line together to keep spinning lure from twisting line. Used most frequently in offshore and big game fishing.

BARBEL: Whiskerlike feelers on mouth of some fish species, mostly bottom-feeders.

BARREL SWIVEL: Device used to join line and leader to prevent twist being put in the line.

BILLFISH: A fish with a bill such as sailfish and marlin.

BLOCK TIN SQUID: Lure molded of block tin in shape of small baitfish.

BLUE WATER: Term applied to far offshore waters because of deep blue color.

BOBBER: Float attached to line to keep baited hook suspended off the bottom.

BOTTOM FEEDER: Term applied to fish that root the bottom for feed.

BRACKISH WATER: Fresh water mixed with salt water. Where rivers and streams flow into salt water.

BRAIDED LINE: Line braided of nylon or Dacron.

BUCKTAIL JIG: Molded lead lure that has a skirt of bucktail tied around it.

BUNKER: Menhaden, an important fish food and bait.

BUTT: The lower section of a fishing rod, also called the handle.

CASTING ROD: Rod specially designed to be used with a casting reel.

CAUDAL PEDUNCLE: That part of the body of a fish in front of the caudal fin.

CHARTER BOAT: Large cabin boat used for private, day, or weekend charter fishing.

CHUM BAG: Mesh bag in which chum is placed and then suspended over the side of the boat.

CHUM LINE: Slick on the water caused by dumping over ground up fish and marine matter. Purpose is to attract school fish in salt water.

CHUMMING: Attracting fish by dumping over ground up fish or marine matter to set up a chum line. Fish follow the chum line to its source.

CHUM POT: Weighted wire basket to put chum on the bottom to attract bottom feeders.

CLICK: Mechanism on reel that sounds a click when line is stripped off.

CLINCH-ON SINKER: A sinker that is held on the line by crimping over ears on each end of sinker.

CORK ARBOR: Cork filler used to increase the diameter of reel spool.

CREEL: Basket or bag used to hold caught fish.

CRUSTACEANS: Animals with hard exoskeletons.

CURRENT: Movement of the water usually caused by tide or wind.

CUTTYHUNT: Linen line.

DEADFALL: Spot that contains brush, wrecks, and the likes that make good fish concentration area.

DEBONER: Metal tube used to remove bone from small baitfish.

DIAMOND JIG: Four-sided lure made of lead and chrome or nickel-plated. Lure is widest at its center and tapers to a point at each end.

DIATOMS: Microscopic algae.

DORSAL FIN: Top and usually largest fin on back of fish.

DOUBLE-LINE: Doubling the end ten to twenty feet of line to increase strength when fishing for big game fish.

DRAG: Device that controls the tension under which a line goes off the reel.

DRIFT: Allowing the boat to be carried freely by the wind or current.

DROP LINE: Handline without rod used for still fishing.

DROP-OFF: Quick plunge of the shoreline when the water goes from shallow to quite deep.

DRY FLY: Artificial lure designed to imitate floating insect.

EAGLE CLAW: Hook in which the point curves back toward the shank. Trade name for hook-type developed by Wright and McGill.

EDDY: Area where small whirlpool occurs on down current side of bridge pilings, rocks, etc.

EELSKIN: Skin of an eel used for bait.

EPILIMNION: Lake thermal stratum above the thermocline.

EXTENSION BUTT: Small extra butt added to fly rod butt after a fish is hooked to give angler extra leverage.

FATHOM: Measure of depth equal to six feet.

FEATHER JIG: Saltwater lure made of metal head with body of feathers.

FEMALE FERRULE: Socket part of a ferrule.

FERRULE: Friction joint in a rod to allow it to be disassembled.

FILLET: Bone-free piece of fish.

FISHING ROD: Piece of equipment designed expressly for catching fish.

FLASHER: Flashing spoon tied above the bait to attract fish.

FLATS: Very shallow water. Areas that are exposed at low tide and flooded at high tide.

FLIES: Small lures to represent insects and bugs.

FLOAT: *See* Bobber.

FLOAT FISHING: Fishing while drifting down stream.

FLOTSAM: Floating objects washed off boats or the shoreline.

FLUKE: Point of an anchor.

FLY LINE: Line designed for fly-fishing. Line is weighted and tapered.

FLYING GAFF: A gaff hook that detaches from the gaff handle when the hook is imbedded in the fish.

FORAGE SPECIES: Small fish upon which other fish feed.

FOREGRIP: Rod hand grip located above the reelseat.

FUSIFORM FISH: Round-bodied fish tapering toward the ends.

GAFF: Large, strong hook attached to a handle for purpose of landing large fish.

GAMEFISH: Fish species that are considered great fighters.

GANG HOOK: Hook with two or more tines.

GANION RIG: A Pacific Coast deep-water bottom-fishing rig on which six or more hooks are used.

GILLS: Membranes that enable fish to absorb oxygen from the water.

GIMBAL: Chair or rod-belt socket to keep rod in upright position at all times.

GIMBAL NOCK: A fitting on the butt of rod so rock can be fitted into gimbal.

GREEN FISH: A hooked fish with too much life to be netted or gaffed. A fish still full of fight.

GRAPNEL: Hook-shaped anchor with four or more tines.

GROUND FISHING: Term applied to fishing for bottom feeders.

GUIDES: Rings attached to fishing rod to guide line in and out from the reel. Term also applied to fishermen who take others fishing on a pay basis.

GUIDE BOAT: Boat used by a fishing guide and equipped specially for fishing.

HABITAT: Environment suitable for maintaining marine life.

HIGH-LOW RIG: A bottom rig with two hooks attached, one on the bottom and the other about two feet above.

HORSE: Term applied to pulling in fish by sheer force.

HYPOLIMNION: A lake thermal stratum below the thermocline.

INLET: Place where small body of water meets a large body of water. An indentation in the shoreline.

I.G.F.A.: International Game Fishing Association.

IMPOUNDMENT: An artificial or manmade body of water.

JIG: Heavy lure that is fished by jigging up and down off the bottom.

JIGGING: Term applied to jig fishing.

JOHN BOAT: Flat-bottomed, square-bowed boat developed for river fishing in the Ozarks.

JUG FISHING: Fishing by tying lines to floating jugs and allowing them to be carried by the current.

KELP: Type of seaweed abundant in the Pacific Ocean.

LANDING NET: A net designed for landing fish.

LAMINATED ROD: Rod constructed by cementing several strips of wood together with the grain parallel.

LEA: Measure of linen line, usually three hundred yards.

LEAD CORE LINE: Line of braided nylon with a thin lead core to make it sink deep.

LEADER: Strand of gut, nylon, or wire between line and hook or lure.

LEVELWIND REEL: Reel with device that spools line evenly.

LIVE WELL: Container in which live bait if contained.

LONG ROD: Term originally applied to a fly rod, now also applied to a long surf rod.

LUNKER: A big fish.

LURE: Artificial bait used to attract fish.

LURE ACTION: Movement of the lure in the water so that it appears to be lifelike.

MALE FERRULE: Insert part of a ferrule.

MINNOW: General term applied to small baitfish.

MIRROR-TYPE LURE: Lure with mirrorlike finish so that it flashes like a spoon.

MONOFILAMENT: Single strand line.

MOSSBUNKER: Small saltwater baitfish often used for chum.

MULTIHOOK RIG: Bottom rig with two or more hooks on the same leader.

MULTIPLYING REEL: A reel geared so that the spool revolves several times for each turn of the handle. Also called a conventional reel.

NODE: Joint or leaf scar on a bamboo cane.

OFFSET HANDLE: Rod handle with the reel set offset for better positioning and ease in casting.

OMNIVOROUS: Fish having a universal diet.

OUTRIGGER: Long poles on each side of boat and used in trolling for big game fish.

PANFISH: Small fish that are sought more for eating than for sport.

PARTY BOAT: Very large fishing boat to accommodate groups of a dozen on up to one hundred.

PERSUADER: A club used to subdue big fish in order to remove hooks.

PILCHARD: Small baitfish popular on the Atlantic and Gulf Coasts.

PLANER: A device attach to the line to cause the bait to plane down to deep water.

PLANKTON: Minute animals that live in the surface layers of water.

PLASTIC FLOAT: *See* Bobber.

PLUGS: Wooden or plastic artificial lures.

POD OF FISH: Small number of fish up to a dozen feeding or traveling together.

POLING: Pushing a boat across shallow flats by means of a long pole made expressly for this purpose.

POPPING BUG: Small surface plug with a concave face that causes lure to make popping sound when jerked through the water.

POPPING PLUG: Same as a popping bug, except much larger in size and weight so it can be fished with casting tackle.

PORK RIND: Pliable rind of pork attached to lures to enhance the action.

PREDACIOUS: Killing other animals for food.

PRIEST: A club for subduing fish. *See* Persuader.

PROPELLER PLUG: Lure with propeller attached fore and/or aft. When retrieved propellers make sounds like those of crippled minnows.

PUMPING: Raising of rod tip, quickly lowering it to reel up line slack, and then repeating procedure again and again to work in big fish.

PULPIT: Platform in the bow of a boat from which to fish or harpoon fish.

REEF: Rocks, coral, or shell on sea bottom, often extending up close to the surface of the water.

REEL DRAG: Reel mechanism that can be set to desired pressure to create drag on fighting fish.

REEL SEAT: Metal seat on butt of rod for mounting of fishing reel.

RIFFLE: Slight disturbance on the surface of the water caused by wind or subsurface obstructions.

RIG: Fishing equipment.

RING GUIDE: Guides mounted along length of rod tip.

ROD BELT: Belt worn for fighting big fish. The belt has a tube or cup to accommodate rod butt.

ROILED WATER: Muddied or disturbed water.

ROLLER GUIDE: Guides with small rollers. They are mounted on rod tip and used mainly in big-game fishing.

RUN: Period when fish is stripping line off the reel.

SAND EEL: Popular middle and north Atlantic Coast baitfish. Also known as a sand launce.

SARGASSUM WEED: A type of seaweed that originates in the Sargassum Sea. Found mainly in the Gulf of Mexico and on Atlantic Coast.

SCHOOLS (OF FISH): Large number of fish, usually of the same species, congregated in a small area.

SCUTE: Bony or horny plate on a fish.

SEAWEED: Leafy green to brown vegetation found in almost all salt water.

SEAWORMS: Marine worms found on our seacoast. Important as fish bait.

SEINES: Nets used in fishing.

SERRATED: Saw-toothed.

SHINERS: Minnows; term often applied to all small shiny baitfish.

SHOALS: Shallow water areas.

SHOULDER HARNESS: Vestlike harness used in big game fishing to take the strain off the angler's arms and distribute it to the back.

SHRIMP: Small marine crustacean that makes excellent bait.

SILT: Fine sediment carried and deposited by water.

SINGLE-ACTION REEL: A nonmultiplying reel.

SINKER: Weight used to carry fishing bait to the bottom.

SKIP BAIT: A trolled bait that is skipped along the surface of the water.

SKITTERING: Drawing the hook through or along the surface of the water with a quivering motion.

SLICK: Oily patch on surface of the water. Can be caused by chum, residue from feeding fish, or from food regurgiated by feeding fish.

SNAGLINE: Line fitted with hooks for snagging fish.

SNELLED HOOK: Hook with short piece of leader material attached.

SOLUNAR: John Alden Knight used the word to describe his theory that living creatures are influenced by the sun and moon.

SPAWN: Eggs of fish and other marine animals.

SPINNER: An artificial lure, a flashing blade that revolves when retrieved through the water.

SPINNING REEL: Reel with a fixed spool instead of revolving spool.

SPLIT RING: A metal ring for connecting lures to leaders.

SPOON: Artificial lure made of metal and resembling a spoon.

SPREADER RIG: Bottom rig of stiff wire to accommodate two hooks.

STAR DRAG: Star-shaped wheel on reel to adjust drag pressure.

STILL FISHING: Fishing without moving.

STINK BAIT: Specially prepared bait used for fish that feed by scent. Most popular in fishing for freshwater catfish.

STRIKE: Describes the fish grabbing the bait. Also the act of tightening the line to set the hook in the mouth of the fish.

STRIP BAIT: Bait cut in strips. Used mostly in offshore and big-game fishing.

STRIP LINE: A fly-fishing term that describes drawing line from the reel for casting.

SURGICAL-TUBE LURE: Lure made by slipping a hook through a piece of surgical tubing. Lure has shimmering action when retrieved through the water.

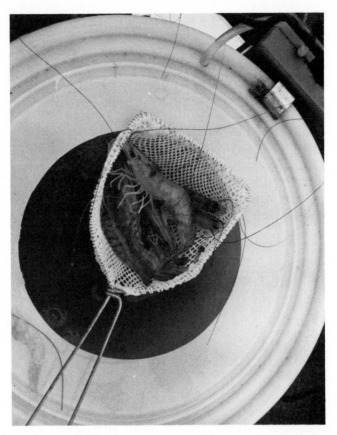

Shrimp are excellent natural bait. They are most appealing to fish when fished live. They can be kept alive and kicking in aeriated bait wells.

SWIMMING PLUG: Lure that has a swimming motion caused by a wobble plate attached to its head.

TAGGING: Use of tags to mark fish.

TAPERED LEADER: Leader that tapers from thick to thin so end creates minimum of disturbance on surface of water. Strictly a fly-fishing term.

TAPERED LINE: Line that tapers from thick to thin to create balance in air when casting. Strictly a fly-fishing term.

TEASER: Any large lure without hooks. Purpose is to attract attention of fish. Used exclusively in big-game fishing.

TERMINAL TACKLE: All tackle—hooks, sinkers, leaders, etc.—at the end of the line.

THREE-WAY SWIVEL: Swivel with three eyes.

THERMOCLINE: Lake thermal stratum in which temperatures are static.

THROW LINE: Line cast by hand for fishing without a rod.

THUMBING REEL: Act of using thumb to control spin of spool in casting or in fighting a fish.

TIDE: Rise and fall of water due to lunar influence.

TIDE RIP: Place where several currents clash.

TIP TOP: Guide ring at the tip end of the red tip.

213

TRASH FISH: Fish not sought by fisherman for either food or sport.

TROLLING: Act of pulling a bait or lure through the water behind a moving boat.

TTROLLING PLATE: Platelike device attached to outboard motor for purpose of slowing the boat's trolling speed.

TROLLING SINKER: Specially designed sinker for trolling.

TROTLINE: Line with many hooks and stretched across a stream or along shoreline between stakes.

WAKE: Water disturbance created as a boat moves ahead in the water.

WASH: Water disturbance created by a passing boat.

WET FLY: Artificial lure for fly-fishing and one that resembles a drowned insect or the larva of an aquatic insect.

WHIP RETRIEVE: Retrieving the lure by whipping the rod tip while reeling to give extra action in the water.

WIRE LINE: Metal line used for deep-water trolling.

WOBBLER SPOON: Spoon attached so it whips and wobbles upon retrieve.

WORKING LURE: Act of imparting action through rod tip to give lure more lifelike action.

X DESIGNATION: Diameter or pound test of leader material, fly lines, and monofilament lines for spinning and baitcasting.

Index

Pages on which illustrations appear are set in boldface.